DATE DUE	
JUN 16 1992		
FEB 25 1993		
MAR 11 1993		
APR 15 1994		

DISCARD

In Celebration of Play

An Integrated Approach to Play and
Child Development

Edited by Paul F. Wilkinson

In celebration of play.
Includes index.
Includes index.
1. Play. 2. Child development. 3. Play
environments. I. Wilkinson, Paul F.
LB1137.I5   1980   155.4'18   80-5283
ISBN 0-312-41078-4

To John and Judy Wilkinson and
Toby and Linda Chown,
in thanks for our childhoods

ST. MARTIN'S PRESS   NEW YORK

Library of Congress Cataloging in Publication Data

Main entry under title:
In celebration of play.
    Bibliography: p.
    Includes index.
    1. Child development — Addresses, essays, lectures.
2. Play — Social aspects — Addresses, essays, lectures.
I. Wilkinson, Paul F., 1948—
LB1137.I5   1980   155.4′18   79-3841

ISBN 0-312-41078-6

To John and Ruth Wilkinson, and
Tony and Luella Ludwig,
in thanks for our childhoods

CONTENTS

Contents

ACKNOWLEDGEMENTS

Credit for the production of any book is never due solely to one person, even if the book is the product of a single author. When the book is an edited collection of papers, however, the list of persons involved grows to immense proportions. The following are some of the people involved in the production of these two volumes: Polly Hill (President), Arvid Bengtsson (Past-President), Muriel Otter (Treasurer), Jane Knight (Secretary), International Playground Association; Cor Westland, Chairman, Conference Planning Committee of the Seventh World Congress of the International Playground Association, and the chairman and members of all of the conference committees; in particular, the members of the Program Committee of the Seventh World Congress of the International Playground Association, of which I was a member — Alexandra Semeniuk (Chairman), Sue Alexander, Pat Artkin, Lynton Friedberg, Herb Gray, Halina Kantor, Paul Kemp, Nancy Mallett, Marilyn Muleski, Les Miller, Karen Oster, Yolanda Pluta, Debra Pepler, Swain Van Camp and Sheila Ward; the Ontario Ministry of Culture and Recreation and the Honourable Reuben Baetz, Minister; Dean Rodger Schwass, Alice Reppert, Betty Peckhover, Al Turner, Donna Lytle, Claire Côté, and other members of the Faculty of Environmental Studies, York University; the authors who contributed their time and effort to these volumes; David Croom for his help and support; Barbara Allan, who acted as research assistant and editorial assistant, and who spent countless hours editing, cutting, pasting, deciphering hand-writing, typing and generally being supportive; Alexandra Semeniuk, who was a constant source of help and inspiration, and who assisted in editing the final manuscripts; Beverley Brady, who typed the manuscripts — including the constant changes and revisions; and Doh and Chris, who put up with me when I could not play because of my reading and writing about play.

PREFACE

This book, *In Celebration of Play*, and its companion volume, *Innovation in Play Environments*, were inspired by the Seventh World Congress of the International Playground Association,[1] held in August 1978 at Carleton University in Ottawa, Ontario, Canada.

The International Playground Association (IPA) was formed in 1961 as an interdisciplinary organization designed to exchange ideas and experiences in the realm of children's leisure and to work for the improvement of play opportunities and play leadership. It is important to emphasize that, despite the name of the association, it is not solely concerned with 'playgrounds' in the formal sense; rather, it is concerned with the wide range of play environments that are — or should be — available to children. It is recognized that play opportunities can exist for the child in and around the home (playrooms, backyards), the school and public park (traditional, adventure and creative playgrounds), the institution (day-care centres, hospitals), and the city *qua* city (the streets, museums, shopping centres). IPA is concerned with all of these environments and, in addition, with the roles that adults play in planning, designing, managing, and providing leadership for those environments.

The theme of the IPA Congress, 'Play in Human Settlements: An Integrated Approach', was directly inspired by the United Nations' Habitat Human Settlements Conference held in Vancouver, Canada in June 1976. One component of the conference was a workshop on 'Children in Human Settlements' sponsored by the Non-Governmental Forum and attended by representatives of a number of co-operating international organizations, including IPA who acted as the workshop organizers.[2] Consistent with the spirit of the United Nations' Declaration of the Rights of the Child Article 7 that 'The Child shall have full opportunity to play and recreation which should be directed to the same purpose as education. . . ' this multi-disciplinary group of experts, practitioners, and citizens concerned with the needs of children in human settlements formulated the following statement:

The child and youth population in human settlements is of prime importance. They are every nation's most valued resource. They comprise over a third of the inhabitants of this planet. Mankind owes the child the best it has to give! Fully endorsing the *UN Declaration of the Rights of the Child* with its all encompassing principles, we emphasize the following points that focus on Habitat issues:

1. Every national government should have a *policy on children* which addresses itself to their total needs and includes the mechanisms and financial resources for its implementation.
2. By 1990 every child should have access to *clean water.*
3. By 1980 every child should enjoy *clean air* through the mandatory elimination of lead in motor fuel and other air pollutants that are known to cause serious brain damage and mutilation in the young.
4. Immediate steps should be taken to ensure *adequate nutrition* for children and mothers in order to eradicate the devastating physical and mental disorders caused by malnutrition.
5. Immediate steps should be taken to reduce the effects of the *killer car.* The child's right to play and move about the community free from danger must be ensured by public transportation solutions, appropriate design and planning, and innovative redevelopment of settlements. The subordination of man to machine must be treated as a disease. This lethal epidemic must be given top priority by all levels of government.
6. The development and redevelopment of settlements must be on a more *human scale.* Children suffer most from the effects of big cities, ghettos of poverty and shanty towns. Children must grow into the Habitat at their own pace — it must be a function of planning to ensure that this happens.
7. The creation of *better balanced communities* with a mix of social groups, occupations, housing and amenities is vital. We must ensure that the total settlement is designed with the child in mind.
8. Changes in *land use policy* should include, along with the essential municipal services, the laying out of spaces for play and family recreation, as well as pedestrian routes or play paths. These should be given the same priority as other elements of infrastructure. At the time of assembling land, moneys for development of play spaces should be set aside until people have moved in and can participate in the designing — children's contributions are particularly vital.
9. *Participation* by the community, including children, in

environmental planning, building and maintenance is the key to meeting the needs of neighbourhood users of different ages, interests and handicaps.

10. *Planning consent* and *financial subsidies* should only be given to family housing composed of suitable housing types which have adequate provision for play and child safety. There is growing substantial evidence that high-rise living and inadequate play provision produce damaging physical and mental effects on children and their parents.

11. All levels of government should recognize that provision for the *out of school* life of children is as serious as formal education. Play is the child's way of learning about, adapting to, and integrating with his or her environment.

12. In addition to adequate sports and recreation facilities, children and youth need a wide variety of opportunities, choices and raw materials that they can use as they see fit for *free, constructive, creative play*.

13. The need for *leaders*, the training of leaders and the stressing of the importance of their role as facilitators for children's play, must be the concern of public authorities. People rather than hardware are what is needed.

14. Child development and environmental planning for children's play must be included in *educational programs preparing people* for all professions concerned with or affecting children in the design and planning of human settlements.

15. *Environmental education* should be an integral part of the school curriculum, to ensure that the citizens of tomorrow do not repeat the mistakes of today.

16. Problems caused by *large concentrations of children* must be dealt with positively, not by imposing additional constraints, guards, locks, etc. . . . but by supplying creative alternatives to boredom, mischief-making and outlets for plain exuberance.

17. *Bold new solutions* that reflect children's real development needs must be found through experimentation, demonstration, adaptations of successful solutions, etc. Not only sewage needs recycling! Unused, poorly designed, static play environments must be recycled into living, learning, happy places to explore.

18. *The cost* of the proposed program can be met by decreasing the current expenditure on arms by 10 per cent.

19. We wish to fully endorse the International Year of the Child. Vitally needed is an advocacy for, and a focus on, the total needs of children and youth on our planet.

The statement endorsed the 1979 International Year of the Child (IYC), which was later formally proclaimed by the United Nations in a General Assembly Resolution of the 31st Session in December 1976. Broadly speaking, IYC aims to provide an opportunity to emphasize the intellectual, psychological, social, and physical development of all children in all countries — rich as well as poor. The Year differs from other recent UN 'Years' in that there will be no UN world conference in 1979. This 'innovative' omission has been widely acclaimed by many who feel that a year-long programme of activities and contributions by people and countries throughout the world without a peak event would better serve the aim of IYC than a jamboree of national delegations. Rather, IYC will consist of a world-wide network of national activities concerning and involving children.

Already committed to holding its triennial world conference in Ottawa, Canada in 1978, IPA decided to adopt the title 'Play in Human Settlements' as the theme of the conference using many of the issues that were highlighted in the Habitat Statement as the organizing framework for the content of the conference. While some of the issues noted in the statement were only dealt with peripherally at the IPA Congress (e.g., pollution, nutrition), most of the issues became foci for papers and discussion sessions at the congress and for contributions to these volumes, including such topics as national policies for children, urban planning, housing design, community involvement in planning, non-traditional play environments, formal and non-formal educational opportunities, environmental education, and implementation strategies. The congress was to serve as IPA's contribution to the preparations for IYC.

This dedication to the aims of IYC was highlighted and reinforced by IPA's 'Malta Declaration of the Child's Right to Play', formulated at a consultation in preparation for IYC held in Malta on 11 November 1977. The declaration stated:

> The Malta Consultation declares that play, along with the basic needs of nutrition, health, shelter and education, is vital for the development of the potential of all children.
>
> The child is the foundation for the world's future.
>
> Play is not the mere passing of time. Play is life.
>
> It is instinctive. It is voluntary. It is spontaneous. It is natural. It is exploratory. It is communication. It is expression. It combines action and thought. It gives satisfaction and a feeling of achievement.

Play has occurred at all times throughout history and in all cultures. Play touches all aspects of life.

Through play the child develops physically, mentally, emotionally and socially.

Play is a means of learning to live.

The Consultation is extremely concerned by a number of alarming trends, such as:

1. Society's indifference to the importance of play.
2. The over-emphasis on academic studies in schools.
3. The dehumanising scale of settlements, inappropriate housing forms; such as high-rise, inadequate environmental planning and bad traffic management.
4. The increasing commercial exploitation of children through mass communication, mass production, leading to the deterioration of individual values and cultural tradition.
5. The inadequate preparation of children to live in a rapidly changing society.

Proposals for Action

Health. Play is essential for the physical and mental health of the child.

1. Establish programmes for professionals and parents about the benefits of play from birth onwards.
2. Incorporate play into community programmes designed to maintain the child's health.
3. Promote play as an integral part of the treatment plan for children in hospitals and other settings.
4. Provide opportunities for initiative, interaction, creativity and socialisation in the formal education system.
5. Include the study of the importance of play in the training of all professionals working with or for children.
6. Involve schools, colleges and public buildings in the life of the community and permit fuller use of these buildings and facilities.

Welfare. Play is an essential part of family and community welfare.

1. Promote measures that strengthen the close relationship between parent and child.

2. Ensure that play is accepted as an integral part of social development and social care.
3. Provide community based services of which play is a part in order to foster the acceptance of children with handicaps as full members of the community so that no child, whether for physical, mental or emotional reasons shall be detained in an institution.

Leisure. The child needs time to play.

1. Provide the space and adequate free time for children to choose and develop individual and group interests.
2. Encourage more people from different backgrounds and ages to be involved with children.
3. Stop the commercial exploitation of children's play, e.g., manipulative advertising, war toys and violence in entertainment.

Planning. The child must have priority in the planning of human settlements.

1. Give priority to the child in existing and projected human settlements in view of the child's great vulnerability, small size and limited range of activity.
2. Ban immediately the building of all high-rise housing and take urgent steps to mitigate the effect of existing developments on children.
3. Take steps to enable the child to move about the community in safety by providing traffic segregation, improved public transportation and better traffic management.

The Malta Consultation

1. believing firmly that the International Year of the Child will provide opportunities to arouse world opinion for the improvement of the life of the child,
2. affirming its belief in the United Nations' Declaration of the Rights of the Child,
3. acknowledging that each country is responsible for preparing its own courses of action in the lights of its culture, climate and social, political and economic structure,
4. recognizing that the full participation of people is essential in planning and developing programmes and services for children to meet their needs, wishes and aspirations,

5. assuring its co-operation with other international and national organizations involved with children,

Appeals to all countries and organizations to consider seriously the implementation of measures to reverse the alarming trends, some of which are identified in this statement, and to place high on its list of priorities the development of long-term programmes to ensure for all time *the child's right to play.*

These three actions — the UN Habitat Statement, the Proclamation of IYC, and the IPA Malta Declaration — were, therefore, the impetus behind 'Play in Human Settlements', the Seventh World Congress of the International Playground Association. These two volumes, *In Celebration of Play* and *Innovation in Play Environments*, are a result of that congress, with most of the papers being formal written versions of presentations made in Ottawa. It should be noted, however, that other papers were solicited by the editor to fill gaps recognized after the conference or to replace contributions from conference participants who were unable to submit formal papers. The volumes have been organized along the lines of the three sub-themes of the congress. *In Celebration of Play*, dealing with 'The Social Significance of Play', concentrates on the developmental aspects of play for the individual child and the importance of play in a social context. Topics explored include: the importance of play, development through play, leadership training, special groups, the role of play beyond the playground, and children and the future. *Innovation in Play Environments* concentrates on the planning and design of play programmes and play environments. It focuses on two of the sub-themes: 'Toward the Perfect Play Experience' deals with such topics as historical approaches to play, play in the home environment, play in institutional settings, handicapped children, planning for play in extreme climatic conditions, and play environments beyond the traditional playground; 'Urban Planning with the Child in Mind' focuses on the child and the urban environment, high-rise residential environments, and the street and the city.

In conclusion, these volumes, therefore, represent not only the personal contributions of the editors and authors to the International Year of the Child, but also the contributions of the International Playground Association, the Canadian Delegation to the International Playground Association, the Ontario Ministry of Culture and Recreation, and the Faculty of Environmental Studies, York University.

Notes

1. Membership in IPA is spread over 30 countries on six continents. In 1975, IPA was granted consultative status with the United Nations' Economic and Social Council (ECOSOC) and Category B status, 'Information and Consultative Relations' status, with the United Nations' Education, Scientific and Cultural Organization (UNESCO) in 1976.

2. The other organizations were: Organization Mondiale pour l'Education Préscolaire (OMEP), United Nations' International Children's Emergency Fund (UNICEF), World Leisure and Recreation Association (WLRA), Foundation for Social Habilitation (FSH), Save the Children Federation Community Development (SCFCD), Rehabilitation International (RI), International Catholic Child Bureau (ICCB).

INTRODUCTION

Nearly twenty-five years ago, Riesman (1954, p. 333) exhorted social scientists to 'pay more attention to play, to study blockages in play in the way that they have studied blockages in work and sexuality'. Since that time, there has been increased interest in the study of play, leisure and recreation — three terms which are often confused. Perhaps the reason for the confusion underlying the use of these terms is that each has usually been examined in the light of the focus of interest of particular disciplines or areas of expertise, including psychology, sociology, geography, education, architecture, landscape architecture and so on. In terms of children and play, rarely has an attempt been made to bring together the concerns, biases and knowledge of the various 'experts'. Because such attempts are few and far between, no strong 'lobby' or organization has come to the fore to represent the interests of *all* persons interested in children and play, and to provide to the world a justification — if that is the proper word — for the importance of play and a set of guidelines suggesting possible approaches to providing opportunities for the development of the full potential of play for all children.

There is a great deal of confusion as to the meaning of the terms 'play', 'leisure', and 'recreation'. It is not the goal of these volumes to enter into this debate — the dialectical, semantical morass is simply too deep and foreboding. Indeed, within these volumes, one may find a number of interesting and often conflicting definitions of the one term that is of particular interest here, that is, play. To end the argument, once, if not for all, the editor uses his privileged position to state that children's play is the freely chosen activity of children; while from the point of view of adults play is a means and may serve several developmental functions, play is undertaken by children as an end unto itself. Play is what children want it to be; therefore, it manifests itself in a variety of forms, including arts and crafts, games, co-operative and solitary behaviour, reading, imitation, fantasy, sports, and so on. The 'equipment required' for play ranges from such simple, common-place items as water, sand, sticks, stones, and food to animals and trees to elaborate, self-built forts and houses constructed out of scrap materials. Given the choice, children would appear to prefer materials that are parts of their everyday lives rather than the mass-produced, expensive, plastic toys and games that bombard them from the television screen. Indeed, adults are frequently dismayed to find that the expensive 'toy' is soon forgotten, to lie abandoned and often broken, in favour of the ball of string, the old wooden blocks and the home-made boat.

If play is so natural to children, why should society worry about it? Why not just let it happen? Will not children simply put what is available to good use? The answer to these questions is that play is too important — both to the individual child and to society as a whole — to let it just happen. It must be nurtured, encouraged and celebrated. Otherwise, it will suffer from benign neglect as it does today in many parts of the world — both rich and poor. An excellent justification for what they call the 'extraordinary power of play' is presented by Caplan and Caplan (1973, p. xi):

> We aim to present a hypothesis of such far-reaching implications that no parent, pediatrician, educator, sociologist, or politician can afford to ignore it. It is our intention . . . that the power of play is all-pervasive. We invite our readers to examine the power of play with us so that we might garner for child play the prestige and wholehearted public support it deserves and must have.
>
> We will set forth how play serves children, and even adults; how it can help to strengthen personality, encourage inter-personal relations, further creativity and the joy of living, and advance learning. We will trace the nature of play and playthings; how one can set the stage for creative play; how play is used to help the emotionally disturbed child; how it reveals the strengths and weaknesses of the child as well as his desires and satisfactions . . . we must take [the readers] through the various ages and stages of development in order adequately to illustrate the many basic facets of growing, learning, and living inherent in the play process.

They go on to provide a series of statements which describe the nature and importance of play:

> We believe the power of play to be extraordinary and supremely serious.
> Playtime aids growth.
> Play is a voluntary activity.
> Play offers a child freedom of action.
> Play provides an imaginary world a child can master.
> Play has elements of adventure in it.

Play provides a base for language building.
Play has unique power for building interpersonal relations.
Play offers opportunities for mastery of the physical self.
Play furthers interest and concentration.
Play is the way children investigate the material world.
Play is a way of learning adult roles.
Play is always a dynamic way of learning.
Play refines a child's judgments.
Academics can be structured into play.
Play is vitalizing.

(Caplan and Caplan, 1973, pp. xii—xvii, *passim*)

(Various papers in these two volumes, and particularly in the first volume, will elaborate on many of these points.)

In addition to the confusion created by conflicting definitions and the entrenched positions of various disciplines as noted above, there are a number of other reasons why play has not been accorded high value in today's life schema. Perhaps the most all-pervasive reason is the dichotomy between play on the one hand and work and learning on the other hand. It is interesting that this distinction can be found in virtually all parts of the world. For example, Caplan and Caplan (1973, p. xviii) note that in the United States,

> puritanical influence has dictated that play and learning are not synonymous. Play is placed at one end of the value scale, with learning and work at the other. Play and playthings have been called 'the companions of a lonely childhood', 'a way of keeping a child out of mischief', 'the discharge of a super-abundance of vital energy', 'the imitative instinct', 'the outlet for harmful impulses', and so on, in the same general vein.
>
> We have been conditioned to think of play and seriousness as antitheses. Most educators make a sharp distinction between academic work and play. . . . Few educators, even today, readily consider play as the art of learning.

Similarly, Hearn (1976—7, p. 145) notes that Marxist political thought has failed to examine the importance of play. In the Marxian perspective, and particularly in its more orthodox interpretations, the realm of freedom — the sphere of play — is contingent upon necessity. According to Marx, beyond necessity begins that development of human power, which is its own end, the true realm of freedom, which, however, can flourish only upon that realm of necessity as its basis. *The shortening* of *the working day is its fundamental premise.*[1] (Selsam and Martel, 1963, p. 269)

Hearn (1976–7, p. 145) goes on to note that, in Marxian terms, play is possible only after the productive forces have been sufficiently developed, when the time for necessary labour has been reduced:

Play as leisure, as free-time during which human capabilities are re-created, is important to the extent that it enhances the productive process. Severed from its instrumental relation to work, play tends to be regarded as inconsequential.

While Marx was apparently seeing play as being synonymous with recreation and leisure, and not speaking directly about children, the results of this philosophy and its implications for children are only too evident today. It is strange how capitalism and communism seem to have converged in theory at this point — the results for children throughout the world have often been disastrous.

This dichotomy between play and work has been carried over into the formal educational system. With the exception of recess time, the educational conspiracy seems to dictate that, after they have completed kindergarten, children are in school to learn and not to play. (Indeed, one may often conclude that the primary purpose of recess is to provide a coffee break for the teachers.)

The rigidity of the set curriculum demands that autonomy and decision-making be turned over to the authority of the teacher. Teaching replaces self-discovery, hatred of school replaces love of learning. The school supplants the environment of pre-school play — which the child can manipulate and affect — with a setting he can no longer control. School bells restrict personal research; stationary desks prevent gross motor exercise; large classes curtail freedom. Mastery of overwhelming and often unrelated subject matter replaces insightful experimenting. The reading of texts and recording of the conclusions of others are emphasized to the detriment of self-learning. The child who feels that he can no longer influence his environment soon loses interest. He ceases to be responsive to academic learning. As a result, he may often require expensive, intensive remedial attention. (Caplan and Caplan, 1973, pp. xviii–xix)

This attitude has developed largely because research has shown that the period of the most rapid increase in learning achievement and growth in certain personality traits occurs before the age of eight. On the other hand, there is no definitive research on the effects of play on the educative process. (There is research on the influence of play on monkeys, rodents, and dogs, but the lack of funds available for research on play and humans seems to indicate a rather strange set of priorities.) One need only examine the curriculum of teacher-training institutions and see the lack of instruction on play and play leadership given to teachers to understand why little attempt has been made to break out of this vicious circle.

The argument presented above applies largely to the developed nations of the world. In Third World countries, it is usually not a matter of political, educational or social development philosophy that has resulted in the lack of emphasis on the provision of play opportunities; it is simply economics. Many countries are so poor that they are forced to concentrate on the provision of the basic necessities such as food, shelter, and health. Play is simply not an issue for many countries. (Unfortunately, this state of affairs often results despite massive expenditures on such anti-human goods as military hardware by many 'poor' countries.)

This lack of money for play and recreation opportunities is not, however, limited solely to the Third World. In these times of inflation and economic uncertainty, most public agencies in the developed countries are sorely pressed for funds. They are constantly being required to justify programmes or facilities. One common result is that they are in effect forced into reinforcing their dependence on activities which have been traditionally successful (e.g., the Canadian penchant for ice hockey for young males). Quite simply, the economics of government do not encourage innovation. (This view is compounded by the complication, because of their very nature, that bureaucracies are rarely innovative.) The problem is more severe for play and recreation facilities and programmes than for other government services (e.g., sewers, transportation) because play and recreation do not lend themselves to cost-benefit analysis.

Because of inflation, increasing taxes, high rates of unemployment, energy shortages, and other assorted crises, it must be apparent to most planners and decision makers that the rules of the game of life are being changed. The phrase 'being changed' seems more appropriate than 'changing' because often the people directly involved in the changes have had no input into the process; the power of external forces is increasing. The implications of such a trend on the provision of social services — including the leisure services delivery system — are potentially great. The impacts are quite evident today. In the face of not-unexpected opposition to rapidly rising taxes, government agencies are drastically cutting back on expenditures on leisure services and even beginning to question the social value of existing services. For example, the Honourable D'Arcy McKeough (former Ontario Minister of Treasury, Economics and Intergovernmental Affairs) recently publicly questioned whether or not the Province of Ontario has devoted too much money to the acquisition of land for public recreation purposes. On another level, the parkland acquisition component of the budget of the Department of Parks and Recreation of the City of Toronto has lost ground to inflation over the last ten years. (More money is spent on replacing worn sidewalks in Toronto than is spent on acquiring new parkland.) But then, perhaps they are correct: what is needed is not *more* parkland, but a higher *quality* of recreation and play opportunities.

Planners and decision makers must recognize that the age of the 'Conserver Society' is imminent if it has not already arrived. In order to maintain the present level of services — to say nothing of increasing the level of services — it will be necessary to re-evaluate completely the present array of available resources and examine potential new resources. Quite simply, the probability is fairly high that recreation agencies, in the face of stiff competition from other social service agencies for a share of a finite resource base, will be forced to do more with less. Such a conclusion is reinforced by the following comment in a recent study of the attitudes of elected municipal officials in the Canadian Province of Ontario toward culture and recreation (Zuzanek, 1977, p. 8):

Generally, the survey revealed rather favourable attitudes of elected municipal officials toward culture and recreation, but when it comes down to decision-making, it appears that the support of culture and recreation is weighed against other social needs which are often perceived as more pressing.

Another major factor is that there is no identifiable profession which can be termed 'play planning' and no body of knowledge which can universally be defined as a 'theory of play'.[2] As a result, planning for play is usually done by professionals from collateral disciplines (urban planning, landscape architecture, social work, etc.). Often their knowledge of play is minimal. When people with an educational background in play are involved, their expertise is usually in the area of programming or research, not planning or design. Given the absence of a recognizable profession of play planning, it would appear appropriate to suggest that the only viable approach to play planning is either (a) an interdisciplinary team or (b) a person with an interdisciplinary education. The problems with the former are manifold, including the difficulty of working as a team and high cost. The problem with the latter is the rarity of such individuals (largely because of the small number of educational institutions that encourage interdisciplinary education and the difficulty involved in mastering and synthesizing all of the necessary fields of study).

Although the following quotation deals specifically with preschool children, it can be argued that its philosophy can be applied equally well to all children:

> Infants, toddlers and preschoolers are a vulnerable group with few past experiences to use as guides for dealing with their constantly expanding world. As well, they are in a period when the physical, mental and emotional patterns are formed which will ultimately influence their behaviour in later years. As such, they need an environment that nurtures, but does not frustrate, their total development. So precious and precarious is our charge as adults, that we must take seriously our responsibility of providing preschoolers with opportunities for healthy growth and learning through play that will give them satisfaction, a sense of competence and the joy of creativity. (Central Mortgage and Housing Corporation, 1976, p. 3)

Adults in general and public agencies in particular have a duty to provide constructive, creative play opportunities for children; out of necessity, they must be innovative. Such a duty has been emphasized in the United Nations Declaration of the Rights of the Child and at the United Nations Habitat Conference held in Vancouver in 1976. Despite the almost universal lip-service that is paid to this duty, Hill (1972, p. 1) notes that

> There is no country in the world, I truly believe, that has given proper priority to the needs of children in the modern city environment, in spite of the fact that the children comprise over 40 per cent of the population and are the biggest potential assets of any country. . . .

All the material gleaned from studies around the world cry out for designed, researched and legislated schemes of a positive, comprehensive nature, which have as their aim to enrich and stimulate the life of the young in mind, body and creative ability, thus preventing the ills that later need expensive remedies or soul destroying custodial care.

The normal child is still in the majority, thank God, but it is the normal child that is most neglected.

She goes on to say that the reason for this short-sighted policy is that the child is not the paying client: the child has no power, political or financial, and no protest voice. The responsibility, therefore, must lie with adults; however, individuals are usually disorganized, unrecognized, and often divided. Public agencies dealing with children, therefore, must accept a large proportion of the responsibility.

It would appear that, nominally at least, many public agencies have accepted their duty. One has only to examine the annual reports of such agencies to see the colourful maps that list all of the parks and playgrounds. Research, however, into the use of urban parks, for example, has shown that the basic characteristic of such facilities is non-use (e.g., Gold, 1972). Two questions arise, the answers to which are closely intertwined: where do the children play; and why do they not play in the parks and playgrounds? The answer is that the children are playing everywhere — in their houses and private yards, on the streets, in vacant lots, in any area that even remotely resembles a 'natural' environment. In other words, they are playing in those environments which have all of the characteristics that most traditional parks and playgrounds do not have: complexity, variety, challenge, risk, flexibility, adaptability, etc. Quite simply, most traditional parks and playgrounds are boring for children. If they do use them, they spend most of their time playing in sandboxes and wading pools — i.e., those elements of the playground which have many of the characteristics noted above — or interacting with other children. The playground equipment is usually ignored, quickly abandoned, or merely incidental to the play experiences.

A basic reason for the continued dependence of most recreation agencies on traditional playgrounds with their static metal apparatus usually encased in asphalt or concrete is simply tradition. Another reason is the lack of sophisticated planning and design skills and a true understanding of the needs of children, characteristics which are particularly common for poorer countries. It would appear, however, that the basic reason is fear — fear on the part of planners and decision makers (especially politicians) that playgrounds are dangerous. They choose traditional playgrounds because they perceive that they are less dangerous than creative or adventure playgrounds. In fact, however, there is strong evidence that the number of accidents and fatalities occurring as a result of the use of playground equipment has been greatly exaggerated. Children do get hurt on playground equipment, but then they can get hurt in many different places and in many different ways. In addition, there is some evidence to suggest that adventure and creative playgrounds are no more dangerous than traditional playgrounds (Wilkinson and Lockhart, 1976). Municipal recreation agencies should be encouraged to go beyond the traditional playground. As Lady Allen of Hurtwood (1968, p. 17) has stated,

It is a rewarding experience for children to take and overcome risks, and to learn to use lethal tools with safety. Life demands courage, endurance and strength, but we continue to underestimate the capacity of children for taking risks, enjoying the stimulation of danger and finding things out for themselves. It is often difficult to permit children to take risks, but over-concern prevents them from growing up. This is all too clearly seen in the dull, 'safe' playgrounds that continue to be devised.

A *creative playground* — which appears to be a North American phenomenon — is a formal playground characterized by apparatus that is designed and created from materials which are more 'natural' (e.g., wood, stone, brick, hills). It is 'creative' in the sense of using more natural materials while at the same time attempting to offer a wider choice and range of alternatives by means of more abstract design. Canadian cities now abound with creative playgrounds, but the problem is that in many cases they are mere transformations of traditional playgrounds, with wood being substituted for metal. It is often painfully obvious that there has been a lack of skilled planning and design.

Adventure playgrounds have often been labelled 'junk' playgrounds, in which children under supervision of trained play leaders are given the opportunity to take part in a variety of self-directed activities (e.g., constructing huts and forts using materials and tools provided at the playground, lighting fires and cooking, camping, keeping animals). Adventure playgrounds are not a recent invention. In 1943 the 'Emdrup Junk Playground' was opened in German-occupied Copenhagen. Now adventure playgrounds are widespread throughout Europe and Great Britain. Despite relatively extensive publicity, however, they have gained little acceptance in North America.

An even more interesting and innovative concept is that of the *playpark*, an integrated complex of activities and facilities which often includes an adventure playground, music and theatre programmes, the planting of fruits and vegetables, sports, outings, the keeping of animals, etc. Such playparks would require a fairly large area (approximately 7,500 m^2) and a year-round trained staff. In 1972, there were 157 such 'parkleken' in Stockholm, usually located adjacent to a residential complex. It would appear that such playparks have not spread beyond Scandinavia.

The above comments apply to both established and new parks and playgrounds. One other area of concern, however, should be noted. With the proliferation of high-rise residential areas and the development of new towns in Canada and many other countries, it would seem essential that research take place into the nature of the leisure service delivery system for such areas. The needs of children in such areas are different from those of children in older, single-family dwelling areas.

One could argue, however, that such facilities as creative or adventure playgrounds and playparks are merely marginal innovations, rather than substantive innovations. Chevalier *et al.* (1974) describe marginal innovation in terms of the management of established trends, which by definition means the reinforcement of the established pattern of interests. Substantial innovation is in terms of the management of new trends, which by definition means a realignment of interests. In effect, the first is within the existing institutional structure and the second is part of structural change.

> Marginal innovation and its consequent reinforcement of interests is a frequent occurrence — a matter of small-scale adjustment to the existing technology or organization of the system. And marginal innovation and reinforcement of interests can also result from the application of advanced technology. In fact, the application of new and highly advanced technology can cut down the possibility of substantial innovation by doing the old job just a little bit better — by making possible a marginal innovation, albeit often at much higher cost. Paradoxically, the higher cost can also have the tendency of reinforcing present interests.
>
> Neither marginal nor substantial innovation, then, is dependent solely on established or new technology, on one hand, or

institutional arrangements on the other. Each is derived from some appropriate new technological—institutional relationship or capacity. This is particularly true in relation to the incorporation of an environmental imperative into technological inventions and its adoption through environmental management procedures. (Chevalier *et al.*, 1974, p. 6)

It can be seen, therefore, that, except at a very basic level (i.e., established interests versus new trends), there is no simple, hard and fast distinction between marginal and substantive innovation. A further complication occurs when more than one decision-making unit is being discussed. For example, what is marginally innovative for one country (e.g., the extension of the concept of adventure playgrounds into playparks in Sweden) may be substantially innovative for another. Marginal innovation, then, is fine-tuning of an existing situation, without comment as to the present 'quality' of that situation. Substantial innovation is the creation of a new situation, which, it is hoped, is an improvement on the present situation.

Many countries — or, at least, parts of many countries — do already have a child-support system which goes a long way towards providing adequate play opportunities for all children. Such systems require only marginal innovation. Examples might include increased emphasis on play in hospitals; greater use of music, drama, games, arts and crafts; play training programmes for parents; etc. Other countries — and parts of even the 'richest' countries — have child-support systems which are woefully inadequate. They require substantial innovation. Examples might include teacher and play leader training; the provision of basic play opportunities; etc.

It is the purpose of these volumes to provide knowledge and incentive to planners, designers, researchers, politicians, parents, and others involved with the upbringing of children that can lead to (1) increased awareness of the importance of play and (2) innovation — whether that be marginal or substantial innovation — in the provision of play opportunities within the context of their own culture. It must be noted that no hard-and-fast solutions, no definitive answers, no concrete plans or programmes are provided here, as each situation must be treated as being unique. Rather, a number of suggestions and possible alternative approaches are put forward which, with careful thought and research, may be applicable to other settings.

Finally, it must be repeated that the push for innovation rarely begins within an institution; it usually comes from an external force.

Quite simply, a lack of access to the planning and decision-making process is characteristic of most public agencies dealing with children. There are two broad levels on which public involvement is required. At the national or regional level, the public should be able to participate in the development of broad goals and objectives for their country or region as a whole. (This can be accomplished through the formulation of a national plan for child development.) At the local level, the public should have an opportunity to become involved in issues in the locality or neighbourhood. Such a process assumes an accurate data base of information on the supply of existing services by the recreation agencies and other agencies, on the nature of the population and its sub-populations, and the nature of their leisure patterns and requirements. It also requires means by which an interested and involved public can participate in decision making about their children and their future.

Notes

1. Emphasis added.
2. Even the work of Piaget is neither universally accepted nor widely known beyond the realm of development psychology. To prove this latter point, try asking a park planner or playground designer about Piaget.

References

Allen of Hurtwood, Lady Marjory. 1968. *Planning for Play*. London: Thames and Hudson.
Caplan, Frank and Theresa Caplan. 1973. *The Power of Play*. Garden City, New York: Anchor Books.
Central Mortgage and Housing Corporation. 1976. *Play Spaces for Preschoolers*. Ottawa: Central Mortgage and Housing Corporation.
Chevalier, Michel, David Morley and Don MacKay. 1974. 'Innovation in environmental management'. A working paper prepared for the Canadian Council for University Research on the Environment, Annual Meeting, Toronto, 27–8 May.
Gold, Seymour. 1972. *Urban Recreation Planning*. Philadelphia: Lea and Febiger.
Hearn, Francis. 1976–7. 'Towards a critical theory of play', *Telos*, 30, Winter, pp. 145–60.
Hill, Polly. 1972. *An Overview of the Needs of Children and Youth in the Urban Community*. Ottawa: Central Mortgage and Housing Corporation.
Riesman, David. 1954. *Individualism Reconsidered*. Glencoe, Illinois: Free Press.
Selsam, H. and H. Martel (eds). 1963. *Reader in Marxist Philosophy*. New York: International Publishers.
Wilkinson, Paul and Robert Lockhart. 1976. *Safety in Children's Formal Play Environments*. Toronto: Ontario Ministry of Culture and Recreation.
Zuzanek, Jiri. 1977. 'Attitudes of elected municipal officials toward culture and recreation', *Recreation Research Review*, 5, 3, pp. 7–11.

1 PLAY IN HUMAN SETTLEMENTS: AN INTEGRATED APPROACH

Ethel Bauzer Medeiros

This book gives reassuring evidence of the continuance of concerted international efforts to promote play in human settlements. It is a significant follow-up to the advance accomplished at the United Nations Conference on Human Settlements, when 'leisure and recreation' were extracted from the vague heading of 'Other social services . . . essential to communities', to be granted separate attention. But even as UN Recommendation C.18 was adopted, the necessity for being unrelenting in our crusade pressed upon all, since we realized, with the Portuguese poet Fernando Pessoa (1913), that 'the day never breaks for those who lean their heads on the breast of dreamed hours'.[1] This book proves this determination and, above all, it demonstrates a solidarity which ignores borders, elevating our hopes for a more humane mankind.

Although play has been a constant dimension of all cultures throughout history and, in our too quickly changing society at present, is amounting to an element of survival, queries about its value continue to be raised. 'Why worry about play when communities both in developing and developed countries are still in the throes of grave problems of health, nutrition, housing, employment, and education?' 'What does play signify to men that makes it deserving of such solicitude?' 'Would so much care not appertain only to the quixotic inhabitants of nowhere?' 'Granting that play is a major natural part of human life, why interfere with its spontaneity by planning and providing for it? Would that not be contradictory?' Briefly, the chronic charges against play are: with regard to the scale of social values, it is not regarded with enough seriousness; in relation to thinking, it is based on utopian ideas; and in reference to practice, it is an exercise in paradox. Merely in the affective domain might play advocates be condoned, owing to their enthusiasm (the term taken in its original sense of 'divine inspiration').

Some support, nevertheless, is won when the focus is put on children, since they play anyhow, even in sickness or poverty. Such endorsement also appears appropriate in a society which purports to be child-loving. In addition, people admit, some physical facilities for their play keep the young out of the path of the ever-diligent adults, thereby allowing

the latter more time to enlarge the Gross National Product . . .
Furthermore, in large centres, play-lots introduce fresh air, sun and
glimpses of broader horizons to high-rise dwellers, counterbalancing
their ever-increasing artificial environment. Such facilities supply
entertaining pastimes and healthy exercise to children, thus hastening
their blooming into hard-working citizens (who indisputably personify
their ideal). In the inner city, in peripheral slums, and in concentrations
of migrant populations, vandal-proof equipment (paternally sprinkled
about) may encourage better social interaction and deter delinquency.
Disadvantaged youth will thus be initiated into social rules and roles, a
turning-point in their enculturation to the adult's 'model' world. Such
images of play might explain its lesser rank in the adults' common order
of priorities.

These ever-recurring contentions will be re-examined in this book,
taking advantage of the richly diverse backgrounds of the authors — a
team of notable experts from various fields, who also compose a
multicultural group. It will hopefully instigate a re-evaluation of the
coherence between practices and professed aims. While so doing,
however, the fundamental questions of who we human beings are and
what our purpose in life is shall eventually be touched. This risky
venture, nevertheless, appears essential, seeing that more cogent
arguments are needed for society to invest time, energy and funds in
play.

Coming from Brazil (one of the so-called developing countries), mine
is a long experience of trying to make the best out of limited means. It
further includes coping daily with sharply contrasting modes of life,
from the traditional relaxed and sometimes patriarchal agrarian ways to
the urban-industrial style of the wheel-borne hurried masses of
consumers. This very predicament, however, facilitates insight into
man's urges. On the one hand, severe restrictions impose a most
thoughtful ordering of priorities: each choice demands cautious
weighing of the renunciations it exacts. On the other hand, actual
participation in diverse systems favours a more objective assessment of
human pursuits: personally experienced contrasts highlight ever-present
cravings.

Of late, these basic drives are surfacing more clearly, as fast planes
and sturdy trucks overcome the last physical distances, brusquely
bringing close together disparate cultures. Meanwhile, truly two-way
telecommunication brings into our very homes the behaviours,
judgements and beliefs of all sorts of people. Under such magnifying
lenses, man's deeper aspirations seem easier to discern. In addition, as

far-reaching transportation and communication means spread to more people and heighten in others the awareness of the technological gap, feelings of deprivation are enhanced and the strongest longing voiced. When vaguely felt needs grow so intense that they develop into demands, massive co-ordination of available resources is claimed to make them function as adequate supplies. Out of this process fundamental motives emerge. Among them stands out self-expression (namely the outlet of inner-pressing thoughts and sentiments) which would seem to rank near food and shelter. Despite the fact that our time-budget studies are just beginning, it is obvious that people do not wait to grow flowers until they have all their vegetables. Also, even in areas where temperatures might exceed 39°C (102°F), television sets outnumber refrigerators, though both cost about the same (antennae sprouting on most rooftops, including slums). Man seems to want more out of life than a purposeless, stultifying, day-to-day struggle to remain alive, which would reduce him to 'a postponed corpse that procreates', in the words of the Brazilian poet Carlos Drummond de Andrade.[2]

Empty, machine-like hours, devoid of an ultimate concern, threaten man's self-concept, the core of his personality, his most precious trait, the fundamental quality which sets him apart from the other nearly two million species on earth. The respect that he owes to himself and that he demands from others, the inherent dignity of his human condition, appears incompatible with meaningless activity. Even in the remotest past, when mass production and automation had not yet so curtailed work satisfactions, senseless occupation equalled punishment. The Greek mythology relates how, after his death, Sisyphus, the cruel king of Corinth, was condemned to keep rolling a huge stone up a hill, merely to see it fall back and have to start anew. Modern urban life reminds Camus (1942) of such penance, and he rejoices when man rebels against it:

> Get up, streetcar, four hours at the office or factory, eat, streetcar, four hours of work, eat, sleep, and Monday, Tuesday, Wednesday, Thursday, Friday, and Saturday with the same rhythm . . . But one day the *why* arises, and everything begins with this fatigue coloured by surprise. . .[3]

Instead of bewailing such grim reality, man can refuse to surrender to hopeless servitude and rally the courage to review his existence. At that, he perceives how many loci of control lie in his own hands, and rises to fulfil the duties commensurate with the rights of belonging to the human race. Not mistaking a worthy life for an apathetic or a plaintive resignation to 'destiny', he uses the privilege of his 'conditioned freedom' (as Merleau-Ponty designates it) to shape the thread of his own life. Though he cannot choose his spinning-wheel and must reconcile himself to the material he is able to secure, he may select the patterns with which to weave his identity.

Unsubmissive to the modern golden calf of technology, he distinguishes between *having* more and *being* more humane (Marcel, 1968).[4] He discriminates labour from work, noticing that the first never ends and leaves no trace of itself as it barely provides for survival, while the second yields permanent (and so, reassuring) results. But along with Arendt (1958), he sees that man's noblest sphere lies in action, served by facts and words. In such area, labour skills or tangible work products are not relevant, for man reveals himself through his acts, as he thinks, wills and judges while relating to others. To this view, I would add that as he ascends from mere subsisting (by ceaseless toil) to existing (on the rewards of his work), and from there to co-existing (in constructive interpersonal relations), he deepens his appreciation of the role of self-expression. Along such upgrowth, play, a satisfying mode of achieving self-expression, mounts in importance to him, irrespective of his age and of the state of development of his society.

Would he wish to delve into the matter, play's impact at the biological level would strike him. Defining health as does the World Health Organization — a state of complete well-being, and not mere absence of disease — he would perceive how play functions, at its very least, as a wholesome activity, for its voluntary engagement of total man. Its physical, mental, social and spiritual benefits can then vindicate play's promotion by any society, regardless of the respective stage of development. More than that, in this swiftly changing age, play fosters health as it helps man deal with the demands posed by incessant environmental modifications. Not to linger on stress, let us just think of health as an expression of fitness to the total milieu. Any alteration of the ecosystem then summons from man new adaptive reactions, which if inadequate entail disease, organic or psychotic. The endless mutations of our times ask successive (and trying) readjustments which endanger man's health. He has 'to keep running simply to remain in the same place', at a forced pace that makes it ever harder for him to balance the intake of tranquillizers and energizers. A French saying underlines such instability, warning that 'good health is a provisional state that heralds no good tidings'.[5] Creative play, inasmuch as it allows man to transform given reality in terms of the demands he places on it (giving him freedom temporarily to modify his surroundings), contributes to man's fundamental ability to cope with unpredictable changes. Furthermore, because some amount of tension and risk seems essential to full growth (Dubos, 1959), play instigates development, as it joyfully offers such conditions. Instead of yielding to daily strains and stresses in Thoreau's 'quiet desperation', man can discover that life may be a chosen adventure, and elect to employ his store of adaptive energies in goal-seeking activites. A life devoted to protection against threats, concentrated on security, lacks the healthy creative qualities found in chosen pursuits. Researchers have shown that even rate, when domesticated, are less capable of withstanding difficulties. Comfort-loving, passive rats — or men — might not then be the most likely to succeed in our competitive society. If work is so regulated that it does not offer much chance for creative activities, leisure hours (perhaps man's only real possession on earth) seem a unique occasion for them. Shunning the evasion provided by mere diversions, man might turn to re-creation and derive the joys of real participation, with its repercussions on his mental growth through happy achievements and increased self-respect. Play would then mean an important factor in survival.

Turning now to the social plane, man observes how play can act as a catalyst of group cohesion — a critical issue in this divided world, where an alarming population explosion multiplies hardships and sharpens competition for finite resources. Crowds so stifle men that they search for privacy, cloistering themselves in what they significantly name apart-ments. There, however, loneliness preys upon them. Painstakingly erecting barriers among themselves, men then deplore indifference. But ignoring all these obstacles, play functions as a *lingua franca*, our last one perhaps in this age of specialists, each with his own outlook and terminology, and more eager than the next to improve on the curse of Babel ('that they may not understand one another's speech'). Play creates a common bond, reminiscent of that found in ancient magical rites, when music, dance, drama, and poetry united men as they looked for loftier realms. Through superb self-control, they rose above petty material concerns, to liberate their innermost powers and contact spiritual beings. One of the oldest texts from India, the Puranas, describes how the Lord created the universe by dancing to the sound of tambours. Then, Shiva Nataraja and his consort, Parvati, taught people how yoga and dance could help them communicate with supernatural powers and feel linked to their Creator. An ancient Hindu manual advises: 'the dancing foot, the sound of tinkling bells, the songs that are sung, and the varying steps. . . , find out these within yourself, then shall your fetters fall away.'

As societies grow in complexity, however, man's basic problems change their focus. If, in the past, control of physical environment was pre-eminent, now that technology dominates the world to an incredible degree, human relations hold the greatest difficulty. Travellers boarding a plane trust its turbines but fear their fellow passengers. Social responsibility has long left the province of alternatives posed to individuals to enter the field of survival.

Leisure, too, as it expands and reaches more people, overlaps personal or even local planes, to integrate social welfare concerns. There it deserves special attention, for it depends on the thorny exercise of freedom. Society should then cater to it, irrespective of its stage of development. The less participating its members, however, the more threatened its solidarity, its traditions, and its further generation of culture. Public support of free-time pursuits would then be rewarding, indeed.

For those obsessed with cost/benefit analyses, additional advantages should be pointed out, particularly in developing countries. Among them is the meagreness of material requirements for play as compared with play's high returns in jobs (found in the manufacture and trade of goods used in play's 'non-productive' activities and in correlated services). There is also the further enlargement of employment opportunities for those for whom play would help improve non-academic skills (such as skills associated with the right hemisphere of the brain). In the early years, stimulating play might reduce the losses incurred through school failures and drop-outs, and the probably related deficient cognitive abilities. Most of all, play's relationship to creativity bears on leadership training and on the development of local know-how, both decisive factors in adapting transferred technology and in advancing towards technological autonomy.

Going beyond biological, mental, and socio-economic domains, to look into culture as an expression of humanity, man would apprehend play's part in it. The universal values which creative play can nurture, as it draws from man's very essence, would amply justify international concern. In times when most beliefs are under attack, when continual change and mass production menace man's feelings of identity, when vandalism, drugs and violence taint even schools, when a few individuals can terrorize entire nations, any contribution to humanistic goals merits high priority. Not to dwell on McLuhan's global village, let us just underscore that, in this increasingly interdependent world, John

Donne's far-sighted warning never to suppose that the bell might be tolling for anyone else has become a platitude. World-scale collaboration is now imperative — if not out of noble sentiments, then purely out of a lucid appraisal of reality. The energy crisis has prompted men to revert to the forces of sun and wind. The humanity crisis might hopefully lead them to rediscover play's potentialities.

Once reinstated in the dignity of human condition, mankind would realize that its best resources are children, and would dedicate itself to them as assiduously as it does to others. Mankind will approach childhood not as an impatient preparation for the future, but as a unique developmental stage with its own cultural patterns, values and needs, to be tended and fostered during its very unfolding. For such ends, man will find abundant research and printed material (as, for example, the interesting iconographic study of Ariès (1960)). Arguing that in the far past the child was a chattel of the family and now is said to be at its heart, Ariès followed through the child's gradual alterations in appearance, clothes, games, and relative placing in family portraits. Starting at the twelfth century, when the child was 'a miniature adult' (dressing and frolicking like the grown-ups since it 'did not count' — as Molière informs us in *Le malade imaginaire*), the French sociologist traced changes up to present times, when the young wear special garments, have their own games, and hold the centre of modern photographs.

Having learned about the growing importance of the child — as a concept — man might ask why the word 'child' continues to be neutral. But if he further inquired into the life of actual children, perplexity would overwhelm him. At home, the smallest chamber is for them, much more space being devoted to the garage and to that compartment named living-room. There, however, children are not very welcome — only being suffered as visitors. Owning colourful toys (ready-bought, naturally), they scarcely know how to play nor are they stimulated to try, lest their clatter disturb too close neighbours (barely protected by paper-thin walls). Mechanical and electronic buttons experts, children act as 'play illiterates', never having learned the old songs and games, nor finding place for them now. Unimaginative, precocious consumers, their days are filled by a succession of images and echoes of other people's first-hand experiences. In large cities, their environment is further impoverished, being devoid of greenery, birds and stars. The moon only noticed as mirrored on rain puddles might symbolize their vicarious life. Those who grow up in high-rise buildings see most things through a disturbing dimension that dwarfs all. Such children are even

more dependent than others on adults' willingness to take them to play
or to let them go down alone, for the streets are dangerous. Fittingly,
larger areas are being given over to automobiles, better to speed the race
between birth and death that some call life. Heartbeats set to the clock,
their parents seldom find time (or patience) to listen to them. Such are
the models offered by grown-ups. Worse than material poverty is such
emotional deprivation, and those who keep silent about it are its
accomplices.

Would man but turn to trivia — like children's bruises — the
enormous numbers of children's non-accidental injuries would shock
him. Severe enough to demand medical treatment, and often to cause
death, they range from cigarette burns to brain concussion. Mostly
inflicted by child guardians (parents included), the incidence is high all
over the world, particularly in infants. First suspected in print thirty
years ago by an American radiologist (Caffey, 1946) who was disturbed
by repeated fractures in the same babies, statistics so mounted that by
1962 they were incorporated into medical dictionaries under the
appalling entry of 'Syndrome of the battered child' (Silverman and
Kempe, 1962).

Observing further child abuse and neglect (frequent enough to
justify, in 1978, a new special journal), it might occur to man that a
more hopeful name for 1979 could be 'The International Year of the
Child's Guardian'. Not a mere substitution of label, it would displace
the accent from the most helpless of beings to those on whom they
entirely depend. Guardians thus set as the target, advertising and
marketing experts could be asked for assistance in disseminating
updated information on play's benefits to all ages and to all societies.
Differently encoding messages according to each group's interests, and
using mass media, we could be listened to and perhaps compete with
commercial amusements. After self-centred adults were persuaded of
the values of creative play to themselves, its particular importance to
the early formative years would be emphasized. Among other
advantages, parents could be shown how play improves competence to
deal with self and environment (thus ridding them of some annoying
tasks. . .).

Our primary goal, however, would lie in the affective arena. As self-
appointed play and children's *ombudsmen*, we would concentrate on
moving guardians, both in the sense of instigating their action and of
touching their hearts, inflaming their emotions. We would hopefully
also attract youth to discover the joy of service to others. The voice of
children, the main clientele, would be listened to, and 'child to child'

programmes would be strengthened. Play's visibility would then increase, and with it its critical atmosphere of social support. Early in the process, the emotional touch of the arts would be enlisted — as it is now, with poetry. Margareth Avison (1960) reminds us that we can recreate our world:

Nobody stuffs the world in at your eyes
The optic heart must venture: a jail-break and recreation. . .
[Things] are desolate toys if the soul's gates seal, and cannot bear,
　　must shudder under, creation's unseen freight.

Saint-Denys Garneau (1937) leads us to those who use their imagination:

Ne me dérangez pas je suis profondément occupé
Un enfant est en train de bâtir un village.
C'est une ville, un comté et qui sait tantôt l'univers.
Il joue.
Ces cubes de bois sont des maisons qu'il déplace et des chateaux
[. . .] Ce ne'est pas peu de savoir où va tourner la route de cartes
Cela pourrait changer complètement le cours de la rivière
A cause du pont [. . .]
Joie de jouer! paradis des libertés! . . .
[. . .] Tout le monde peut voir une piastre de papier vert
Mais qui peut voir au travers si ce n'est un enfant
Qui peut comme lui voir au travers en toute liberté
Sans que du tout la piastre l'empêche ni ses limites
Ni sa valeur d'une seule piastre.

Notes

1. 'O dia nunca raia para quem encosta a cabeça no seio das horas sonhadas.'
2. 'Um cadáver adiado que procria.'
3. 'Lever, tramway, quatre heures de bureau ou d'usine, repas, tramway, quatre heures de travail, repas, sommeil, et lundi, mardi, mercredi, jeudi, vendredi, et samedi sur le même rhythm . . . Un jour seulement le *pourquoi* s'élève et tout commence dans cette lassitude hantée d'étonnement. . .'
4. 'Au fond tout se ramène à la distinction entre ce qu'on a et ce qu'on est.'
5. 'La bonne santé c'est un état provisoire qui n'annonce rien de bon.'

40   *Play in Human Settlements*

References

Arendt, Hannah. 1958. *The human condition*. Chicago: Chicago University Press.
Ariès, Philippe, 1960. *L'enfant et la famille sous l'ancien régime*. Paris: Librairie Plon. (English translation. 1962. *Centuries of Childhood: A Social History of Family Life*. New York: Alfred A. Knopf.)
Avison, Margareth. 1960. 'Snow', in Robert Weaver and William Toye (eds), 1973. *The Oxford Anthology of Canadian Literature*. Oxford: Oxford University Press, p. 15.
Caffey, John. 1946. 'Multiple fractures in long bones of children suffering from chronic subdural hematomas', *American Journal of Roentgenology and Radiology Therapy*, 56, pp. 163–73.
Camus, Albert. 1942. *Le mythe de Sisyphe*. Paris: Gallimard.
Dubos, René J. 1959. 'Medical utopias', *Journal of the American Academy of Arts and Sciences, Daedalus*, 88, 3, pp. 410–24.
Garneau, Saint-Denys. 1937. 'Jeu', in *Regards et jeux dans l'espace*. Montréal: Fides.
Marcel, Gabriel. 1968. *Etre et avoir: journal metaphysique (1928–1933) Tome I*. Paris: Aubier-Montaigne.
Pessoa, Fernando. 1913. 'O marinheiro', in *O eu profundo e os outros eus; seleçao poética*. 1972. São Paulo: Biblioteca Manancial, p. 119.
Silverman, F. N. and C. H. Kempe. 1962. 'The battered child syndrome', *Journal of the American Medical Association*, 181, pp. 17–24.

Part One

THE IMPORTANCE OF PLAY

2 PLAY AND EARLY CHILDHOOD

Otto Weininger

Introduction

Since the time of Plato educators and philosophers have pointed to the necessity of including play in the educational opportunities provided for young children. The value of play has been summarized by Sapora and Mitchell (1961) as 'proportionate to its power to interest the player, absorb his attention, and arouse him to enthusiastic and persistent activity'. The works of Piaget (1951, 1952) have explicated how the child attains knowledge by means of active construction and activity. Because the activity of the child is play, the most natural and most efficient way for a child to acquire competency in any curricular area is through activity and play.

Prior to coming to school, the young child has played at home for five to six years. Out of his self-chosen pursuits, he has acquired a series of physical, socio-emotional and language competencies. By analysing the way these were developed through play skills and abilities, those who are involved in the education of the young can see how the school curriculum may best continue these natural, exploratory modes of learning and inquiry.

Young children between birth and school age play to their heart's content at home. At first, in infancy, they play with their sight: they observe, watch, discriminate patterns, shapes and people. This is done in an exploratory way, and children are usually not pushed to perform this activity faster or better, nor are they told that they are not seeing things correctly, nor to 'see it this or that way'. A period of time lapses during which the consolation is in saying that the infant is a 'neuropsychologically immature organism' and so he or she is given the time to explore and play with the sense of sight. Even when the infant reaches the level of discriminating between mother and father, he is allowed to continue to play and is helped to play at different kinds of activities by enriching and changing the environment, usually when he is ready for such changes. Print is added to the wall, a trinket to the mobile that is hanging above the bed, or a plastic bottle and clothes pegs of different colours are provided for him to play with. As the child is involved in these activities, he or she shows changes in co-ordination and exercises responses over and over again. We watch the young child pass his hands over his eyes, play with his fingers, maybe even suck them, pull off his socks, play with his toes; turn his head, roll on his side; turn over. The child is not only encouraged, but usually indulged in this play. It is believed that the growth and development of infants are dependent upon play. Play is a learning process through which infants learn about themselves and what they can do. Growth should go along naturally but, unless activity continues, a general dampening and slowness will start to make its appearance in the child's response to environmental stimuli.

Studies of a baby's exploratory play during the first year of life show it to be not merely random behaviour; the playing baby develops the rudiments of directedness, selectivity and persistence (Murphy, 1969; Piaget, 1952). Babies do this as they seek out many opportunities to investigate their total surroundings and find many different kinds of material with which to play. Through baby play, which seems to be mainly a manifestation of curiosity drives (Harlow, 1973), the foundation is laid for later emergence of logical thinking, creative behaviour, and abstract problem solving.

For very young children, all activity is play, and from all play they learn. The desire to play, the absorption in play, and the concentration in play activity are signs of a healthy child. The child who does not play is a child who needs to be encouraged and stimulated.

In 1960 at the Nebraska Symposium on 'Motivation', Robert White said, 'Play may be fun, but it is also a serious business in childhood. During these hours, the child is steadily building up his competence in dealing with the environment.'

All children show a strong drive to play and need to make use of curiosity, exploration, organizing, planning and doing, to clarify the potential uses of their thinking (cognitive) resources and to discover feelings of success and mastery by putting ideas together in new and interesting ways (Weininger, 1972).

Teachers of young culturally disadvantaged children who were not given much opportunity to play and experiment with their home environments have noted that these children come to school with a different linguistic, perceptual, and cognitive repertory from children who had a rich play life (Smilansky, 1968). They may not communicate as much, and they may not see toys and play materials as things to be manipulated. They are accustomed to 'less language' in their homes and are often children who have been told, 'Don't touch — you'll break it.' Their natural drive to touch and to understand their world has been smothered by their environment. They have learned that in their home they have to behave in a certain way and to do otherwise is to risk rejection, hurt or deprivation. As these young children come to school there is no reason why they should think that the teacher, another adult, is not going to behave in just the same way as all the other adults. The children are then restricted in what they may do and practically have to be helped to play and to explore. It is as though the teacher has to give the child 'licence' to play. The teacher has to create the kind of environment which will be sufficiently safe for the children so that they may risk their prior understanding that to play is dangerous. The teacher certainly cannot say, 'Go and play.' This is rather meaningless to children who already know that they cannot or must not. The teacher must help these children to bridge the gap between the home and the school by providing 'home-like' materials, by using the materials, by becoming involved with the play, and by inviting the child to 'come and do things with me'.

It is important that the children feel comfortable not only with the play materials, but also in communicating. This means that the children should be encouraged to talk in whatever way is 'available' to them — if the children talk in phrases without verbs, or if the words are always in the 'imperative', or if the children ask single word questions, it is suggested that the children should not only be allowed but encouraged to use these forms of language. The teacher answers in his/her own language, but does not attempt either to complicate his/her speech form or to correct the children's speech. It is by imitation, modelling, identification, and through the relationship with the teacher that the children's language and communication patterns will change. If change is demanded, then learning appears to slow down and the opportunity for creative play with language lessens.

It is recommended that children be treated as individuals and that their heritages be appreciated. If this is done, the children will be able to apply themselves fully to the play at hand and 'produce' to the best of their capacities at that moment. The teacher's language, conduct, ethics and ideas — in short, the teacher's standards — will become those of the children if he/she permits them to build upon what they have and not upon what 'should have been there'. Recognition, understanding and encouragement at each stage of learning allow children to succeed in the process of educating themselves (Weininger, 1972a).

Play, then, is an integral part of the child's being. It is the business of childhood and it has a unique and vital role in the whole educational process. As Joseph Lee (1915) noted, play to children is growth, since

46 Play and Early Childhood

only through play can they take on, absorb and assimilate experiences – physical, social or intellectual – in meaningful ways. It is through play that they grow, and the growth in turn acts as a stimulus to change through play, which is learning. The relationship is a reciprocal, totally integrated one: play and growing – growing and play.

The Adult's View of Child's Play

Does growing up mean giving up play? Many adults play golf weekly, and weekly insist they do so 'only for their health' or 'to keep those old pounds off'. They seem to need to provide a safe reason for their play; to enjoy themselves seems to impose a feeling of guilt. They do not seem to realize that limits have been imposed on their thinking; they are hardly aware of the fact that if they could really play and feel comfortable about playing, they would have fun, learn about the game, enjoy companionship and thorough relaxation. Play is essential to growing children if they are to mature and learn effectively. Too often parents, lacking an understanding of the importance of play, place undue emphasis on premature maturity, on giving up play – in short, on 'playlessness' – or they bolster their own defences against playing by either not allowing it in their children or imposing limits on it.

Unfortunately, Western society seems to have a tradition of saying that it is all right to play once the children's work has been finished, that it is not all right to play until they have done what we (some adults in our society) consider important for them to do. Too often adults assume that they know exactly the right time and place for the children to do something; they think that, since children are small and are socially, intellectually and emotionally unable to cope with many things and situations effectively, they have no awareness of their own needs. Adults too often assume that children need to be pushed into this or that activity – because it is 'good for them', or because 'they are lacking' or because it's 'what other children his/her age are doing'.

The inherent assumption that adults always know what is good for children is, in fact, to say that adults know everything about the developing child – but they do not. It is not in any way suggested that teachers or adults absent themselves from the 'growing child', but rather that the adults recognize that the play in which children are engaged is their way of growing, and that to insist on some other form is to arrest their development.

The adult must be able to recognize the time at which children are able to use new materials, for it comes at a point in their lives when they are receptive to a change in the environment, to a new bit of nformation, to a new way of handling something. This timing is generally up to the children and it is the important business of the adult to be able to help the children at this time, when they are open o and accepting of new thoughts and information.

If children ask why mountains are big when they have been sorting bottle caps into different shapes, it is not for the adult to say, 'Let's finish this, and then I'll answer your question.' Rather, it is for the adult to give an explanation that is understandable to the children, to follow the questioning until it stops and then to allow the children to continue with the activity. The adult will quickly see how the explanation has become integrated into the children's activity, for later the bottle caps may be piled in pyramid fashion to simulate a mountain. If the adult or teacher adds to the environment by adding play landscapes, the play activity will change and the children will then try to understand and assimilate information about how mountains are made.

If children persist at one kind of play endlessly, then the adult should try to understand why they are so inflexible. Perhaps they are frightened, perhaps they are coerced at home to come to school to learn something' and their anxiety about returning home takes on the form of endlessly repeating the same activity. Or perhaps the children are unable to use other materials in the room because they are too unfamiliar, or may need some interaction and involvement with the teacher in their play; maybe they have to be allowed to move backwards' and play with materials that seem to be appropriate for much younger children. Whatever the reason, children should not be forced out of their play by punishment, deprivation or sarcasm, but rather should be made to feel as comfortable as they can be. The teacher should come to them and talk with them about their play — not to distract them, but to find out if there is something bothering them — and then help them by giving the freedom, the licence, to continue with their play and the assurance they can come and talk with the teacher whenever they wish. Perhaps the children need to be recognized, but often the fear of being scolded is so great that they rigidly repeat one pattern in order to avoid anxiety. The anxiety prevents learning, the anxiety prevents play, and it is the role of the teacher to participate with the children in order to help them get on with the business of play.

Biber (1951, p. 19) has summed up the problems of play and of teacher in the following. If play in school is to be a learning experience,

it requires a skilled guiding hand, especially where children are collected in groups as they are in schools. There is a way of setting the stage and creating an atmosphere for spontaneous play. Most important in this atmosphere is the teacher's sensitive understanding of her own role. Sometimes the teacher needs to be ready to guide the play, especially among the fives, sixes, and sevens, into channels that are beyond the needs of the nursery years. But she must guide only in terms of the children's growth needs. Her guidance may be in terms of her choice of stories, materials, trips, experiences. It may function through discussions. Without skillful guidance, a free play program for successive years can become stultified and disturbing to children.

Biber goes on to point out that teachers have to be helped to know how much, when, and how to get involved in the children's play. The teacher is no longer someone relegated to 'teach this in this way', but still has to find out when are the best times to step in and offer new materials to the child to enrich the play. The teacher cannot take over the play, for that would be the same as having him/her as the only source of information in the classroom. Biber puts the question this way: 'Are we stimulating and developing the child by our active teaching, or are we becoming so active that the children are overwhelmed and restricted by the flood of our bright ideas?'

Play and the Educational Process

Some assume that when play is a central method for education, the educational process will stop when learning becomes difficult or threatening — that is, the children will cease learning when the activity is too difficult. If, however, children are allowed to make use of the learning materials in a safe way, and are not expected to accomplish at the same time as another child but permitted a uniqueness so that they learn at their own rate, the learning is not threatening or difficult. Allow them time to integrate and synthesize; do not assume that learning has gone on simply because we have presented the opportunity once. It cannot be assumed that all children integrate at the same time. Allow the children to go back over materials; allow them to have the safety of known facts and help them to learn the new material in relationship with the known facts. If we do not then we stop play and arrest learning.

If learning is thought of as the acquisition of kinds of competencies given through experience, as a way of providing knowledge which helps to clarify thinking and sharpen images in a child's mind, then the provision of open-ended experiences is essential to the process. Too often, educators are intent on imparting a framework within which they expect children to operate, forcing them to learn what questions to ask when, rather than helping them explore how something operates or helping them deal with everyday realities in an open, natural fashion. The tendency is to provide a total concept for children before they have a chance to explore the ideas around it sufficiently, and this leads to premature concept formation, limited understanding, and rigid or circumscribed conceptualization preventing further exploration or expansion in the face of increasing thinking or knowledge. We must begin seriously to question whether we want to lock children into an educational system which discourages connections with everyday realities and limits the possibilities for creativity and mind expansion.

It is suggested that the aspects of activity manipulation and exploration, all aspects of play, must be the way in which children build up their conceptualizations. Skills and competencies cannot be considered as belonging to one subject-matter area, to one subject description, but rather the information provided to children must be made to flow from one area to another. Reading is not learned by just looking at books. It requires visual-motor play, body-image understanding, black-white sequencing, straight-line conceptualizing, and so forth. Children must be given the opportunity to explore the fullness of their life space, to make many of their own connections, to find out what they can do with their materials and what the materials can do for them. They are essentially setting up a kind of map of their world and taking pieces of it to explore and to play with chosen materials. In the same way, subject matter does not really belong in isolated categories, particularly in early childhood, but rather some of the information from one area helps to understand the information from another. It is difficult, if not impossible, to say that it is known how children 'hammer out' (Murphy, 1956) their understanding of the areas of knowledge. Therefore, to separate the areas might, in fact, not allow them to 'hammer' through their conceptualizations effectively or even fully for their ages.

When the classroom programmes involve play, the concepts at which children arrive will be used to make further sense of their world. There is no other kind of activity in which children engage that allows them to begin to test and then to expand their sense of competence.

At play, children are constantly moving, touching, listening and looking. Therefore, at play they practise and learn physical skills and sensory discrimination. At play, they are constantly talking and thus practise their vocabulary and concepts. At play, they are constantly exploring and questioning, increasing their knowledge, skills and vocabulary. At the same time, they practise ways to relate to people, learning the complicated business of human relations. Through imaginative and dramatic play, children make models of the real world and play out situations in order to understand and gain mastery over what they know about the world. By acting out what they have seen people do, they learn to comprehend and understand male and female roles. Play also allows them to act out their fantasies, fears, needs and wants. Thus play, a learning activity, also makes a great contribution toward personality development, mental health and emotional well-being.

An example of a play situation in a classroom could be as follows: 'John has been playing by himself for quite some time with a toy car. He is simply talking to himself and manipulating the car.' What are the learning possibilities for John in this situation? He can discover and learn concepts about space, such as high, low, around, far, near. He can discover and learn concepts about speed, such as fast, faster, slow, stop. He can discover and learn concepts about direction, such as forward, backward, left, right, up, down. At the same time, he can practise and learn sensory discrimination from the sound and feel of the car, and he can learn how to co-ordinate his movements to make the car go as he pleases. He can explore the role of a bus driver and play out this role. In doing this, he can practise, consolidate, and gain mastery over his vocabulary and the concepts that have to do with cars, buses, safety, policemen and so on, that this model of the real world evokes for him. He can learn to direct himself, think for himself and solve his own problems, to put his past knowledge to work and to adjust to new experiences which the teacher introduces gradually to him.

This example points up two important facts. First, John's play is free play because he was allowed time, material, freedom and opportunity to explore, manipulate and test. This is the kind of play needed at school, a minimum of direct control but a teacher-created climate and an atmosphere of catalytic guidance, so that each child can concentrate and learn at his own level of readiness, at each stage of his development.

Second, a casual observer would likely be fooled by the apparent simplicity of what John is doing. He is learning what no one could teach him. Teachers must not be casual observers of play, but rather careful students of play. They must recognize that play can seem idle and aimless when all the while the child is really seeking to discover the basic dimensions and physical operations of the actual world and learning its space-time properties and physical relationships. They must remember, even if play appears purposeless, that the child may be endlessly rehearsing and practising what will later become a directive for many of his activities.

Play helps children to think more clearly and to begin to manage and control their feelings more successfully. As children develop clear thinking, they will have more skill in managing their environment, they will have greater confidence in their abilities and will be able to participate actively in the world around them. Children who are encouraged to play will be active, happy, exploring, sociable and creative.

Purposes and Achievements of Play

Play helps children to make use of their growing muscular skills and helps them co-ordinate the developing muscle systems, both gross motor movements and fine motor co-ordination. Play that helps this muscular co-ordination includes such activities as climbing, skating, jumping, running, playing ball games. Small manipulative activities such as Lego, bolt boards, puzzles and breaking eggs, are just a few of the experiences which help fine motor movement.

With such games as hiding an object behind a screen and letting the child touch it, guess its nature and tell the group what the thing is, not only is social interaction facilitated (for they get lots of social encouragement), but also sensory development (for they use kinesthetic and haptic senses in co-ordination). This touch system is of vital importance to learning.

Play helps to clear up cognitive confusions which all growing children meet during the day. Sometimes their play will help the teacher recognize the variance between school values and home values; at other times play will help the teacher recognize the confusion in social roles, in presented fact, and in concept formation. For example, a child observing two yellow bean plants he is growing — one in the light and one in a dark cupboard — notices that the one in the dark cupboard is yellow. He/she concludes that the stem and leaves of that plant are yellow because it has grown from a yellow bean seed. This confused concept is overcome by comparing the colour of the plant in the cupboard with the plant growing in the light. There is no need to go through a formal lesson; the cognitive confusion has been clarified through play. The child has been given the opportunity at his/her time and in a circumstance meaningful enough to him/her to alter the concept.

Again, in playing make-believe children may emulate the teacher's role and the parents' role, and help themselves not only to express their confusions as to the meanings of the role, but, once the role has been acted, to allow for change through the interpersonal responses from their peers. In other words, they do not just go along with what they think they know, but they begin to clarify through play.

Play helps to relieve and release experiences which are painful to the child and which often have prevented the learning process from continuing. If children are afraid, if they have been hurt, then they approach learning situations with these fears in mind and the fears crowd out learning. In play, an opportunity is provided for children to re-enact and relive the experience. The children play out both fearful family feelings and the satisfying ones. Activities of 'playing house', carrying on the baby role, the mother role, the father role, going on picnics, of being scolded, punished, of being afraid of being lost, of being afraid of being left behind, are activities that explore and relive the experiences.

As children play through these experiences, time and again they explore and relieve themselves of the painful things and find new ways of handling situations, all under their own steam and in their own time. To rush them in this activity or arbitrarily to set a time limit would only be saying that the children must conform to the adult's pattern, that adults know the amount of time children need in which to understand and release their feelings in order to learn what they can go on to learn. Nonsense!

Along with the release of emotions which might block learning, play helps to further self-understanding. Children are expressing things their way, and so they gradually gain confidence in their ideas. They see that they can work, and this helps to lead them to explore new situations which previously they would have avoided out of anxiety.

With self-understanding children acquire a sense of independence; they can explore the idea of being alone, think of themselves as the captains of a ship with or without a crew. They direct the activities, sail for North, issue orders and send messages, but just what do they learn? Some of the concepts they make use of are directional (North, South, West, East, up, down, around), some are mathematical (sending 2 messages, 3 orders), and keeping track of the messages, where they go and who deals with them and how they are dealt with — that is, social judgement, reasoning, remembering, abstraction. The captain also draws maps, plots courses, steers the ship — again, concepts one finds in geometry, arithmetic, geography, deductive and inductive reasoning, drawing lines and printing words, and so on.

Just because these activities take place in a play situation, are they not learning material? Children play hospital, playing out feelings of fear, anxiety and anger. Children who are afraid to go to the hospital because they do not know what will happen are also angry because they have a sense of being ignored by the adults in their world. They work out all these in play. The children can reassure themselves about new or old situations and, if they can reassure themselves about primary experiences, they will be able to reassure themselves about the new business of learning in school.

Play extends the exploratory drive of children. Compare children in playpens for most of the day with only a limited amount of toys and children who are free to crawl around and watch and touch the things which attract their attention. The children who are free to play and to move explore an increasingly large area of the room, coming back to the familiar and the safe when they need to, gaining in mobility and independence at their own rate. The children who are penned up or, later, the children whose play is restricted to certain physical areas or types of behaviour, lack the same ability and desire to move farther afield and learn about different things. These children are likely to be more passive in play.

Play increases the sensory input which, in turn, increases cognitive awareness of the environment. Children who are free to explore see, hear, feel, touch and sense more of the world around them; they become practised in noticing and being aware of their environment; they have more fuel for thought, as it were.

Play is a major achieving pattern of children. Look again at very young children who will stack the rings on a post and them dump them off and do it again, varying the order, the colour, the size, repeating the game until they feel that they have mastered it. The children repeat this pattern of attempt, practice and mastery daily in their play, adding to the store of things they feel sure of and safe with, reducing the uncertainty of the large and often inconsistent adult world. Thus slowly they gain confidence to begin to investigate novel or complex stimulation, as long as the safety of the established pattern can be returned to whenever they need to feel secure in themselves again. This is why it is wise to have familiar objects, experience-events, or routines to surround children with before bringing them into a new situation. Children should be helped to make the same kind of transition from old to new that they instinctively make in their play experiences. In the classroom, understanding of this concept means starting from that which is known to the child and moving to that which is novel and different at the rate at which the child can assimilate the new experiences.

Play increases a child's creativity. This refers specifically to children's capacity to perform a task which requires ingenuity in formulating an answer not readily suggested by the materials themselves or by another person. If posed with a problem of building a tower, and making sure that it stands, young children will test the blocks and planks of wood first, and find out that they can get the planks to stand upright if they brace them with blocks at the base. Creative or ingenious children will find a way to use the materials to solve their problems. For many years, educators have assumed that there is a high correlation between intellect and creativity; this, in fact, may be a spurious relationship. Research (Ford and Renzulli, 1976) has indicated that creativity is related to several factors other than intellect. For the adult this means it is impossible to assume that because children are not particularly bright, they will not be very creative, and therefore provide fewer creative opportunities of less stimulation. It is interesting to note that for years teachers for the mentally retarded have been insisting that their students were in fact very creative in many ways, and have been patted on their heads rather patronizingly by those who have felt secure in their knowledge that only intelligent children are creative!

The Use of Space and Materials to Encourage Play

The following section examines the use of space and materials to encourage play activities, especially in the classroom. If it is desired that children make room for certain concepts in their heads, then they must be given room to acquire these concepts by giving them the space to work in. They cannot sit at a desk and work; they need to move. They cannot use fine motor movement as do adults; they need to explore much more of their gross motor activities. They need space in which to run, to climb, to jump, to push, to roll, to do thousands of gross motor activities before they can be expected to sit and have an attention span at a desk. First allow gross movement, then encourage 'involvement time' and children will develop because allowance has been made for activity which is meaningful to developing children.

Thus, classrooms need space; they need central open areas where activities can go on, activities needed by the developing child, such as walking, running, sitting, rolling, looking, climbing, holding, touching and smelling. Children then need 'bays' where they can take their play and extend it in quietness and where they and their teacher may be able to discuss some aspects of their play without interfering with the activities of other children. Children may not be ready to share what they have done. They need time to master the concepts and then, and only then, will they share them in a confident way.

Adults are often concerned about teaching children in the above kind of classroom atmosphere, and perhaps an example of how one teacher approaches the teaching of mathematics may help to clarify this position. Several ways are used by this teacher to increase the ease of the child in learning number concepts and recognition. Tally and concept of mathematical sign are at first provided by playing a game of catch and tallying the individual throws and catches, playing a game of telephone calling and tallying the number of calls that have been made, and so forth. Children, given a pad and pencil, will tally just about anything that comes to hand! As they tally and count to reach a total, they are talking to other children and to the teacher, learning how to relate in a language way the numbers and number concepts they are learning. They imitate other children and the teacher as well. At about this time they are ready for a number line, a simple chart built up in equal units to show how many catches they made today, yesterday, the day before, how many telephone calls they made yesterday and today, and how many days have gone by this week.

Next comes the problem of recognition of numbers, which the teacher can facilitate by setting up the classroom so that the child becomes aware of the different numerals. For example, the teacher may have a calendar on which he/she circles today's date, or counts the days on a pad until the arrival of special events, or he/she may have a clock on which hands can be set for special times (like recess or lunch) for the children to compare with the real clock.

The teacher also sets up learning bays where the children are able to experiment in meaningful ways with meaningful numbers. The store is about the best way to acquire number concepts. Children can buy from the store, sell to their peers, make change, and keep records of the transactions. They learn number recognition when another child asks how much something costs. The children learn addition and subtraction by making change. They learn the concepts that go with terms like more than, greater than, less than. They help others to read because they ask what is for sale. They learn at their own speed with the ready help of the teacher and other children.

Another useful device for understanding numbers is a simple pair of scales. Children weigh objects and record numbers; they compare weights of various objects; the children begin to understand the relationship of volume to weight because they fill containers with sand, water, pebbles, acorns, or sticks, and weigh them. They begin to find out the difference between heavy and light, big and small and smaller, all in a context which is meaningful to them.

As the children make use of these games and materials, they are learning to write numbers because they are meaningful and necessary to them in their play. They are learning verbal concepts such as one more, one less, heavier than, bigger than, in a way that makes sense to them because they have been used in their play. The teacher is there to direct, ask questions and extend their thinking and play so that they begin to learn concepts that are quite complicated, such as things weighing the same although they are of different sizes. They are stimulated to explore and experiment when they come upon an occurrence or event they do not immediately grasp.

Soon the children are ready to make use of games which require them to use mathematics, they can play with dice or dominoes, keep track of scores in snakes and ladders, and play bingo. Best of all, they enjoy what they are doing — they enjoy learning.

What kinds of materials, raw and ideational, best accomplish the learning through play? Should the materials be of the finished, polished variety, or should they be of the 'raw' variety, things like clay, paper, sand, tree bark, stones, or dolls, trucks, dishes? What balance should there be between variety of materials? When should the materials be used? These are questions to which there are no ready and easy answers. Again, there need to be study and experimentation with the ways children use their materials. Teachers need to be helped to make use of their own skills at play and at being able to see the child's developing needs. At one point, clay will be used by very young children, but soon some children will gradually be able to use paper and move towards this medium. The teacher can help by having a sensitivity to the needs of the child and by being prepared to bring out materials at the appropriate times: not to stultify, not to over-stimulate, but to move along at the developing rate of the child.

Outside the classroom, adults often try too hard to provide the 'right' materials. If a group of young children is observed playing in a backyard — one which is in a low socio-economic area — many of their activities will be seen. Among these activities are:

1. *Communication* — using language which is relevant to them. There is brevity of speech; no long, drawn-out talks.

2. *Leadership encounters* — either in single pattern leadership or else a multiple and changing leadership. Leadership stays until ideas are exhausted, or until the children move on to another area.

3. *Play* — using the broken and dirty materials of a backyard, pieces of chairs, bedsprings, glass, poles, cardboard and wood. These pieces are fashioned into other objects: the chair becomes a bridge, or the paper

becomes a dress. The children are learning by play how to relate the objects to other uses, learning the dimensions of form, task involvement, even arithmetic. They learn through play how to interrelate the materials of the next child to their objects, and then how to make their own objects either fit in with the other child's or make a new one for the next child.

They learn social relationships. Children move in and out of the game. They add different aspects to it and then it alters. Children who cannot keep up or who wish to play the game differently either stay with their material or game until they are ready to move on, or if they are threatened by the move, they may become bullies to preserve their safety.

The backyard scene is used here only because it demonstrates that children just need space — they bring their materials with them. Too often the middle and upper socio-economic playground has too much equipment designed by someone who thinks he/she knows how children will make use of materials. Unfortunately, they are wrong too often. Then the children have to alter the materials so they can play with them — they convert hardware into childware.

An Atmosphere for Learning

As well as providing space and certain materials to encourage play, adults must provide the emotional atmosphere in which a child can discover, make mistakes, correct them and go on to acquire principles — in short an atmosphere which allows for learning. The teacher in such a classroom must provide guidelines and safety (which sometimes means instruction) so that the child can use materials and space in an innovative, creative way.

'Culturally deprived' or 'culturally satisfied', children cannot learn when their environment is such that the materials are unknown to them. They must examine in their own way, with help from a guiding and responsive — non-threatening — person. Difficult play does not mean cessation of play, nor does difficult material presentation mean cessation of learning — as long as it is recognized that the child has the need to review, to re-experience the known, to integrate, to synthesize, to evaluate, and then to adapt. This all goes on in play.

When the teacher is 'open' as opposed to 'closed' (i.e., when the teaching situation is 'low-controlling' as opposed to 'high-controlling') then he/she is significantly more conducive to growth in the students' creative behaviour (Wodtke and Wallen, 1965). In a learning environment where the teacher is an idea-seeking person, 'open', 'low-controlling' of the limits of information — as opposed to one where the teacher categorically gives all the information and ideas — children are more creative, make better use of materials, and seem to retain and move on towards more complex learning.

Again, where judgement on an activity is deferred, creative learning patterns are encouraged. If children are permitted to postpone judgement on their activities, then they are no longer afraid of their ideas, they no longer fear that each end-point will be criticized, they become able to make full use of their associative processes (Johnson and Zierbolio, 1964). When children are not afraid to explore their ideas and materials and recognize that no specific judgement will be made at the time, they make more use of and express a greater variety of ideas. Play helps children explore ideas because:

1. this is a way of life of which they are not afraid;
2. the teacher is sensitive to their growing needs for change and encouragement in materials and information handling; and
3. they recognize that no judgement will be made by the teacher. This does not mean unresponsiveness on the part of the teacher, for a growing relationship with the teacher is needed; rather, it means that guidance and even criticism is given without making final statements. The teacher does not judge, but helps the children evaluate their own productions in order that they can see their play activity evolve into learning concepts which gradually stimulate more play and further concepts.

Creativity and Learning

Creativity and learning cannot be increased by reward (Ward and Kogan, 1970). Creativity is derived from internal capacity, and this capacity is stimulated into action by:

1. an unstructured environment which has guidelines — for, as Piaget suggests, structured play may not be sufficient for learning to proceed; and
2. an environment which takes into account their emotional attitudes, that is, their self-concepts.

When the classroom does not provide the opportunity for children to make use of their constructive and creative tendencies and capacities, they respond to that classroom with a relative degree of boredom. If the classroom does not permit or encourage play activity, the class is empty and full of monotony and the children are prevented from making comparisons, organizing experiences, trying to make a study of their expanding awareness of the world about them. The cognitive-thinking aspects of play involve block construction, puzzle solving, painting, drawing, rolling, moving, pushing (objects), telling stories, showing things. Children experience activities by doing them and by participation in the 'doing' of others: painting a story together and finding out how other children feel and experience things; building a block house together and deciding how high walls are to go; placing weights on a scale together and finding out who has the heavier objects; measuring each other and then grouping the results; numbering the children in each class and finding out how many people there are in the school; taking a piece of string and finding the perimeter of the teacher's chair top, of the animal's cage, of the sink, and of the classroom. All these activities are called 'cognitive'. As group play activities, they are also social learning experiences. Basically, however, these are all play activities and, as with all play, children learn from these experiences.

These activities go on in a classroom where play is encouraged, that is, in a classroom where the children are allowed and encouraged to work in activities which are meaningful to them. Learning then results, but the teacher may not realize it unless he/she is sensitive and aware. When children have to make use of media or relationships which are meaningless to them, or for which they care very little, then they do not learn; they copy without developing insights. The teacher, however, may be able to see what little the children have learned.

Take, for example, toys and the business of play. Some schools have accepted the idea that children need to play and have bought them some very beautiful and perhaps even expensive toys. They have argued — perhaps validly — that toys are the objects which encourage children to play and therefore these things must be made available and plentiful.

Perhaps the school is in a poor area of the city and now the children are supposed to get the 'enriched environment' plus the effective 'human warmth' they desperately lack: lo and behold, however, they do not make use of the toys! Why? The teachers may be put off at this point, feeling that the children are ungrateful (and all people feel this when they think that their efforts are unappreciated). The teacher may withdraw and say that the children need to learn how to make use of the toys. Perhaps this is true, but more important is the fact that the children are unable to respond to this new atmosphere because they do not find anything in the situation which is familiar to them. They have no transfer from home to school. They play at home — maybe — but they use very different materials. Now they come to a nice shining class with a young, eager teacher. They have not had this experience before and may be confused by the strangeness of the situation. Studies have shown that children who come from working-class homes often have parents who are at a loss to see the educational functions of play or toys. These children come to school to 'learn' and now they are expected to play. How should these children know that playing is learning, when they have been told that they go to school to 'work' and not to 'play'? The conflict of values is enormous and often creates a serious learning problem.

Parents

We advocate play, yet we do not help parents understand the value of play in the total educational system. Parents must be reached and helped to understand that play is a natural activity of children and that this activity permits development and acts as a vehicle for all learning. Without this natural behaviour robot-like learning may be produced, but it will not develop the student who will perhaps invent a new way of looking at things — perhaps a more effective way to communicate with people!

In addition, it should be noted that middle-class parents are not so different from working-class parents. The former may understand the value of play, but generally they do not approve (Bernstein, 1967). These people think of school and 'hard work' as the necessary ladder of success in the economic world. In their zeal for success, they often forget the ingredients vital in successful learning, if not for business: social experiences, a sense of autonomy, the capacity to deal with various life situations, and the motivation to continue developing thinking-cognitive skills. Most parents have yet to be shown that play is not something quite different from work. Bernstein (1967) has noted that

> Many middle-class mothers (parents) think that the child gets enough 'play' at home; at school he should learn the basic skills so that he can proudly take his place in the 'A' stream. Some middle-class mothers (parents) are aghast if their children are not 'early' readers and upset if their children cannot docilely repeat tables. In the coffee groups of the suburbs they complain to each other of their children's apparent lack of progress. They go to see the teacher,

frequently, in order to discuss their children's failure to master mechanical skills, pointing out how young they were when they could accomplish more than their child. Some middle-class homes are pseudo-educational pressure-cookers, forcing houses for skills thought to be of examination rather than of educational relevance.

Thus, the problem is many-pronged. First, adults, parents and teachers alike have to be helped to understand that play is the essence of learning for children. The purposes it serves are manifold: not only promoting academic learning and concept formation, but also social interaction and self-understanding and acceptance. Second, educational goals must be made relevant to parents so that children will be able to make use of their drive to learn and explore and not be made to feel anxious and different from their parents. Third, school administrators and teachers must become more aware of the need to provide the space and materials which encourage play and an emotional atmosphere which promotes it.

Learning Equals Play Equals Fun

It will be hard for many to accept the premise that the curriculum which is the eventual goal of education can be arrived at through cops and robbers, cowboys, space pilots and frogmen. Much of the carefully structured and rather rigid curriculum planning and classroom timetabling devised over the past years will need to be reconsidered and some of it discarded.

Most important, however, the firmly embedded Puritan equation that learning equals work equals playlessness must be cast aside. The idea that one must agonize to learn now and suffer to triumph later is patently ludicrous. Think of the look on a two-year-old's face as he carefully fills containers with water and empties them into each other; of the four-year-old constructing vast empires of buildings with blocks; of the six-year-old examining a wriggling worm in fascination; of the eight-year-old bouncing a ball as hard as possible to see how high it will go. These are children at play, exploring the world of which they are a part and learning more than adults can begin to catalogue from their constant investigations and questions, learning more than adults can begin to teach in all their careful curricula. These children are playing, learning, enjoying at the same time. Is this not what life is really about? Can a new equation not be written that will allow children to grow into less restricted adults, adults who can say 'I play golf because I love being outside, moving freely, looking at the sky and feeling the grass beneath my feet, laughing and doing well at something and getting to know other people better?'

Let us begin to say learning equals fun. Let us watch our children grow in joy and expand in their awareness of the human potential for wonder.

References

Bernstein, B. 1967. 'Play and the infant school', *WHERE*, Supplement II, 'Toys', Christmas.

Biber, B. 1951. 'Play as a growth process', *Vassar Alumnae Magazine*, 37, 2, pp. 18–20.

Ford, B. G. and J. S. Renzulli. 1976. 'Developing the creative potential of educable mentally retarded students', *The Journal of Creative Behaviour*, 10, 3, pp. 210–18.

Harlow, H. F. 1973. *Learning to Love*. San Francisco: Albion Publishing Company.

Johnson, D. M. and D. J. Zierbolio. 1964. 'Relations between production and judgment of plot-titles', *American Journal of Psychology*, 77, 1, pp. 99–105.

Lee, J. 1915. *Play in Education*. New York: Macmillan.

Murphy, G. 1956. 'The Process of creative thinking', *Educational Leadership*, 14, pp. 11–15.

Murphy, L. 1969. 'Children under three: finding ways to stimulate development', *Children*, 16, 2, pp. 47–52.

Piaget, J. 1951. *Play, Dreams, and Imitation in Children*. New York: W. W. Norton and Company.

——, 1952. *The Origins of Intelligence in Children*. New York: International Universities Press.

Sapora, A. V. and E. D. Mitchell. 1961. *The Theory of Play and Recreation*. New York: Ronald Press Company.

Smilansky, S. 1968. *The Effect of Sociodramatic Play on Disadvantaged Preschool Children*. New York: Wiley.

Ward, W. C. and N. Kogan. 1970. 'Motivation and ability in children's creativity'. Reprinted from The Proceedings of the 78th Annual Convention of the American Psychological Association. American Psychological Association, Washington, DC.

Weininger, O. 1972a. 'Help stamp out playlessness', *Educational Courier*, 42, 6, pp. 8–15.

——, 1972b. 'How is a rabbit?' *Involvement*, 4, 4, pp. 16–21.

White, R. 1960. 'Competence in psychosexual stages of development', in M. R. Jones (ed.), *Nebraska Symposium on Motivation*. Lincoln: University of Nebraska Press, pp. 97–141.

Wodtke, K. H. and N. E. Wallen. 1965. 'Teacher classroom control, pupil creativity and pupil classroom behavior', *Journal of Experimental Education*, 34, 1, pp. 59–63.

3 EDUCATION FOR LEISURE: IS IT OUR RESPONSIBILITY?

Catherine Cherry and Robert Woodburn[1]

Introduction

A society unprepared for leisure will degenerate in relatively prosperous times.

Aristotle

A recent study, reported in *Society and Leisure*, comparing the work, time and leisure patterns in the United States, Czechoslovakia, France and Great Britain makes clear that the changing distribution of time and the increasing importance of the use of free time is a world-wide phenomenon in industrial society. These findings have wide-ranging implications for the citizens of Canada. One of the major points from this study is that the time block of youth, essentially disengaged from the labour market, is creating within it new values and life-styles which have as their fundamental source leisure in all its dimensions. This group, the retired population, and others who have experienced an increase in the blocks of free time available to them, are referred to as a vanguard movement — a 'sub-culture of leisuring'. Although this trend is not new, it has definitely accelerated in the past few years.

The most important question is: what is being done with this expanded opportunity for leisure? Is it truly an opportunity for most people or is free time a problem? The latter view is expressed by Cousins:

> For there still remains the biggest problem of modern man — perhaps even bigger than war: what to do with himself. As he ceases to be a creature of endless toil, poverty, and famine, he is apt to find himself liberated into nothingness. His free time can become more of a curse than the plagues of old. (Corbin and Tait, 1973, p. 13)

It would appear that many people are already experiencing this 'liberation into nothingness' as their free-time pursuits are often costly, somewhat stressful and more of an attempt to fill time than to pursue something personally meaningful.

What is leisure? Is it free time? Many can have free time without experiencing leisure. Then is leisure an experience of well-being evolving from the pursuit of meaningful and satisfying experiences? Ultimately, we believe that a definition of what a leisure experience is rests personally with each individual. The prerequisites to leisure are often the same for everyone, namely: the freedom to choose — to discover one's potential and to enjoy life in a joyful and creative fashion; and the intrinsic motivation to choose. The experience of leisure, therefore, can include aspects of work, study, family life and recreational activity.

Dr John Neulinger, of the Leisure Institute in New York City, has stressed that the distinction between free time and leisure is important to understand. It will affect the philosophy and therefore the approach to educating people for leisure. Instead of associating leisure with time (as in the oft-used phrase 'leisure time') one must appreciate leisure as an experience — an ultimate goal of life — which one strives for through meaningful behaviours. Life is pursued not only for the accumulation of possessions or for the occupation of time, but for the development of character and for the pursuit of those things that provide a reason for living. The pursuit of leisure is not a problem of what to do with free time, but of what one wants to do in order to live enjoyably and fully.

To date, many have perceived leisure as no more than time or activity. If we have free time, then, we often conclude that we must merely fill it. If we choose to recreate and recreation is commonly seen as activity, then we choose to learn a recreational activity. Unfortunately, however, recreational activities and programmes often leave individuals still feeling unsatisfied and searching for something else. Perhaps, on the other hand, if we see leisure as an experience for well-being, then we, as professionals, would want to facilitate individuals in the selection and pursuit of those experiences that are most meaningful and rewarding, whatever area of life they may be in — work, education, social life, family life, or community life, to mention a few. Our services would go beyond skill instruction in recreational activities to the facilitation of human satisfaction.

Free time, however, is big business today and the pressure to buy and consume our way to happiness is readily endorsed by the media. The statement 'I've got to buy tickets, equipment or memberships before I can participate' is frequently echoed. Free-time behaviours are also affected by the work ethic. Many people bring a 'busy and productive' mind set to their free time. For instance, we hurry to try everything or we compete to be number one. The result is a tendency to fill up free time with obligations and tasks which, in fact, resemble work. In these cases, our free-time experiences may not bring satisfaction and may even prevent us from developing a healthy life-style.

It appears, then, that there is a need to help prepare individuals for leisure. People are often unprepared for leisure, not just physically, but psychologically, socially, emotionally and creatively. We are not naturally endowed with an understanding of how free time can be effectively used to experience a state of well-being. We must learn the value of leisure and must learn positive attitudes and habits towards free time. Schools and governmental and leisure service agencies have, however, lagged behind in exploring the most effective methods of educating for leisure. This presents a leisure society with a social network that is not sufficiently prepared to meet this challenge.

The Role of the School

While no single agency is responsible for the entire programme of educating for leisure, the education system has a major role to play in the process. A number of philosophers, educators and social scientists have been advocating such a function for schools for many years. For example, the Ontario Provincial Committee on Aims and Objectives of Education (1968) stated:

> Today's child is facing a new world of work and leisure. Job descriptions unknown twenty years ago appear in advertisements every day. Automation dictates . . . new job requirements and a flexibility heretofore unrealized; added to this, leisure is growing in importance. The question of whether we live to work or work to live becomes increasingly relevant. . . . We are also beginning to recognize that preparing oneself to cope with leisure time is as important as preparing oneself to cope with a job.

The schools have recognized a need to educate for leisure as indicated and as outlined in recent curriculum guidelines published by the Ministry of Education. However, in practice, few teachers really understand what it means 'to prepare individuals for the meaningful pursuit of leisure'.[2] The importance of trained educators is critical to the type of interdisciplinary and developmental approach that is required.

The Role of Recreation Agencies

Recreation agencies in Ontario are beginning to take responsibility for developing professional training resources on education for leisure and for co-ordinating training sessions on the topic. Agencies providing play facilities and services could also significantly contribute to this need.

There is no doubt that all agencies have expended much effort in providing facilities and leisure environments and in teaching skills in the arts, crafts and physical education. None the less, there is more we can do and should be doing. We must now not only stress skill instruction but also emphasize the beliefs and values that are necessary to encourage people to act on and take responsibility for finding leisure.

Recreationists are beginning to understand the symbiotic relationship between values and behaviour change. A person's willingness to learn certain free-time activities will be enhanced when personal values and commitments are present. Skills are important and can help satisfy a craving for a sense of adequacy, but are only part of the picture. Values are critical. The interdependence of values, skills and interests can be used to motivate and sustain a balanced and rich use of free-time. Also, if values, skills and interests are not developed in a person's early years, then they become extremely limited in their adult leisure outlook. It is to this particular concern — the value of leisure — that play agencies must address themselves. Perhaps play leaders will also want to choose their role as facilitators of human growth and, therefore, will want to provide human services that go beyond the management of playgrounds, activities and skills.

Leisure Education

Leisure education is an enabling process that can be accomplished through a variety of approaches. It is all those experiences and personal relationships that help prepare individuals to enjoy and reap maximum personal fulfilment from their lives. The objectives include the discovery of confidence, interests, values, skills and knowledge to satisfy the current and future life-style needs of each person.

Values Clarification

Too often, children do not choose meaningful free-time pursuits because they do not know what it is they need or what is important to them. A key to leisure education is helping children become aware of their needs and of the creative options available to help them meet those needs.

Making choices and decisions depends on values, and values need to be priorized and clarified. An authority in this area of concern, Dr Sid Simon, has noted:

> It is indeed a matter of values. In effect, a person does what he values and what he values he does something about. The gap between what one says, and what one does, is probably never more blatantly visible than how one actually allocates his time in relation to the values he claims to cherish. Consequently, one of the aims of leisure education should be to help students understand this. (Davis, 1976, p. 30)

Values clarification is an important part of leisure education and is not too 'intellectual' for even the youngest child. Certainly, young children can tell you why they enjoy doing one thing rather than another. Perhaps they have a social need — to be liked or wanted by friends. You can help them to find ways of meeting this need through healthy leisure pursuits. You can also help them find how this element can be achieved within other interests. You want to help children verbalize and clarify their needs and affirm their responsibility for meeting these needs through leisure pursuits. Asking children what they like and dislike; what is important to them; and what they need to feel happy is the basis of values clarification.

Cultivating Participation Habits

Direct participation in a wide variety of activities is also very important at a young age. Too often children select unfulfilling activities because of a lack of skill in the wide range of available choices. The lack of even basic skills in a few interest areas inhibits future explorations. Children must have positive reinforcement for all types of leisure pursuits. This will increase the likelihood that they will be able to build on these skills at a later date. These are just a few of the objectives of leisure education. There are others and there are many different ways we can accomplish these objectives.

Before we try to prepare others for leisure, however, it is essential that we come to terms with our own personal philosophy of life and leisure. This will help us better to understand the process of self-development and growth. If each of us were to spend the next few months considering our own leisure and our own needs and priorities, then we would have significantly progressed towards becoming a competent leisure educator.

The challenge is real, the task a difficult one. It calls for openness to creative and flexible approaches, pilot programmes and resource materials. By valuing leisure as a topic worthy of serious discussion, education for leisure can become an exciting and dynamic component of life – both for the play leader and for the child.

A Leisure Education Programme

The Ontario Ministry of Culture and Recreation has established a Leisure Education Programme to encourage the growth and development of leisure education as it pertains to individuals, community groups and leisure service agencies, the business sector and the education system. The main goal of this programme is 'to enhance the quality of life for Ontarians through preparing individuals to enjoy and reap maximum personal fulfilment from their leisure opportunities'. To this end, the consulting resources of this programme are pointed towards:

Raising awareness of the need for, and potential of, leisure education; communicating an understanding of the concept of educating for leisure; initiating and encouraging leadership development in leisure education in three sectors: education, recreation and business; and establishing a network of human resources that will assume responsibility for the continuing growth and development of leisure education.

Begun in 1976, the initial focus of this programme has been the school system, K-13. A major task in this area has been the development and publication of *Leisure: A Resource for Educators* (Cherry and Woodburn, 1978). The resource book is designed to give teachers a concrete understanding of the process of educating for leisure. It is frequently used in conjunction with professional development workshops and as a basis for curriculum or programme planning.

The task is a huge one. Plans include not only the educational target group but also recreationists and leisure service agencies. A few of the programme activities for 1978–9 are:

1. to publish the results of a 'State of the Art' survey completed for the leisure services field;
2. to develop a leisure education resource package for recreationists;
3. to develop, implement and evaluate pilot demonstration projects in education settings;

4. to conduct professional development workshops with both education and recreation personnel.

The Ministry would be interested in learning of related efforts that may be going on in your area and are willing to correspond with anyone interested in this area of concern. Enquiries should be directed to either of the authors.

Notes

1. This paper is based on Cherry and Woodburn (1978) which is available for $4.50 Cdn. from the Ministry of Government Services, Public Service, 880 Bay Street, 5th Fl., Toronto, Ontario, M7A 1N8. Cheques or money orders should be made out to 'The Treasurer of Ontario'.
2. Summary of Provincial Survey to determine the Status of Leisure Education in Ontario Schools. Leisure Education Project, Ministry of Culture and Recreation, 1977.

References

Cherry, Catherine and Bob Woodburn. 1978. *Leisure: a resource for educators.* Toronto: Ontario Ministry of Culture and Recreation.
Corbin, H. Dan and W. J. Tait. 1973. *Education for Leisure.* 3rd. edn. New York: Prentice-Hall.
Davis, Joan. 1976. 'Valuing: a requisite for educating for leisure', *Journal of Physical Education and Recreation,* American Alliance for Health, Physical Education and Recreation, March.
Levy, Joseph. 1977. *A Recreation Renaissance.* Ottawa: Canada Parks/Recreation Association.
Neulinger, J. 1978. 'Leisure: the criterion of the quality of life: a psychological perspective'. A paper presented at the Harold K. Jack lecture at Temple University, Philadelphia, April.
Strom, Robert. 1975. 'Education for a leisure society', *The Futurist,* April.
Tourism and Outdoor Recreation Planning Study Committee, 1978. *Tourism and Recreational Behaviour of Ontario Residents — Volume 5: Preference and Constraints.* Toronto.

Part Two

DEVELOPMENT THROUGH PLAY

4 ROADBLOCKS TO CREATIVITY THROUGH PLAY

Claudine Jeanrenaud and Doyle Bishop

Introduction

A cherished belief among many play specialists is that play enhances
the development of creativity. The fact is that the paths to play have
many dead-ends, detours and debris that discourage instead of enhance
the development of creativity. These conditions are numerous and often
not easily visible until it is too late. The traffic engineers, road crews
and patrolmen who manage the journey through play (e.g., parents,
teachers, recreation leaders, therapists) must work hard to remove these
roadblocks. Otherwise, play experiences will almost certainly help to
make non-creative children and later adults.

The authors propose to demonstrate these roadblocks with a general
model of the stages, or choice-points, involved in play. This model is the
authors' integration of diverse ideas about play as well as some that, up
to now, have not been closely linked to play. The model is the result of
the authors' many discussions between themselves and with students
in their 'Theories of Play' courses. The detailed ideas included in the
model are not novel; they have been borrowed from previous research
and theory. What is original is the particular ways in which the ideas
were integrated to provide one view of play and its link to creativity.

The main ideas from previous work are: Hutt (1966), and Linford
and Jeanrenaud (1970), who laid the groundwork for viewing play as a
series of critical stages; reinforcement theorists, such as Hull (1951)
and Skinner (1953), whose principles of learning help to show how
movement through the stages of play can be enhanced or retarded;
arousal theorists, particularly Berlyne (1960), and Fiske and Maddi
(1961), whose ideas about concepts like novelty, complexity, curiosity
and exploration help to define the distinctive crossroads on the path
through play; personality and development theorists like Piaget (1951),
Harvey *et al*. (1961), and Eysenck (1967), whose ideas illustrate how
different combinations of persons and environments, for both players
and managers, can produce different outcomes at the different stages
of play; and some investigations of play and creativity such as those by
Torrance (1964), Lieberman (1965), Sutton-Smith (1967), and Bishop
and Chace (1971), which have demonstrated that play is a powerful

medium for inhibiting or enhancing creative potential. The purpose of this paper is to outline the model and its implications for play, not to display or defend the theoretical development of the model, which is being done in a more formal paper.

A Journey Through Play

Figure 4.1 shows a journey through play:

1. *The attention stage* comes first. In order to begin learning anything, the person must first pay attention to some object or situation. No attention, no learning. No learning, no creativity.

Novelty, or the extent to which an object differs, relatively or absolutely, from what has occurred before, helps to gain one's attention. So does the intensity of the object or situation — how much it stands out from the rest of its environment. Things that are familiar or plain will not grab attention very often or for very long. People with an economic motive, like toy manufacturers, understand very well the necessity of attracting attention. There is the too common example of children in a department store, grasping towards brightly coloured toys and throwing temper tantrums because their mothers are trying to pull them away.

2. *Curiosity*, or the *approach–avoidance conflict*, must be resolved into approach if play is to occur. Novelty and intensity also make a person approach or avoid a play object or situation, but their effects are a little different from those at the attention stage. Novelty and intensity are increasingly related to attentiveness: the more of them, the greater the attention, but they have an 'inverted U' relation with avoidance–approach, as shown in Figure 4.2 (*page 76*). More novelty or intensity, up to a certain level, increasingly makes the person want to approach the play thing or situation. Beyond this critical level, adding more novelty or intensity produces greater avoidance. This effect seems to happen because too much novelty or intensity creates fear, not wonder.

Approach does not have to mean literally moving toward an object. It can also mean sustained interest, or not actively avoiding the object. This is an important distinction for spectator forms of play, where the play thing or situation is supposed to do something to the person, instead of him/her to it. Approach (or avoidance) can be psychological as well as physical. Also, the distance between player and object and the presence of barriers between them can affect the amount of approach or avoidance. In summary, if children are presented with optimum amounts of novelty, intensity, distance and barriers in a play situation,

Figure 4.1: Model of the Behavioural Stages and Blocks to
Creativity through Play

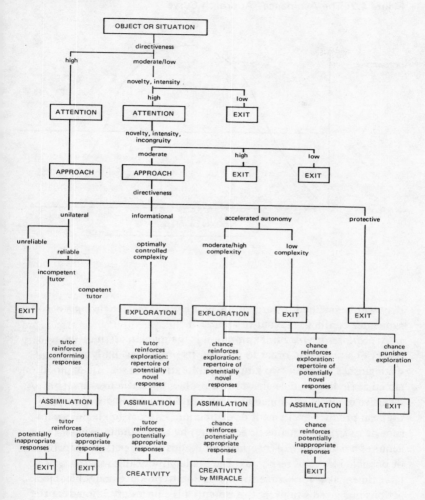

Figure 4.2: The Avoidance—Approach Curve

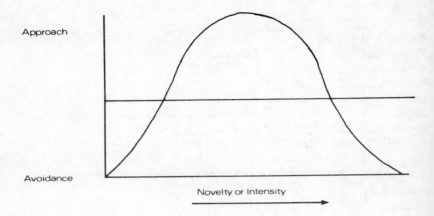

they will be inclined toward curiosity; they will resolve the approach—avoidance conflict in favour of approach.

3. *Exploratory play* or exploration is the manipulation of the new object or situation in order to discover its properties. Berlyne distinguishes between two kinds of exploration: (a) specific exploration, aimed at finding a single answer to a problem or challenge; and (b) diversive exploration, aimed at finding in the environment elements that can produce excitement or distraction. Exploration is the means (not necessarily conscious or deliberate) by which the individual acquires a wide range of information; it adds to the person's repertoire of possible ideas and responses. The availability of this repertoire at a later time makes it possible for the person to produce many ideas or actions in a given situation; this potential is a necessary, though not sufficient, condition for creativity to occur.

The complexity of the play thing or situation determines how much the person will explore it. A complex thing has many different parts and/or unusual arrangements or combinations of parts; so certain kinds of novelty affect exploration too. An object or situation that has many things to see, hear, touch, smell, taste and manipulate, especially in unusual ways, is more complex than one with fewer of these features and is more likely to encourage exploration.

These rules about complexity and exploration hold, of course, only if the parts of the object did not produce so much intensity or novelty that an avoidance reaction occurred. Given that approach takes place, then complexity should be increasingly related to exploration.

4. *Assimilation or consolidation play* is the repetition of behaviours or situations, which, during the exploratory stage, appeared challenging or were reinforced; such repetition permits the child to assimilate or master the behaviour or situation. As a rule, unless other people impose the constraints that will be discussed later, the child's assimilation play does *not* involve 100 per cent repetition. Complete repetition of behaviour, all the time, would seem to discourage the development of creative abilities. The natural tendency of children, according to Freud and Piaget, would be to make subtle transformations in their play or the situation. These transformations are the child's attempts to bring the object or situation within his/her range of comprehension or ability. These attempts are not diverse exploration, but are forms of specific exploration that result in mastery. This word, although a good one to describe the outcome, does not necessarily mean that the child is diligently striving to master some specific skill, as a high-school student strives to memorize the parts of the body for an anatomy course. If exploration is not interfered with, mastery or comprehension tend to follow, not necessarily by the child's design or intent, but often simply as a result of practice.

Assimilation play, along with formal training, helps the individual acquire proficiency in various responses; this proficiency is the other necessary condition for creativity.

5. *Creativity* is the production of novel responses that have an appropriate impact in a given context. If several truckloads of 'creativity' were dumped in one's frontyard, this definition probably would not help one to identify it. The definition, however, does neatly summarize, if somewhat cryptically, the essence of a great deal of research and writing about creativity. It probably summarizes, too, most people's thinking about creativity; most people would probably agree that redundancy of ideas or products is not creative, but neither is novelty for novelty's sake; if the idea or product does not resolve some problem or affect established beliefs or practices, it is regarded as not appropriate and thus not creative, for the given context, although it might be appropriate in another place or time.

The concern here is to outline the general conditions that are likely to enhance or, more often, inhibit the person's ability to make novel *and* appropriate responses. According to the definition, if either of these abilities fails to develop, the person will be incapable of creative performance.

The first condition for creativity, the ability to make novel responses, comes primarily from the exploratory-play experiences of the person; the attention and approach experiences are critical as well, but mainly because exploratory play cannot occur without them. In exploratory play, children learn the many different things that the environment can 'do' and the many things that they can do to it. Over time, in many exploratory-play situations, they accumulate a repertoire of potential responses that can be called upon, if and when needed. The more responses they accumulate, the greater the probability that at least one of them will be novel in some context, sometime. Also, the more there are, the greater the possibility of combining several to yield a novel pattern of behaviour, even though one response would not be novel in the given context. In short, exploratory play, by providing many potential responses, helps make the person potentially creative, in that he/she is able to emit those responses in some future context.

Exploratory play probably also increases people's motivation to make novel responses, or at least reduces their fear of making them. Studies of humans and other animals suggest that fear of novelty is an acquired drive and that it is greatest in animals whose early environmental experiences are impoverished. Piaget said that 'the more a child has seen and heard, the more he wants to see and hear'. It should be added that this probably applies to the stimuli produced by the child's own responses.

The second condition for creativity, the ability to make appropriate or useful responses, comes primarily from the assimilation-play experiences of the person. It is during assimilation play that people develop, through repetition and transformation, specific, known skills. They are not trying to find out all the things that the environment can do or that can be done to it, as in exploration, but are perfecting, within the limits of their existing abilities, their understanding of or skill at some particular situation or task. They are figuring out how to hammer a nail, throw a football, ride a bike, or why mother insists that food be eaten with a fork, not the hands, why it is necessary to go to the dentist, or later how a barometer, carburettor, or electric motor works.

In short, there is a kind of learning, distinct from exploration, that results in the acquisition of particular performance skills that are, or are intended to be, thorough and permanent. The more thorough and permanent the skills developed in a given domain of performance, the more likely it is that the person can make appropriate responses, and thus is potentially creative, in that domain. The more frequently specific-skill learning is concentrated in one domain, the less potential creativity the person has in other domains: it is not likely that a professional novelist will help to invent a new breed of computers or that an electronics engineer will win the Nobel prize for literature.

This completes the summary of the major stages. By successfully progressing through these stages repeatedly, on many encounters with the environment during development, the person would become creative. Progression can be blocked, however, by environmental, social and personality factors; the more often this happens, the less creativity will develop. It has been seen how the degree of novelty, intensity, incongruity and complexity affect these stages. Some other factors that can block the development of creative ability will now be examined.

Other Factors Blocking the Development of Creative Ability

Control can be exercised by parents, older friends or relatives, teachers etc. For the lack of a better word on which most people can agree, they will be referred to as 'tutors'. Tutors, then, can exercise control either directly on the child by means of directives and/or reinforcements (rewards and punishments), or indirectly through manipulation of the child's play environment, including its degree of novelty, complexity, intensity and incongruity.

Control can be exercised with over-directiveness, under-directiveness, or moderate directiveness. Over-directiveness can take several forms. The tutor can draw the child's attention against his/her will, and demonstrate how to handle an object or situation before the child has had time to be curious about it or to explore it.

For instance, the tutor may say this to the child: 'Here, come with me, I want to show you something: see this airplane? I want you to play with it, and I'll show you how to hold it. . .' This condition is called unilateral since all the information passes from the tutor to the child, and none from the child to the tutor. If the airplane flies and does not crash, the condition is considered as being reliable.

Under this form of over-directiveness, reinforcement is contingent upon conformance to directions. So punishment might sound like this: 'How many times must I tell you not to hold your ball with your left hand?'

Because both curiosity and exploration were circumvented, the behaviours displayed during assimilation play are limited to the motions dictated by the tutor. Consequently, the child becomes fearful, dependent upon his tutor's instructions, imitative, conforming and non-creative.

If the tutor's directives are unreliable (i.e., produce undesirable outcomes or contradict previous directions), the child faces a multiple conflict; following directions does not necessarily lead to desirable outcomes; not following them certainly leads to punishment. Unfortunately, having missed exploration, the child has no alternative solutions to the tutor's instructions. Consequently, he/she reacts with distrust and anger towards the tutor, and might try to oppose him/her. Often, therefore, behaviours that are opposed to directions and that escaped punishment are perceived as being rewarded, even though they may be regarded as inappropriate by society. So, the child might become rigidly anti-authoritarian and/or non-conforming, but not creative.

Tutors can also provide unnecessary assistance. For example, they might say this: 'Here, this is too hard for you, I'll do it!' Under these protective interpersonal conditions, the tutor is over-responsive to the child's wants.

While tutors might interfere at any stage of the child's experience, they tend to do so mostly when the child meets his/her first obstacle during exploratory play, thus preventing assimilation play. Therefore, while the development of novel responses might not have been impaired as severely as under unilateral conditions, acquisition of proficient responses, whether appropriate or not, will have been inhibited.

One response, however, will have been fully explored and assimilated: manipulation of the tutor in order to elicit assistance. The child might, therefore, become an expert at social manipulation, but without confidence in his/her own ability to achieve anything. So, he/she remains dependent on others to be creative instead.

Under-directiveness occurs when the tutor exercises no control over the child. This is considered to be the accelerated autonomy condition. Spontaneous attention, curiosity, exploratory and assimilation play all occur, but in the absence of any guidance by the tutor. Reinforcement is dispensed by the environment. Behaviour is rewarded whenever environmental consequences are pleasant, and punished whenever environmental consequences are adverse. For instance, a child's attention has been caught by a toy which is lying on a table. The child decides to explore the toy. Because he/she is too small to reach it, he/she grasps the table cloth and pulls on it until the toy falls on the floor. If the toy breaks, the child's behaviour has been punished. If not, the child's behaviour has been rewarded and table cloth pulling might become a favourite play activity. As this example illustrates, the absence of adult guidance makes it difficult for the child to learn about society's sense of appropriateness. So while he/she might have developed a wide repertoire of novel responses, few of them will be appropriate, thus limiting creativity.

Moderate directiveness, as in the interpersonal informational condition, is most likely to lead to creativity. The tutor manipulates the environment so as to provide the child with 'a series of graded experiences which the child will almost certainly follow because of the way the environment is programmed' (Harvey *et al.*, 1961). Although the child's approach and exploration are experienced as spontaneous, they actually follow a predetermined path leading to the discovery of appropriate responses. For instance, if the tutor decides that the child will learn about co-operation, he sets up a game where success depends directly on the degree of co-operation between the players. He/she does not tell the child what to do. The child's desire to succeed motivates him/her to test alternative approaches, including the co-operative one. The consequences of the various approaches are compared. This information is stored and thus becomes available for combination with previously stored information, so that conceptual links can be drawn. In other words, the seeking of alternative solutions has been elicited, and concept formation made possible.

To that, the tutor may add social reinforcement by congratulating profusely the child for co-operating or initiating exploration. So the behaviours likely to be learned during assimilation play are those rewarded during exploration as well as exploration itself. The child thus develops a wide range of appropriate and novel responses, the two necessary skills for creativity.

In summary (see Figure 4.3), of the control conditions discussed

Figure 4.3: Illustration of the Skills Developed under Each Control Condition, and the Resulting Creativity

| | Creative Skills | | Resulting |
Control Conditions	Novelty	Appropriateness	Creativity
Unilateral			
reliable	−	+	−
unreliable	−	−	−
Protective	+	−	−
Accelerated Autonomy	+	−	−
Informational	+	+	+

Note: + means existing skill; − means absent skill.

above, only the last one offers the opportunity to develop both novel and appropriate responses. The unilateral condition, by bypassing exploratory play and emphasizing assimilation play, encourages the development of appropriate responses (at least when the tutor is competent), but discourages the development of novel responses. The protective condition allows some exploration, but no assimilation. Therefore, while some novel responses might develop, neither appropriate nor inappropriate learning occurs. Finally, in the accelerated autonomy condition, exploration and assimilation both take place, but the absence of guidance results in the learning of many inappropriate responses.

Personality of Player and Tutor

The environmental effects and tutoring practices that have been outlined are probably determined, in part, by the personality characteristics of both learner and tutor. Some effects of personality are undoubtedly independent of what is actually present in the environment or what the tutor intends at any given time. On the other hand, the stages that have been discussed obviously help to shape the personalities of people in some ways. So movement through the stages and the participants' personalities are in a dynamic relationship; they influence one another. This dynamic interplay continues throughout development, which, though concentrated in one's early years, probably is a lifelong process.

The player or learner will be motivated or able to notice, approach, or explore things depending, in part, on his/her past experience in doing so. Some children will approach and explore things that other children will not even notice or will be frightened by. Piaget's phrase, 'the more he will want to see and hear', is highly relevant to this point; so is the added notion: the more he/she will *be able* to see and hear. Fiske and Maddi's (1961) idea of high- and low-activation people (seekers or avoiders of stimulation) could be an example of a pertinent personality characteristic, which presumably develops out of experience.

Eysenck's (1967) introverted and extraverted types, characteristics which he believes are largely inherited, are other examples. The introvert has a nervous system characterized by high levels of cortical arousal and low levels of reactive inhibition (mental fatigue or boredom); the extravert is just the reverse. These differences suggest that introverts should be less impulsive, more conscious of details, more persistent at various tasks, and more capable of long-term memory than extraverts; these hypotheses have been supported by a variety of studies. Extraverts, because of their high boredom potential, presumably would attend to and approach novel stimuli more than introverts, but would engage in less detailed exploration and less consolidation play. This reasoning would conclude that, given the same developmental circumstances, introverts have a better chance of becoming creative than extraverts.

Now consider the personality of the tutors. Even with the best of intentions, what can actually be done will be partly dictated by their own personality. In fact, their intentions — what they think should be done — will be somewhat preconditioned by their personality. This is a vital point for the management of play experiences: tutors (e.g., recreation leaders) cannot simply decide to manage play for the betterment of the player and expect to do so entirely on the strength of personal motivation and game skills. Their personalities might be such that they cannot recognize or manage the delicate balance between exploratory and consolidatory play. If the aim is the enhancement of creativity, they will almost certainly fail. For example, a highly extraverted tutor (if Eysenck's meaning of extraversion is correct) would probably emphasize a great variety of novel but — for learning purposes — superficial experiences in play. This approach, if prolonged or used often enough, seems likely to produce a jack-of-all-trades-but-master-of-none kind player. Though often interesting, such persons are hardly models of creative production.

Because tutors were once players and learners, their personalities have been shaped by the developmental experiences that have been described above. The previously outlined methods of control used by tutors were derived largely from the childhood training conditions described by Harvey *et al.* (1961). These authors claim that the different training conditions produce distinctive adult personalities, ranging from the highly concrete, authoritarian, rigid person to the highly abstract, open-minded, adaptive one. What this means, in the terms of this paper, is that tutors who were frequently exposed to directive, unilateral methods of control in their development are likely to become concretistic, authoritarian personalities who, as tutors, will employ directive, unilateral methods of control.

In this section, no attempt has been made to present a precise and exhaustive rendering of relevant personality characteristics. Rather, the importance of personality, for both player and tutor, was pointed out and a few directions for further thought and research were suggested.

The reader might have concluded by now that, in order to promote creativity in others, tutors must be creative themselves. The authors do not disagree with that conclusion. Unfortunately, telling would-be tutors to 'be creative' is about as helpful as telling alcoholics that they really ought to stop drinking. Clearly, it is easier said than done.

Summary

A model of stages of play, which is really a view of developmental experience adapted to play, has been presented in order to reveal various roadblocks to creativity. The major points are: (a) the critical stages of play, or more generally, development; (b) the dynamics between these stages and personality development; and (c) the many roadblocks to creativity as well as the nature of the singular path that is likely to lead to it.

Recreation rhetoric sometimes extols the joys and wonders of play and its role in creative development. Researchers, including the authors, have often looked to play as one source of creative behaviour. It is not the authors' wish to squelch pleasant thoughts or discourage positively oriented research, but perhaps an alternative view should be heard and researched: if the model is somewhere along the right lines, the greater miracle is that anybody at all ever becomes creative.

References

Berlyne, D. E. 1960. *Conflict, arousal and curiosity*. New York: McGraw-Hill.

Bishop, D. and C. Chace. 1971. 'Parental conceptual systems, home play environment and potential creativity in children', *Journal of Experimental Psychology*, 12, 3, pp. 318–38.

Eysenck, H. J. 1967. *The biological basis of personality*. Springfield, Illinois: Charles C. Thomas.

Fiske, D. W. and S. Maddi. 1961. *Functions of varied experiences*. Homewood: Dorsey Press.

Harvey, O. J., D. E. Hunt and H. M. Schroder. 1961. *Conceptual systems and personality organization*. New York: Wiley.

Hull, C. L. 1951. *Essentials of behaviour*. New Haven: Yale University.

Hutt, C. 1966. 'Exploration and play in children', *Symposium of the Zoological Society of London*, 18, pp. 61–81.

Lieberman, J. N. 1965. 'Playfulness and divergent thinking: an investigation of their relationship at the kindergarten level', *Journal of Genetic Psychology*, 107, pp. 219–24.

Linford, A. G. and C. J. Jeanrenaud. 1970. 'A behavioral model for a four-stage play theory', in G. S. Kenyon (ed.), *Contemporary Psychology of Sports*. Chicago: Athletic Institute, pp. 447–50.

Piaget, J. 1951. *Play, dreams and imitation in childhood*. London: Routledge and Kegan Paul Ltd.

Skinner, B. F. 1953. *Science and human behavior*. New York: Macmillan.

Sutton-Smith, B. 1967. 'The role of play in cognitive development', *Young Children*, 22, pp. 361–70.

Torrance, E. P. 1964. 'Education and creativity', in C. W. Taylor (ed.), *Creativity: Progress and Potential*. New York: McGraw-Hill, pp. 49–128.

5 AN INVESTIGATION OF IMAGINATIVE PLAY AND AURAL LANGUAGE DEVELOPMENT IN YOUNG CHILDREN, FIVE, SIX AND SEVEN

Thomas Daniels Yawkey[1]

Introduction

Play, and playing processes in the context of aural language development, has been of theoretical importance only within the past 15 years. Prior to the recent interest in child's play and aural language growth from empirical perspectives, play, and its varied relationships to development and learning, was largely left to intuitive hypothesizing (Hartley, 1952; Isaacs, 1935; Weber, 1969). Classical theories of play such as the surplus-energy theory (Spencer, 1896), recapitulation theory (Hall, 1916), and representative others focused on the causes of and provided a rationale for play behaviours that were replete with non-testable and inferred states. Classical theories of play considered thematic content of the child's play as irrelevant to explicating its causes (Yawkey, 1977). Although historically more recent than the classical paradigms, traditional theories of play, derived largely from catholic psychoanalytic and neo-Freudian models, examined both the causes and effects of play in human organisms. The traditional theories of play, however, rested largely on data gathered by clinicians on 'hallucinating' adults and personality 'deviates' in institutionalized settings. Trying to infer 'normal' traits from 'abnormal' subjects contributed little to the understanding of play and its relationship to cognitive development and to language growth. With the recent consideration of the young child, the importance, thematic content, and cause-and-effect relations of play and playing processes were investigated on a more empirical basis.

Given increased research funding, two contemporary areas of research in young children contributed significantly to researcher and practitioner interest in play and its relationships to cognitive growth and/or language development. One contemporary area of research on play derived from Genevan epistemology was developed by Piaget (1962) and his associates. It viewed ludic play in relation to evolving cognitive structures of human organisms. Piaget's view of ludic play, a contemporary theory of play, postulated that ludic playing processes were crucial to cognitive growth. Symbolic play, described as representations (or imaging) projected upon environmental objects, is, in fact, a basic and necessary condition for the development of thinking structures. Simply stated, Piaget noted and hypothesized a connection between representational thought and imaging, and between representational thought and the child's play. In this instance, symbolic play is viewed as a vehicle for inducing the organism to image. In support, Pulaski (1971, p. 213) observed that, '. . .the relationship of play to symbolization or mental representation is in theory the foundation for relating play and languaging'.

The second area of current research was more behavioural in orientation than Genevan epistemology and represented investigations based upon paired-associate learning paradigms. Current paired-associate learning studies viewed play as a process vehicle or mediator that aided the child's acquisition of selected learning skills. Although Genevan epistemology linked play to cognitive development, and paired-associate paradigms viewed play as a mediator for learning, both areas of research supported the importance of play and playing processes to cognitive growth and learning. From these contemporary areas of research on play as cognition and learning, three specific lines of empirical research on play emerged: (1) investigating qualitative levels of play and their relationships to cognition (Lieberman, 1965; Pederson and Wender, 1968; Pulaski, 1971; Wolfgang, 1974); (2) studying the improvement of cognitive performance relative to various play pre-training conditions (Feitelson and Ross, 1973; Lovinger, 1974; Sutton-Smith, 1971); and (3) particular play-like behaviours and their effects on cognitive abilities (Smilansky, 1968; Wolff and Levin, 1972; Wolff *et al.*, 1972).

Investigating qualitative levels of play and their relationships to cognition was classified as the play behaviour research group. These experimenters hypothesized that the levels of play in which the subjects were engaged at any point in time were directly related to their cognitive abilities. For example, Lieberman (1965) rated young children on both the quantity and quality of five specifically defined traits of playfulness. The subjects were then administered three divergent thinking tasks: ideational fluency, spontaneous flexibility and originality. The correlations between the divergent thinking tasks and playfulness were 0.36, 0.26, and 0.23, respectively. In similar research fashion, Pulaski (1971), working with primary-grade children, administered the Barron's Inkblot and Singer's play interview, and scored them for low and high fantasy. With the data from the Barron and Singer tests and the drawings, she grouped the subjects into high or low fantasy groups. Recording the subject's ongoing play behaviours, Pulaski then rated these protocols for organization, variety of themes and concentration — all cognitive-verbal indicators. The results showed that high fantasy subjects significantly outperformed low fantasy subjects on cognitive-verbal indices. Both Lieberman's and Pulaski's results suggested that the type (rather than the level) of play was related to oral language and cognitive behaviours. Similarly, the results of Pederson and Wender (1968) and Wolfgang (1974) consistently showed that play of young children was associated with cognitive abilities and linguistic behaviours.

Studying the improvement of cognitive performance relative to various play-training conditions was labelled the external-control play-like research group. These researchers investigated play-like performance in young children. Initially pre-testing, then training subjects on tasks using adult-directed play-like behaviours, and finally post-testing, the investigators initially focused upon differences between various play-like actions and how these actions affected other cognitively related behaviours. By training the subjects on specific play-like behaviours, it was predicted that cognitive performance would improve relative to the pre-training. For example, Sutton-Smith (1971), using the classical pre-test and post-test paradigm, employed a formal game as a treatment condition and found that five-year-old subjects significantly improved their abilities to conserve on number arrays. In a similar fashion, Feitelson and Ross (1973) pre-tested five-year-olds on creativity and thematic play, administered a treatment of thematic play to four groups, and noted a significant difference between pre-test and post-test on thematic play. Their analyses also confirmed their initial prediction that qualitatively enriched thematic play increased performance on creativity relative to the assessments used. Similarly, Freyberg (1973), Lovinger (1974), and Rosen (1974) provided experimental treatments of play-like behaviours and similarly concluded that play was a viable strategy for facilitating performance and was useful for acquiring selected cognitive and/or language skills.

Researching particular play-like behaviours and their effects on cognitive abilities was categorized as the internal-reality play-like research group. These investigators predicted that play would facilitate paired-associate learning and general cognition. This group, unlike the two other mainstreams of research, was focused largely on imagery and its role as a mediating strategy through paired-associate learning paradigms. Using play as a tool for imaging, three sub-areas of research using paired-associate learning paradigms emerged: (1) the form (e.g., perceptual versus symbolic) that imagery takes (Fleming, 1977); (2) the facilitating effects of imagery given task performance; and (3) the eliciting of imagery through varying task instruction (Levin, 1977). For example, Wolff *et al.* (1972) examined the relative effects of visual and tactual conditions in play of kindergarten children. The results showed that subjects who used action play with objects outperformed those who employed abstract (i.e., 'thinking things through') and pantomime play on paired-associate learning tasks. Wolff and Levin (1972), with kindergarten and third-grade subjects, assigned them to various conditions differing on the form of play. The results were that older subjects outperformed younger subjects on each of the forms of play. More importantly, however, the subjects employing action play with objects and those seeing play performed by others manipulating objects performed significantly better than abstract play and the control treatment on paired-associate learning tasks. Other studies using play from paired-associate perspectives (such as Varley *et al.* (1974) and Bender and Levin (1976)) consistently reported that action play using concrete objects effectively facilitated learning. Smilansky (1968), exemplifying a non-paired-associate design and the internal-reality play-like group of studies, examined a particular play-like behaviour on the young child's cognitive ability. Noting differential performance between children from low and high socio-economic status (SES) groups on play and verbal abilities, Smilansky trained low SES subjects on play behaviours reflective of high SES subjects. With various control and experimental treatments, the results indicated that low SES subjects in the adult-guided play group who received training on play behaviours reflective of the high SES subjects, and those who received additional life experiences to extend the training, changed their play behaviours relative to the high SES subjects. In addition, subjects who improved on play behaviours also significantly improved on mean frequencies of: (1) words used in a sentence; (2) contextual words; and (3) non-repeated words compared to baseline language samples recorded prior to the treatment conditions. From non-paired-associate perspectives, Smilansky further supported the notion that active play facilitated cognitive and language learning. The major hypothesis of the internal-reality play-like group was that specific play-like behaviours facilitated cognitive and language learning on tasks compared to non-play-like behaviours.

Outside the domain of current play research, investigations have explored aural language comprehension and the role of imagery. For example, Lesgold *et al.* (1974), using children and adults, found that the subjects on imagery treatments outperformed those subjects in the non-imagery conditions on the ability to recall aspects of a story after having listened to it. In addition, the imagery subjects outperformed the non-imagery subjects on retention and type of story. Working exclusively with children, Lesgold *et al.* (1975) also observed that those in the imaging training group performed better than the control subjects on recall of story content after both groups listened to a story.

From both Piagetian developmental and paired-associate learning perspectives, the young child's play was crucial to cognitive growth and language. Whether viewing play as a mediating mechanism for facilitating abilities such as language, or seeing play via its connections with representational thought and imaging for cognitive growth and oral language expression, the young child's play was a necessary, basic and fundamental condition for the evolution of intellectual and language systems. From research investigations on aural language and the role of imagery, results showed that imagery was an effective mediator on recall in aural language learning situations.

In the context of the research examined on symbolic play and its relation to cognitive and language systems from Piagetian and paired-associate perspectives, and investigations on the facilitative effects of aural language production using imaging, the hypotheses for the research investigation were:

1. There will be no statistically significant differences between play treatments requiring subjects to display self-action play and those required to demonstrate puppet play to represent a story on recall in young children.

2. There will be no statistically significant differences in young children between a play treatment requiring subjects to demonstrate play after and one requiring them to display during a story on recall.

3. There will be no statistically significant differences between age groups, five, six and seven given treatment conditions on recall of a story.

4. There will be no statistically significant differences between experimental and comparison groups on aural language growth in young children.

Method

There were 240 subjects (Ss), ages 5, 6 and 7, employed within the study. All the subjects were pulled from the same geographic area, basically rural in nature and agricultural in occupation, and attending schools which qualified for and were supported by Federal funds.

Since all the children in the study qualified for supportive services and were in fact supported under these Federal poverty programmes, the subjects individually and as a group represented a low socio-economic population. Having been randomly assigned to experimental and control groups by use of a random number table, 120 subjects comprised each of the groups. The restrictions placed on random sampling were numerical equivalency on age and sex by treatments. Thus, each treatment had 40 subjects per each of three age groups with 20 subjects per sex by age.

A 200-word selection from *The Biggest Bear* (Ward, 1952) was read to the Ss. The passage was selected because it was action-oriented, one with which subjects could easily identify, described a rural setting, and portrayed the main characters with non-racial biases (Yawkey and Yawkey, 1976). The reading and listening levels of the passage selected were calculated by Bormuth (1968) to be appropriate to five-year-old children. In addition, a tape recording of the passage was used to assess aural language comprehension — the dependent variable in the investigation. One puppet was also used with the Ss in the puppet-action treatment groups. The puppet represented a boy and was of the standard hand-operated variety made from cloth and stuffed.

After random assignment to experimental and control groups and within experimental to self-action during, self-action after, puppet-action during, and puppet-action after, each subject was individually tested in a classroom devoid of distracting stimuli in each of the co-operating elementary schools. There were two phases basic to the investigation: the play and language, and the assessment phases.

Play and Language Phase

The play and language phase — given the experimental group and its four treatment conditions — had four differing sets of procedures. In the self-action during, S listened to the passage and after every third sentence of the narration was asked by the experimenter (E) to 'use your body to act out the story'. E introduced the game situation to S in the condition by stating:

We are going to play a game. I am going to read you a story and you are going to pretend that you are in the story. I want you to listen to the story very carefully. I will stop at different times in the story. When I stop reading, let's pretend that you are in the story and you will show me what happened in it. The story is about Johnny. I would like you to pretend that you are Johnny. Now we're going to start the story. Remember to listen carefully so that you can do the things in the story.

E read the story and stopped after every third sentence. E stopped and said, 'Now pretend that you are Johnny and show me what happened in the story.' E used neutral prompts to encourage S to respond. The neutral prompts used in this and the three other experimental treatment conditions were: (1) 'Tell me what happened'; and (2) 'Did anything else happen?'

In the self-action after, S listened to the passage and upon completion of the passage was required by E to 'use your body to act out the whole story'. Introducing the game-like situation to S in the condition, E noted:

> We are going to play a game. I am going to read you a story and you are going to pretend that you are in the story. I want you to listen to the story very carefully. At the end of the story, let's pretend that you are in the story and you will show me what happened in the story. The story is about Johnny. I would like you to pretend that you are Johnny. Now we are going to start the story. Remember to listen carefully so that you can do the things in the story.

E read the story completely through. E stopped and said, 'Now pretend that you are Johnny and show me what happened in the story.' E again used neutral prompts to facilitate responding.

In the toy-action during, S listened to the passage and after every third sentence of the narration was asked by E to 'use the puppet to act out the story'. In this experimental condition, E introduced the game situation to S by saying:

> We are going to play a game with puppets and a story. I am going to read you a story and you are going to play with a puppet. I want you to listen to the story very carefully. I will stop at different times in the story. When I stop reading, I would like you to use the puppet and show me what happened in the story.

E showed S the boy puppet and continued:

> This puppet is Johnny. He's the one we are going to read a story about. Now we are going to start the story. Remember to listen carefully so that you can make Johnny do the things in the story.

E read the story and stopped at the end of every third sentence. Then E said, 'Now show me what happened in the story.' E gave neutral prompts when the subject did not respond.

In the toy-action after, S listened to the passage and at the end of the entire narrative S was asked by E to 'use your puppet to act out the story'. In this treatment condition, E introduced the game situation to S by commenting:

> We are going to play a game with a puppet and a story. I am going to read you a story and you are going to play with the puppet. I want you to listen to the story very carefully. At the end of the story I would like you to use the puppet and show me what happened in the story.

E showed S a puppet and continued:

> This puppet is Johnny. He is the one we are going to read a story about. Now we are going to start the story. Remember to listen carefully so that you can make Johnny do the things in the story.

E showed S a puppet and continued:

> This puppet is Johnny. He is the one we are going to read a story about. Now we are going to start the story. Remember to listen carefully so that you can make Johnny do the things in the story.

E read the story completely through. When E finished the story, E said, 'Now show me what happened in the story.' E again used the neutral prompts.

In the control treatment group, E said to S:

> I am going to read you a story about Johnny. I want you to listen to the story very carefully. At the end of the story you will be asked some questions. Now, we are going to start the story. Remember to listen carefully so that you will be able to answer the questions on the story asked at the end.

Assessment Phase

Regardless of experimental or treatment groups, and upon completion of respective procedures in each group and condition to which he/she was assigned, S was immediately and consistently administered the assessment phase of the investigation. The assessment phase consisted of listening to the tape recording of the story, *The Biggest Bear*. The taped story was approximately 10 minutes in duration. Every tenth word of the story was deleted. In place of the word, a 'buzz' occurred on the tape. After the ten-second 'buzz' terminated, the tape was stopped and S was required to fill in the missing word. The words filled in by S in turn provided a basis for assessing aural language comprehension. E said:

> We are going to listen to the same story again. This time instead of hearing it from the book, we are going to listen to it from a tape recorder. As we listen to the words in the story, we will also hear a 'buzz'. When we hear the 'buzz', I will stop the tape. I will ask you to insert the word that went in the blank. Let's practise hearing the 'buzz' and inserting your name.

After E practised with S to ensure understanding, the tape recording commenced, and when the 'buzz' began E turned off the recorder and asked, 'What word fits in the buzz or blank space in the sentence?'

At the completion of the assessment phase, S was asked how he/she liked the game and told to select a prize from a prize bag containing trinkets (e.g., toy figures, animals, etc.) for playing the game and doing so well. After the prize selection, S returned to his/her classroom.

Experimental Design

There was an experimental and comparison group. For the experimental group, three independent variables were examined: (1) forms of play (i.e., self-action; and puppet-action); (2) timing of play (i.e., play actions performed during and after the story); and (3) age (i.e., five-, six- and seven-year-olds). The dependent measure for the experimental group was the total number of words S filled in and scored correctly in the assessment phase. Based upon absolute scoring, the range of possible points per S was 0 through 20 — given the passage of 200 words in which every tenth word was left blank and the 'buzz' inserted. Each of S's word responses were scored either as correct (and given 1 point) or incorrect (and given 0 points). The over-all analysis for the experimental group was a $3 \times 2 \times 2$ multi-classification analysis of variance. Consistent with the design, the factors were: (a) age (3 levels); (b) form of play (2 levels); and (c) time of play (2 levels). Following the procedures outlined by Winer (1962) for multi-classification experiments, factors A through C were entered as mixed effects. Scheffé procedures were used for *post hoc* analyses. For the comparison group, the two main variables of age (i.e., five-, six- and seven-year-olds) and treatment groups (i.e., comparison and experimental) were analyzed.

Table 5.1: Forms and Timing of Play and Frequency of Ss per Cell for the Experimental Group

Groups	Age (in years)			Total
	5	6	7	
Self-Action				
During	10	10	10	
After	10	10	10	60
Puppet-Action				
During	10	10	10	
After	10	10	10	60
Total	40	40	40	120

The dependent measure and scoring procedures for the second main analysis were the same as the first analysis. The over-all analysis used was a 3 x 2 multi-classification analysis of variance. For purposes of analyzing treatment effects between comparison and experimental groups, scores between forms and times of play within the experimental group were collapsed. Given the design, the factors were (a) age (3 levels), and (b) treatment (2 levels). Following the procedures outlined by Winer (1962) for multi-classification designs, factors A and B were entered as mixed effects. Scheffé procedures as *post hoc* analyses were again employed.

Results

Of immediate concern in the experimental group were the effects of the age of the Ss, forms of play, and temporal proximity of playing on aural language comprehension. The ages of the Ss, forms of play, timing, and the number of Ss per cell for the experimental group are illustrated in Table 5.1.

For the comparison group or the secondary analysis, the number of Ss by age and group are important and are shown in Table 5.2.

For the experimental group, significant main effects were found for the factor of age.[2] The results demonstrated that five-year-old Ss differed significantly from six- and seven-year-old Ss on performance.[3]

Table 5.2: Ages, Groups and Frequency of Ss per Cell

Groups	Age (in years)			Total
	5	6	7	
Comparison	20	20	20	
Experimental	20	20	20	
Total	40	40	40	120

Table 5.3: Summary for Analysis of Variance for Main and Interaction
Effects of Forms and Timing of Play and Age of Ss

Source	df	SS	MS	F
Forms of Play	1	20.18	18.07	1.37
Timing of Play	1	15.36	14.00	1.04
Age	2	228.06	114.03	8.55*
Forms x Timing	1	8.73	6.72	
Forms x Age	2	41.76	20.88	1.56
Timing x Age	2	10.57	5.28	>1
Forms x Timing x Age	2	93.11	46.56	3.49*
Residual	108	1440.16	13.33	

*$p < 0.05$

The three-way interaction between age, forms of and timing of play
showed significant differences.[4] Table 5.3 illustrates the results of the
main analysis.

For the second major analysis, performance between the
comparison and experimental groups was observed collapsing scores
between forms of play and timing of play in the experimental
conditions. The treatment groups significantly differed from each
other with the experimental Ss outperforming the contrast Ss.[5] Also,
the age groups differed significantly from one another.[6]

Table 5.4: Summary for Analysis of Variance for Main and Interaction Effects of Treatment Groups and Ages of Ss

Source	df	SS	MS	F
Treatment Groups	1	911.24	822.40	3.91*
Age	2	793.28	296.64	18.42*
Treatment Groups x Age	2	68.68	34.34	2.61
Residual	224	2110.63	212.23	

*$p < 0.05$

Table 5.4 above shows the results of the main effects.

Discussion and Conclusion

Given the results of the analyses, the variables were of significant interest. With the results of age in the initial analysis differing between five- versus six- and seven-year-olds, imaginative play facilitated older children's play to a greater degree than younger children's play. When the results of the combined analysis were analyzed, the experimental subjects outperformed comparison subjects not using play on aural language growth. Thus, it appeared that older subjects benefited from play more than younger subjects and that imaginative play was a facilitator of aural language comprehension in children five through seven relative to the non-play comparison group. The results supported both Genevan epistemology and selected paired-associate learning studies showing that imaginative play was a facilitator of development and learning. Piaget (1962) and neo-cognitivists such as Pulaski (1971), Smilansky (1968), Sutton-Smith (1971), and Yawkey (1978) have generally postulated that ludic representations in 'as if' form were primary to basic cognitive structures. The investigation, with its results of older children outperforming younger children on aural language growth through play, was also in support of the results of paired-associate studies such as Lesgold *et al.* (1975). In particular Lesgold *et al.* (1975) noted that imagery through play facilitated older children and adults, but hindered younger children on paired-associate learning tasks.

In the experimental groups, the main effects of forms of play and timing were not statistically significant. On aural language comprehension, it appeared that self-action play and puppet-action play were similarly facilitating. Although the present study did not find differential effects between forms of play, Varley *et al.* (1974) noted that various forms of play as main effects were not similar on performance of paired-associate learning tasks. Basic differences between the present investigation and Varley *et al.* (1974) might be accounted for on basic research designs — the latter being an exemplar of paired-associate learning designs and the former representing non-paired-associate models. However, when performance between experimental and comparison groups was contrasted, subjects using play outperformed those not using play on aural language comprehension. It appeared that play was better than no play on the aural language growth of young children. The main variable of time showed that regardless of whether play was introduced during the story or at the end, temporal proximity had similar facilitating effects on aural language growth. Perhaps the length of time required to complete the entire passage before testing began demanded more concentration abilities and higher cognitive capacities than was characteristic of the sample. Lower capacities for concentrating, cognizing, and pretending in subjects from low SES vis-à-vis middle to high SES populations have already been observed in studies such as Lovinger (1974) and Rosen (1974). Given that the subjects represented a low SES population, it could have been that information stored by these subjects plus duration of the task quickly 'washed-out' over time as 'surface information'.

The interaction effect of play forms, timing and age in the initial analysis was also of interest. Although older subjects outperformed younger ones regardless of play forms and timing used, it appeared that five-year-olds using puppet-action during and self-action after significantly outperformed five-year-olds using puppets after and self-action play during the story. The results suggested that five-year-old subjects benefited more from puppet-action during and self-action after than from puppet-action after and self-action during. Especially for five-year-olds puppet-actions during required the projection of play schemes on to another object and served to facilitate recall and re-enactment of the story as well as maintain their concentration abilities. On the other hand, puppets employed after the story may have been treated as toy tangibles, i.e., something to be played with. With the possibility of surface information loss, puppets after could have been remotely connected with content. Self-action after required projection of schemes back on to the child. In this instance, self-action after demanded that the subject become directly and immediately involved with the entire story even though information loss may have been present. Brown's (1976) notion that children performed better through direct cuing and/or through direct cuing with organizers presented after passages might be applicable if puppets during and self-action after were thought of as direct cues and organizers after passages for involvement aiding recall rather than objects used as toys or physical movements of the body made in disjointed fashion.

Possible limitations in the study included: (1) duration between beginning and ending of the timing, and (2) the low SES population employed by the research. Possible additional research might answer related questions such as: (1) What are differential performance effects on language growth used in play during and after between subjects from low and middle SES population?; (2) Are there differential effects between play conditions of puppet-action, self-action, pantomime, and abstract-action play on language growth of young children?; and (3) Are there any differential effects between individual and dyadic groups of children on language growth through play?

Notes

1. The researcher gratefully acknowledges the financial support from The Spencer Foundation, Chicago, Illinois for the study, and the contributions of Dr Steven B. Silvern, currently Assistant Professor of Early Childhood Education, Auburn University, Auburn, Alabama for prior Research Assistantship responsibilities to the research project.
2. $F = 8.55$; df $= 2/108$; $p < 0.05$.
3. Using the Scheffé *post hoc* analysis.
4. $F = 3.49$; df $= 2/108$; $p < 0.05$.
5. $F = 7.45$; df $= 1/224$; $p < 0.05$ using the Scheffé *post hoc* analysis.
6. $F = 30.19$; df $= 2/224$; $p < 0.05$.

References

Bender, B. G. and J. R. Levin. 1976. 'Motor activity, anticipated motor activity, and young children's associative learning', *Child Development*, 47, pp. 560–2.

Bormuth, J. R. (ed.) 1968. *Readability in 1968*. Champaign, Illinois: National Council of Teachers of English.

Brown, A. L. 1976. 'The construction of temporal succession by preoperational children', in A. D. Pick (ed.), *Minnesota Symposia on Child Psychology* (vol. 10). Minneapolis: University of Minnesota Press.

Feitelson, D. and G. S. Ross. 1973. 'The neglected factor – play', *Human Development*, 16, pp. 202–33.

Fleming, M. L. 1977. 'Sensory versus symbolic aspects of imagery processes'. Paper presented at the American Educational Research Association Annual Meeting, New York, April.

Freyberg, J. T. 1973. 'Increasing the imaginative play of urban handicapped kindergarten children through systematic training', in J. S. Singer (ed.), *The Child's World of Make-believe*. New York: Academic Press.

Hall, J. S. 1916. *Adolescence: Its Psychology and Its Relations to Physiology, Anthropology, Sociology, Sex, Crime, Religion, and Education* (vol. 1). New York: Appleton.

Hartley, R. E., L. K. Frank and R. M. Goldenson. 1952. *Understanding Children's Play*. New York: Columbia University Press.

Isaacs, S. 1935. *Intellectual Growth in Children*. New York: Harcourt, Brace.

Lesgold, A. M., M. E. Curtis, H. DeGood, R. M. Golinkoff, C. McCormick and J. Shimron. 1974. *The Role of Mental Imagery in Text Comprehension: Preliminary Studies*. Pittsburgh: Learning Research and Development Center, University of Pittsburgh.

———, C. McCormick and R. M. Golinkoff. 1975. 'Imagery training and children's prose learning', *Journal of Educational Psychology*, 67, pp. 29—34.

Levin, J. R. 1977. 'Imagery processes in children's prose learning'. Paper presented at the American Educational Research Association Annual Meeting, New York, April.

Lieberman, J. N. 1965. 'Playfulness and divergent thinking: an investigation of their relationship at the kindergarten level', *Journal of Genetic Psychology*, 107, pp. 219—24.

Lovinger, S. L. 1974. 'Socio-dramatic play and language development in preschool disadvantaged children', *Psychology in the Schools*, 11, pp. 313—20.

Pederson, F. A. and P. H. Wender. 1968. 'Early social correlates of cognitive functioning in six year old boys', *Child Development*, 39, pp. 185—93.

Piaget, J. 1962. *Play, Dreams, and Imitation in Childhood*. New York: Norton.

Pulaski, M. A. 1971. *Understanding Piaget*. New York: Harper Row.

Rohwer, W. *et al*. 1974. *Understanding Intellectual Development*. New York: Holt, Reinhart and Winston.

Rosen, C. E. 1974. 'The effects of sociodramatic play on problem solving behavior among culturally disadvantaged preschool children', *Child Development*, 45, pp. 920—7.

Smilansky, S. 1968. *The Effects of Sociodramatic Play on Disadvantaged Preschool Children*. New York: Wiley.

Spencer, H. 1896. *Principles of Psychology* (vol. 2). New York: Appleton.

Sutton-Smith, B. 1971. 'The role of play in cognitive development', in R. E. Herron and B. Sutton-Smith (eds), *Child's Play*. New York: Wiley, pp. 252—60.

Varley, W. H., J. R. Levin, R. A. Severson and P. Wolff. 1974. 'Training imagery production in young children through motor involvement', *Journal of Educational Psychology*, 66, pp. 262—6.

Ward, L. 1952. *The Biggest Bear*. Boston: Houghton Mifflin.

Weber, E. 1969. *The Kindergarten: Its Encounter With Educational Thought in America*. New York: Teacher's College Press.

Winer, B. J. 1962. *Multiclassification Experiments*. New York: McGraw-Hill.

Wolff, P. and J. R. Levin. 1972. 'The role of overt activity in children's imagery production', *Child Development*, 41, pp. 537—47.

———, J. R. Levin and E. T. Longobardi. 1972. 'Motoric mediation in children's paired-associate learning: effects of visual and tactual contact', *Journal of Experimental Child Psychology*, 14, pp. 176—83.

Wolfgang, C. 1974. 'An exploration of the relationship between the cognitive area of reading and selected developmental aspects of children's play', *Psychology in the Schools*, 11, pp. 338—43.

Yawkey, T. D. 1977. 'Role playing and the young child', *Research in Education*, December, pp. 1—34.

———, 1978. 'Symbolic play and early reading and language growth in five year olds'. Research paper presented at the Research and Development Association for Education, American Educational Research Association Annual Meeting, Arlington, Virginia.

——— and M. L. Yawkey. 1976. 'Racism, sexism, socioeconomic status, and story location of characters in selected picture books for young children', *Elementary English Journal*, 53, 545—8.

6 FREE-PLAY BEHAVIOURS OF NURSERY SCHOOL CHILDREN IN AN INDOOR AND OUTDOOR ENVIRONMENT

Michael L. Henniger

Introduction

Play is an important part of the lives of young children. Beginning with the first few months of life, this complex set of behaviours can be observed in nearly any situation in which children are present (Collard, 1972). The grocery store, a laundromat, an alley behind the house, a playground, the home, the school classroom — these are some of the many environments in which children play.

Just as the settings in which children's play occurs are many and varied, the play behaviours themselves come in many forms. Garvey (1977, p. 2) presented the following purely imaginary dialogue between a mother and her six-year-old son to describe some of the many behaviours that are often classified as play:

Tom, I want to clean this room. Go out and play.
What do you mean 'go out and play'?
You know what I mean.
No, I don't.
Well, just go out and do whatever you do when you're having too
    much fun to come in to dinner.
You mean toss the tennis ball against the garage? Finish painting my
    bike? Practice standing on my head? Tease Andy's sister? Check
    out the robin eggs?

From this complex array of settings and behaviours, a more limited set was chosen for analysis in the present study. The play of four- and five-year-old nursery school children was compared in the indoor and outdoor environments. The study was conducted to develop a clearer understanding of the similarities and differences in young children's play in these two environments.

Beginning with the pioneering work of Parten (1932), the free-play classroom behaviours of young children have been carefully studied. Parten's social play research, along with the more recent work of Barnes (1971) and Rubin *et al.* (1976) centred on the indoor play

100

choices of young children. Findings from all three studies indicate that these social play behaviours follow a developmental pattern moving from simple to more complex as the child matures.

Piaget (1962) has added further insight into the play of young children with his discussion of cognitive play and its developmental nature. Piaget states that children pass through a series of stages of cognitive play, beginning with simple repetitive muscle movements (functional play) and moving to progressively more complex play in which games with prearranged rules are used. Rubin and Maioni (1975) used Piaget's cognitive play categories to code the classroom play behaviours of preschool children. Their results support Piaget's hypothesis that cognitive play is developmental in structure.

Parten's social play categories and Piaget's cognitive play categories, then, have been used to assess the indoor play behaviours of young children. On the other hand, outdoor play behaviours and their relationships to indoor play have been largely ignored. A review of the available literature found few research studies designed to compare the indoor and outdoor play behaviours of young children.

The purpose of this study, therefore, was to analyze in greater detail the play behaviours of young children, comparing indoor and outdoor play using modifications of Parten's and Piaget's social and cognitive play categories.

Review of Relevant Research

The major emphasis of this research is a comparison of the indoor and outdoor play of young children. This review of the literature, then, will focus on research analyzing social and cognitive play in these two environments. A discussion of research looking at the social and/or cognitive play of children indoors will be followed by a discussion of similar research studies done in the outdoor environment. The studies that have used both environments in assessing the social and/or cognitive play of young children will end the review.

Research Using Indoor Environments

Parten (1932), in an early piece of research on the play behaviours of young children indoors, developed a scale of social play categories to describe the extent to which children participate in social interactions. These categories were defined as follows:

Solitary independent play. The child plays alone and independently with toys that are different from those used by the children within speaking distance and makes no effort to get close to other children. He/she pursues his/her own activity without reference to what others are doing.

Parallel activity. The child plays independently, but the activity chosen naturally brings him/her among other children. The child plays with toys that are like those which the other children are using, but plays with the toy as he/she sees fit, and does not try to influence or modify the activity of nearby children. The child plays *beside* rather than *with* the other children. There is no attempt to control the coming or going of children in the group.

Associative play. The child plays with other children. The conversation concerns the common activity; there is a borrowing and loaning of play material; following one another with trains or wagons; mild attempts to control which children may or may not play in the group. All the members engage in similar if not identical activity; there is no division of labour, and no organization of the activity of several individuals around any material goal or product. The children do not subordinate their individual interests to that of the group; instead each child acts as he/she wishes. By the child's conversation with the other children one can tell that his/her interest is primarily in associations, not in activity. Occasionally, two or three children are engaged in no activity of any duration, but are merely doing whatever happens to draw the attention of any of them.

Co-operative or organized supplementary play. The child plays in a group that is organized for the purpose of making some material product, or of striving to attain some competitive goal, or of dramatizing situations of adult and group life, or of playing formal games. There is a marked sense of belonging or of not belonging to the group. The control of the group situation is in the hands of one or two of the members who direct the activity of the others. The goal, as well as the method of attaining it, necessitates a division of labour, a taking of different roles by the various group members, and the organization of activity so that the efforts of one child are supplemented by those of another.

Unoccupied behaviour. The child apparently is not playing, but is occupied with watching anything that happens to be of momentary interest. When there is nothing exciting taking place, the child plays with his/her own body, gets on and off objects, just stands around, follows the teacher, or sits in one spot glancing around the area.

Onlooker. The child spends most of the time watching the other children play. The child often talks to the children whom he/she is observing, asks questions, or gives suggestions, but does not overtly enter into the play. This type differs from the 'unoccupied' in that the onlooker is definitely observing particular groups of children rather than anything that happens to be exciting. The child stands or sits within speaking distance of the group so that everything that takes place can be seen and heard.

Parten's findings indicated that there is a general trend towards a decrease in solitary and parallel play with increasing age and a corresponding increase in associative and co-operative play. Parten's work has had considerable influence on the more recent research in this area. Her social play categories have been used with little or no modifications in the research of Shure (1963), Barnes (1971), and Rubin *et al*. (1976).

The more recent work of Barnes (1971) is an attempt to replicate the findings of Parten. The sample of children matched those in Parten's study in terms of age, occupational class of parents and family size. Barnes' sample, however, was from a small Canadian community, whereas Parten's subjects were from an American urban environment. Barnes found basically the same patterns of social interactions as did Parten. That is, solitary and parallel play tended to decrease with age, while associative and co-operative play increased. Barnes also found, however, considerable differences in the observed quantities of more socially oriented forms of play. He concluded that present-day preschool children are much less socially oriented than were their contemporaries of forty years ago. This latter result may be questionable, however, because of the sample differences.

Shure (1963) modified slightly the categories of social play proposed by Parten by adding a seventh category called *solitary-same* and specifying more clearly behaviours which could be coded in the remaining six categories. Shure defined solitary-same play as occurring when the child plays alone and independently with toys that are the same as those used by the surrounding children.

In addition to improving upon Parten's play categories, Shure was interested in determining if different areas of the classroom tended to stimulate specific types of social play. She found that play involving a single child (either solitary or solitary-same) was exhibited most frequently in the block and games areas. Play that displays awareness but lack of social interaction (onlooker or parallel) was exhibited frequently in the art and book areas. Complex social interaction (associative or parallel play) was found to occur most often in the doll corner.

A specific social play category proposed by Parten, that of solitary play, was more closely analyzed by Moore *et al.* (1974). Parten found that the frequency of solitary play decreased as children grew older. This led her to conclude that solitary play was a less mature form of play. Moore *et al.* came to different conclusions in their study of the solitary play of kindergarten children. Rather than seeing it as indicative of less mature play, they discovered that

> the majority of solitary play involved active, goal-directed activities such as blocks and arts and crafts, large muscle play, and educational play, such as challenging puzzles, workbooks or reading. Thus, most solitary play appears to be independent task-oriented behavior which is functional in school situations and indicative of maturity rather than immaturity. (p. 834)

The work of Buhler (1951) led play research in a different direction from that taken by Parten. Buhler described many of the cognitive changes that occur in children's play as they mature. She (p. 82) discussed the cognitive levels involved in the child's use of play materials by defining the differences between play and work: 'Play is that activity with or without materials in which bodily movement is an end in itself. We define work as the systematic effort to create a new entity.' Buhler also talked about how children later use play materials at a higher cognitive level to represent other objects:

> Something can be made out of some material other than that actually necessary to make the real object. This substitute material stands for the real material, since it has been named after it and it is possible in this way to make any number of things very easily that in reality could never be made. (p. 108)

Finally, Buhler discussed school-aged children and their need to be members of a group.

Children of this age enjoy the organization of, as well as participation in group life. Clubs and other organizations are founded, whose rules, or laws, require the performance of certain duties and responsibilities. Skill in social and competitive games is also emphasized. (p. 150)

The above-mentioned work of Buhler laid the groundwork for Piaget (1962) and the development of his cognitive play categories: functional play, symbolic play, and games with rules. It is interesting to note that each of these play categories has its roots in the earlier work of Buhler.

Based on the work of Piaget, Smilansky (1968, pp. 5–7) described a series of four cognitive play categories that children pass through as they develop:

Functional play. At first the play of a child consists of simple muscular activities based on his need to activate his physical organism. He/she repeats actions and manipulations, imitates them, tries new actions, imitates them, repeats them, and so on.

Constructive play. This form of play introduces the child to creative activity and thereby to the personal joy of creation. He/she moves from functional activity to activity that results in a 'creation'. From the *sporadic* handling of sand or bricks the child moves to *building* something from these materials that will remain after he/she has finished playing.

Dramatic play. The child takes on a role: he/she pretends to be somebody else. While doing this, he/she draws from first or secondhand experience with the other person in different situations. He/she imitates the person, in action and speech, with the aid of real or imagined objects.

Games with rules. Here the child has to accept prearranged rules and to adjust to them. More important he/she learns to control his/her behaviour, actions, and reactions within given limits.

Smilansky notes that dramatic play is actually composed of two major parts: dramatic play in general, and the more complicated socio-dramatic play. She defines four components that make an incident dramatic play:

    1. the child undertakes a make-believe role and expresses it in imitative action and/or verbalization;

    2. the child uses movements or words in place of certain real objects;

    3. the child uses verbal descriptions to represent actions or situations; and

    4. the child continues in the play episode for at least ten minutes.

To these four criteria that make a situation dramatic play, Smilansky adds two more for it to be socio-dramatic:

    1. there must be at least two players interacting in the framework of the play episode; and

    2. some verbal interaction related to the episode must occur.

Another study, by Rubin and Maioni (1975), used Smilansky's (1968) cognitive play categories in observing preschool children's play preferences and then compared these to scores of egocentrism, popularity and cognitive development. The results indicated a strong correlation between several categories of play and certain cognitive measures. The least mature level of play (functional) was negatively related to the child's ability to classify. Dramatic play, on the other hand, was positively correlated with classificatory ability. Furthermore, a negative relationship was found between the frequencies of functional and dramatic play. These results support the hypothesis that Piaget's cognitive play categories are developmentally ordered and that there is a relationship between play development and the development of cognition.

The relationship between play and cognitive development was discussed in an article by Rubin *et al.* (1976). The authors used both the social play categories of Parten (1932) and the cognitive play categories of Piaget (1962) to assess the differences in play behaviours of middle-class and lower-class preschoolers. Results indicated that middle-class preschoolers engaged in significantly less parallel and functional play and significantly more associative, co-operative and constructive play than did their lower-class counterparts. In other words, middle-class children tended to participate in higher levels of both cognitive and social play than did the lower-class children.

Research Using Outdoor Environments

An early piece of research analyzing the play of young children outdoors is the work of Johnson (1935). Her work involved two surveys of the play of children on three separate playgrounds, once before and once after a variation occurred in the play equipment. Results indicated that bodily exercise and play with materials ranked high in amount on all playgrounds when compared to games and undesirable activity, and did not appear to be entirely dependent upon extensiveness in equipment. Findings also showed that play on the more extensively equipped playgrounds was characterized by: (1) a greater amount of bodily exercise and play with materials; (2) smaller numbers of social contacts in games; and (3) less undesirable social behaviour. Play on the playground with a reduced amount of playground equipment showed less bodily exercise and play with materials and a greater number of social contacts and social conflicts.

The only other study of young children's use of outdoor space in their play is the research of Harper and Sanders (1975). Results indicated that, when free to choose between the indoor and outdoor environments, these children spent approximately one-half of their play time outdoors. Boys, in general, spent more time outdoors than girls. Boys used between 1.2 and 1.6 times as much space and entered significantly more areas than girls. In terms of equipment choices, boys played consistently more than girls in sand, on a tractor, on a climbing structure, and about an equipment shed.

Research Using Both Environments

The earliest piece of research to use both the indoor and outdoor environment in assessing children's social play was the work of Green (1933a, 1933b). Observations were made outdoors during warmer weather and indoors when the weather was cold. Unfortunately, these two sets of data were collapsed for an analysis of the differences in social play. Although results may well be confounded by including data from both the indoor and outdoor environments, Green found that the amount of group play increased regularly with age. Also, in 42 per cent of the observations the play was solitary. Broken down by age, the two-year-olds played alone 61.5 per cent of the time, three-year-olds spent 52 per cent of their time alone, four-year-olds only 35 per cent, and five-year-olds 30.3 per cent.

Sanders and Harper (1976) have compared the free-play fantasy behaviour of nursery school children in an indoor and an outdoor environment. Results indicated that children spent between 0.2 per cent and 6 per cent of their time in overt make-believe play. Boys and older children were found to spend more of their time in fantasy play than girls or younger children. Over all, boys devoted a greater amount of time to solitary fantasy play than did girls, and older children displayed significantly more interactive fantasy than the younger ones. Girls were shown to devote more time to co-operative role taking than did boys. Boys engaged in more fantasy play outdoors than girls, and older children spent proportionately more of their outdoor time engaged in fantasy play than did younger children.

Tizard *et al.* (1976a, 1976b) observed a total of 52 working-class and 57 middle-class nursery school children, balanced for sex, in three different types of preschool centres: traditional nursery schools with trained teachers; nursery schools with a language programme emphasis and trained teachers; and nurseries not staffed with trained teachers. The three- and four-year-old children had free access to the indoor and outdoor environments during the observation period. Two-thirds or more of the play of three-year-old children and over half the play of four-year-old children was solitary or parallel play. Associative play, the next most frequent category, totalled 21 per cent of the play. Co-operative play was observed in only 16 per cent of all the play observations. About 30 per cent of all play was found to be symbolic. Sex differences were found in choice of play materials, with girls spending considerably more time than boys playing with fixed physical equipment, such as climbing frames and swings, while boys more often played with wheeled vehicles and larger outdoor construction materials. Boys were also involved more often with miniature cars and garages and less often with miniature domestic equipment and dolls than were girls.

Tizard *et al.* (1976b) also cite some interesting results for children's play indoors and outdoors. A striking social class difference was found. There was a consistent trend for the play of working-class children to be more mature outside than inside. The solitary and parallel play of working-class children showed a substantial decrease outdoors as compared to indoors, while their mean score for social play increased outdoors. There were also differences in verbal communication indoors and outdoors for working-class children: outdoors they talked much more to other children and less to the teaching staff. Similar findings were not established for the middle-class children.

It is clear from the research reviewed here that play is an extremely important part of the lives of young children. The social and intellectual growth of the early childhood years is intimately bound up in this phenomenon. Therefore, despite the difficulties inherent in defining and describing play, it is important to understand the factors influencing its various aspects.

Two of the factors influencing play are the indoor and outdoor environments. Although children's play in indoor environments has received considerable attention, little research has been done outdoors and even less has been done in comparing children's play choices in both environments. The present study attempts to add needed research in this area by making an in-depth comparison of the free-play behaviours of nursery school children in indoor and outdoor environments.

Method

Setting

Children. A total of 28 nursery school children from the two morning groups in the University of Texas Child Development Laboratory were observed for the study. Seven boys and six girls from the older group (mean age 5.0 years) and eight boys and seven girls from the younger group (mean age 4.0 years) made up the sample. The children were predominantly Caucasian and came from middle-class families.

Environment. The indoor environment in the nursery school consisted of eight activity centres in which different materials were placed each week. These centres included a dramatic play area, a manipulative toy corner, a housekeeping centre, a music area, a science table, a block area, and a quiet/puzzle area.

   The outdoor environment contained a variety of fixed and moveable equipment. Stationary equipment included a treehouse platform with slide and steps, a jungle gym, a sandbox, a concrete bike path, a water play area, and a swing set. Moveable equipment, which was rearranged and/or changed each week, consisted of a boat, a steering wheel mounted in a box, metal triangular climbing structures with ladders, a teepee-type climber, large wooden crates, metal barrels, and an assortment of wooden boxes and tyres. Storage facilities outdoors provided children with ready access to tricycles, numerous sand toys, water-play materials, shovels, rakes, balls, chairs, ropes, traffic signs and wagons.

Procedure

Play Categories. The cognitive play categories as defined by Smilansky (1968) were used to assess children's cognitive play in the two environments. In addition, the social aspects of their play were evaluated using modifications of Parten's (1932) social play categories. Many of the ideas of Iwanaga (1973) were used to restructure these social play categories as follows:

Solitary play. The child's play takes place without the involvement of his/her peers. There is an absence of attempts to make social contacts with other children. Verbalizations and gestures are primarily egocentric and not directed towards others. The child shows no prolonged interest in looking at other children and may attempt to exclude these children from joining the play.

Parallel play. Two or more children are engaged in a similar activity. There is a maintained awareness of and contact with these other children by frequently looking at, talking to, and/or touching them. Maintained awareness may also be indicated by the frequent checking and showing of each other's work.

Complementary play. The child initiates and engages in play activity where differentiated roles are assigned to self and others. These roles are acted out independently as the children play together. The children involved develop and agree upon a general play plan, assign specific roles for each of the participants, and then proceed to enact their specific role with little additional concern for the play of the rest of the group.

Co-operative play. The child initiates and engages in play activity where either differentiated or undifferentiated roles are assigned to self and others. The quality of visual, verbal, and physical contacts indicate that children are aware of changes in peer behaviours. There is a greater adjusting of each child's behaviour in response to the shifts and adjustments of the behaviour of others. The respective roles are not carried out independently, but rather are developed and modified in interaction with other children as they play their roles.

Observations. A prepared checklist with children's names and the social and cognitive play categories was used to observe each child during free play for a 30-second time interval. After a child had been observed and his/her play behaviours coded, the researcher moved to the next name on the checklist for observation. Each day the order of observation was changed. Children were observed a total of 20 times indoors and 20 times outdoors over a six-week period. A minimum of ten children had to be present before observations could be made and no observations were made when the head teacher was absent. The author was the sole observer during data collection.

Table 6.1: Indoor and Outdoor Means for the Social and Cognitive Play Categories (Including *t*-Tests Showing Significant Differences)*

| | Group | | | | | | | | | |
| | Total (n = 28) | | Older (n = 13) | | Younger (n = 15) | | Male (n = 15) | | Female (n = 13) | |
Category	In	Out	In	Out	In	Out	In	Out	In	Out
Social										
Solitary	4.07	3.25	3.83	4.15	4.67 ($t = 3.21$ $p < 0.01$)	2.47	4.47	3.20	3.61	3.30
Parallel	8.36 ($t = -3.44$ $p < 0.01$)	10.32	8.38	9.15	8.33 ($t = -4.86$ $p < 0.001$)	11.33	8.33 ($t = -2.43$ $p < 0.05$)	9.87	8.38 ($t = -2.45$ $p < 0.05$)	10.84
Complementary	1.00	0.79	1.00	0.92	1.00	0.67	0.67	1.13	1.38	0.38
Co-operative	2.46	2.39	2.54	3.38	2.40 ($t = 2.23$ $p < 0.05$)	1.53	2.47	2.80	2.46	1.92
Cognitive										
Functional	0.43 ($t = -11.72$ $p < 0.001$)	6.79	0.15 ($t = -7.69$ $p < 0.001$)	5.15	0.67 ($t = -10.33$ $p < 0.001$)	8.20	0.40 ($t = -8.64$ $p < 0.001$)	6.07	0.46 ($t = -8.61$ $p < 0.001$)	7.61
Constructive	6.86 ($t = 5.42$ $p < 0.001$)	3.18	7.30 ($t = 2.87$ $p < 0.05$)	3.62	6.47 ($t = 5.56$ $p < 0.001$)	2.80	7.47 ($t = 6.48$ $p < 0.001$)	2.33	6.15	4.15
Dramatic	8.29	6.36	7.38	8.00	9.07 ($t = 4.57$ $p < 0.001$)	4.93	7.73	8.13	8.92 ($t = 5.42$ $p < 0.001$)	4.30
Games	0.29	0.36	0.38	0.77	0.20	0	0.33	0.47	0.23	0.23

* *t* was not computed when both the indoor and outdoor means for a category were less than 2.

Data analysis and results. The first task of data analysis was to tally the number of play behaviours each child exhibited for each of the play categories both indoors and outdoors. The mean number of observations for each play category was then computed for both environments. These indoor and outdoor means were analyzed for significant differences using a t-test for the 40 correlated means, with the total sample being grouped by age and sex. Tests for correlated means were run. Table 6.1 (*page 111*) presents the indoor and outdoor means for each of the play categories.

Discussion

It is important to emphasize the fact that the children and settings used to compare indoor and outdoor play in this study are not typical of most nursery school programmes. Both environments have a wide assortment of equipment and materials to enhance the play of young children, highly skilled teachers, and a low adult:child ratio of 1:5. This situation is thus an optimal one for observing play. Despite the fact that this optimal setting may limit the author's ability to generalize from the study, important conclusions can still be made about children's play in this situation.

The most comprehensive statement that can be made about play compared indoors and outdoors is that both environments are valuable in stimulating the various play types. While, for example, constructive play was enhanced more by the indoor environment, the outdoor environment stimulated more functional play. For other types of play, such as co-operative play, observations indicated that nearly equal amounts occurred in the two environments. Thus, one environment should not be favoured over the other; the settings complemented one another by stimulating different important play types.

Indoors

Traditionally, the indoor play area has been considered the most valuable environment for the development of the child. One indication of this is the amount of research generated in this environment compared to the outdoor setting. Other indications are the amount of materials present in the indoor environment and the percentage of the budget often invested there.

This study has raised serious questions about the validity of placing so much emphasis on this environment. Despite the undeniable values of free play in an indoor setting, this environment is limited in its ability to stimulate certain important play types and is only equivalent to the outdoor environment in stimulating some others. The limitations of the indoor environment should be kept in mind while reviewing the benefits of this setting.

The indoor environment seemed to foster three types of desirable play behaviours. The incidence of indoor dramatic play was significantly larger for both the girls and the younger children. Since dramatic play is viewed as an important vehicle for the development of social relationships, this finding seems very important. Garvey (1977, p. 81) saw dramatic play as important to the child's understanding of '. . . classes of individuals and their relationships of categories and types of goals, and of the possible actions and sequences of action that can be employed to accomplish these goals'.

In addition to stimulating dramatic play in girls and younger children, the indoor environment should be structured to enhance this type of play in boys and older children. Perhaps new equipment would help meet the needs of these groups. Teachers should renew their efforts to encourage the boys, especially, to become involved in dramatic play indoors. Given the importance of this type of play, even small increases in imaginative play indoors would yield positive results.

The indoor environment had a strong effect on constructive play as well. The groups observed showed a consistent trend to engage in more constructive play indoors than in the outdoor environment. Since this play type helps in the development of fine-motor skills and provides children with the opportunity to develop their creative skills, the indoor environment provided another fertile situation for growth.

It should be emphasized that the nursery school teachers took considerable time in planning and changing the materials and equipment placed in the indoor and outdoor environments each week. This careful planning influenced the amounts of constructive play observed in each environment. If their planning had included more woodworking or art activities outdoors, the differences observed in constructive play in the two environments might have been eliminated.

Finally, this environment had a tendency to stimulate more solitary play among the nursery school children. Although significantly different from the outdoor environment only for the younger group of children, the trend was for more of this play type to occur indoors. Although a primary goal of most nursery school programmes is to develop in children the skills necessary to interact with other children, it is also important for children to feel comfortable playing alone. Every person needs a healthy balance of both social time and time spent alone. A positive relationship between solitary play and high intelligence has been proposed (Strom, 1976), and with further research the values of solitary play will be more clearly understood.

Outdoors

The outdoor environment has received far less attention from researchers and practitioners interested in children's play. The results from the present study, however, seem to warrant a re-evaluation of its importance. It seems quite possible that given the right equipment and careful teacher planning and encouragement, any desired play type could be stimulated in the outdoor environment. This setting has definite advantages over the indoor environment for certain types of play and for certain children.

The outdoor environment, for example, stimulated nearly all of the functional play observed in the nursery school setting. These repetitive muscle movements are valuable in developing motor skills and in developing feelings of success and self-worth for certain children. The outdoor setting provides an excellent situation for the physical development of the child.

The outdoor environment stimulated social play as well. Co-operative play, the highest level of social play, was observed in nearly equal amounts in both environments. The only significant difference for the groups observed was the younger children's preference for co-operative play indoors. When the needs of individual children are considered, finding no significant differences in co-operative play in the two environments may be particularly important. It is very possible that some children are more inhibited socially in the indoor environment. For example, the space, floor covering and noise levels prevent the occurrence of the more active play that often encourages many boys to get involved in the higher levels of social play. Providing a stimulating outdoor environment for these children, then, could encourage this important type of play.

The dramatic play of the boys and the older group of children was strongly influenced by the outdoor environment; both groups engaged in somewhat greater quantities of this play type outdoors. Especially considering the boys' preference for more active dramatic play roles, the outdoor environment seems to be an important stimulus situation. Boys' preferences for the more active dramatic play roles were enhanced by the activity-producing materials and greater freedoms found in the outdoor environment. Dramatic play for older children also may be stimulated by the outdoor environment because of the wide varieties of dramatic themes available there; the equipment and materials provided outdoors are often less detailed, giving the older child the option of using them in a variety of ways to meet his imaginative needs and interests.

Implications and Recommendations

The results from the present study, which indicate that the indoor and outdoor environments studied differ in their ability to stimulate various important types of play, add important insights into the play of nursery school children. From these results, specific recommendations can be made that have important implications for curriculum planning and future research.

Curriculum Planning

In planning a curriculum for a nursery school, it must be remembered that both the indoor and the outdoor environments are important in stimulating a variety of play types and that each should be given considerable attention. Functional play, for example, helps develop large-muscle co-ordination and should be encouraged in a well-organized outdoor environment. Co-operative play is another highly desirable type of play which can be planned for in the outdoor environment. Traditionally, the indoor environment has been given first priority in planning, equipment and materials. This practice should be discontinued, giving the outdoor environment more attention and consideration than it has received.

The additional attention and planning given the outdoor environment could be used to provide a safe, yet relatively free, environment with ample equipment and materials, so that children would have the opportunity to explore new roles and situations not possible in the indoor environment.

This study raises an important question for curriculum planners at the nursery school level: how much of each play type is desirable in each environment? Due to the apparently strong influence of equipment on children's play choices, it seems likely that either or both of these environments could be restructured in such a way as to stimulate more or less of certain play types. The questions then facing curriculum planners are: how much of each play type is desirable?; and how should each environment be structured to encourage this quantity? The solution is not an easy one, and will require greater insight into the developmental needs of the nursery school child.

In restructuring both the indoor and outdoor environments to encourage specific types of play, three general options appear available:

1. both environments could be structured so that similar amounts of each type of play were stimulated in each environment;

2. the indoor and outdoor environments could be arranged so that different play types occurred in each setting with little overlap;

3. each environment might be organized so that it stimulated different types of play while at the same time allowing for considerable overlap.

This last option seems most workable; the differences in the two environments would maintain interest and provide needed variation, while the similarities would allow children to engage in similar types of play in two different settings.

Future Research

In reviewing the results of the current study, two categories of play were consistently excluded in both environments because the social play category of complementary play and the cognitive category of games with rules were observed very few times.

There are two possible reasons for the low number of observations of complementary play. Either it did not occur often in the play of the nursery school children observed or, more likely, the time interval of observation was not long enough truly to identify this play type.

Future researchers wishing to use this play category may wish either to observe individual children for longer intervals in order more accurately to code this play behaviour, or to eliminate this category altogether.

The games with rules play category was observed with very low frequency in both the indoor and outdoor environments. This finding is consistent with Piaget (1951, p. 142) who stated that 'games with rules rarely occur before stage II (age 4–7) and belong mainly to the third period (from 7–11)'. Unless the researcher has a particular interest in these early examples of games with rules, it is recommended that this play category be excluded in studying the play of nursery school children.

In the future, new research on play using both the indoor and outdoor environments should consider these settings as variables. For at least the functional, constructive and dramatic play categories, these environments have a strong influence on children's play. Researchers should avoid collapsing data collected in both settings to prevent confounding the results due at least in part to potential environmental effects.

Additional research is necessary for the individual play categories of solitary, co-operative and dramatic play in both environments. Research needs to focus on the potential benefits of solitary play and on how it may change as the child matures. The effects of equipment, teacher involvement and peer interaction on co-operative and dramatic play also deserve further research.

Little research has been carried out on analyzing the effects of various pieces of outdoor equipment on the play of young children in that environment. To date, the effects of such factors as amount of space, size, placement of equipment and the variations in weather have received little emphasis. As the importance of this environment becomes more evident, research in this area would be of considerable benefit to both researchers and practitioners.

Another little-understood factor for both the indoor and outdoor environment is the influence of teachers on children's play. Little has been done to measure this potentially significant variable. Tizard *et al.* (1976a) mention teachers as possibly influencing the play of young children in their study and suggest that this be analyzed. Intuitively, there is reason to believe that in addition to structuring the environment, teachers guide and stimulate the play of young children and strongly affect the play behaviours exhibited by them.

Finally, additional research is needed comparing the indoor and outdoor play of children across a broader age range and for different socio-economic groups and cultures. An understanding of how these different groups play in the two environments would provide additional important information needed to structure supportive environments that meet the needs and interests of young children.

The results presented for the current study were consistent with the findings from previous research and at the same time added new insights into an understanding of the play of nursery school children. The findings should provide a sound base for future researchers interested in analyzing play, using both the indoor and outdoor environments.

References

Barnes, K. 1971. 'Preschool play norms: a replication', *Developmental Psychology*, 5, pp. 99—103.

Buhler, C. 1951. *From birth to maturity*. London: Routledge and Kegan Paul (Sixth impression).

Collard, R. 1972. 'Exploration and play in human infants', *Journal of Health, Physical Education, and Recreation*, 43, 6, pp. 35—8.

Garvey, Catherine. 1977. *Play*. Cambridge, Massachussets: Harvard University Press.

Green, E. H. 1933a. 'Friendships and quarrels among preschool children', *Child Development*, 4, pp. 237–52.

——, 1933b. 'Group play and quarrelling among preschool children', *Child Development*, 4, pp. 302–7.

Harper, L. V. and K. M. Sanders. 1975. 'Preschool children's use of space: sex differences in outdoor play', *Developmental Psychology*, 11, p. 119.

Iwanaga, M. 1973. 'Development of interpersonal play structure in three, four, and five year old children', *Journal of Research and Development of Education*, 6, 3, pp. 71–82.

Johnson, M. V. 1935. 'The effect on behaviour of variation in the amount of play equipment', *Child Development*, 6, pp. 56–68.

Moore, N., C. Evertson and J. Brophy. 1974. 'Solitary play: some functional reconsiderations', *Developmental Psychology*, 10, pp. 830–4.

Parten, M. B. 1932. 'Social participation among preschool children', *Journal of Abnormal and Social Psychology*, 27, pp. 243–69.

Piaget, J. 1951. *Play, Dreams, and Imitation in Childhood*. London: William Heinemann.

——, 1962. *Play, Dreams, and Imitation in Childhood*. London: Norton.

Rubin, K. and T. Maioni. 1975. 'Play preference and its relationship to egocentrism, popularity and classification skills in preschoolers', *Merrill-Palmer Quarterly*, 21, 3, pp. 171–9.

——, T. Maioni and M. Hornung. 1976. 'Free play behaviours in middle and lower-class preschoolers: Parten and Piaget revisited', *Child Development*, 47, pp. 414–19.

Sanders, K. M. and L. V. Harper. 1976. 'Free-play fantasy behavior in preschool children: relations among gender, age, season, and location', *Child Development*, 47, pp. 1182–5.

Shure, M. 1963. 'Psychological ecology of a nursery school', *Child Development*, 34, pp. 979–92.

Smilansky, S. 1968. *The Effects of Sociodramatic Play on Disadvantaged Preschool Children*. New York: Wiley.

Strom, R. 1976. 'The merits of solitary play', *Childhood Education*, 52, 3, pp. 149–52.

Tizard, B., J. Philps and I. Plewis. 1976a. 'Play in preschool centres – I. Play measures and their relation to age, sex, and IQ', *Journal of Child Psychology and Psychiatry*, 17, pp. 251–64.

——, J. Philps and I. Plewis. 1976b. 'Play in preschool centres – II. Effects on play of the child's social class and of the educational orientation of the centre', *Journal of Child Psychology and Psychiatry*, 17, pp. 265–74.

7 THE PRIVACY BEHAVIOUR OF PRESCHOOL CHILDREN: MECHANISMS AND FUNCTIONS IN THE DAY-CARE ENVIRONMENT

Ellen Jacobs

Introduction

Although the concept of privacy is not commonly associated with young children, the research of Schwartz (1968) and Wolfe and Laufer (1974) has pointed to the existence of developmental trends in the expression and comprehension of privacy. Schwartz maintains that infants express a desire for privacy by squirming and wriggling away from an adult. Wolfe and Laufer discovered that children of 4 to 5 years of age possessed a basic understanding of privacy but could not provide a verbal definition of the concept in the way older children could.

The importance of recognizing a young child's need for private moments is indicated by the functions which privacy performs. It has been postulated that privacy is influential in the development of self-identity (Simmel, 1971), self-esteem (Ames, 1952), self-evaluation (Westin, 1970), self-respect and self-freedom (Chapin, 1951).

The advent of the day-care centre has created a trend in which young children are away from their home environment for protracted periods of time each day. Therefore the possibility arises that the population size and the communal nature of the day-care centre will combine to limit the child's opportunity for privacy in time and space.

If privacy seeking is a natural occurrence in the young child's development, then the mechanisms which regulate privacy should be very much in evidence in a situation in which the natural opportunity for privacy is reduced and/or denied. Altman (1975) states that desired levels of privacy are regulated by the mechanisms of personal space and territorial behaviour and studies have shown that both of these mechanisms exist in the behavioural repertoire of the young child (Lomranz *et al.*, 1975; McGrew, 1970; Paluck and Esser, 1971a, 1971b).

An observational study conducted by Jacobs (1977) in a day-care setting verified the existence of these behaviours at the preschool level. This paper explores the link between the development of a rudimentary concept of spatial organization, a sense of self, and the concepts of personal space, territoriality and privacy in the preschool child, and presents realistic provisions for privacy in the design of day-care centres.

Development of a Concept of Spatial Organization

In a review of the development of spatial cognition, Hart and Moore (1973) present the specific theory of the development of the concept of space in accordance with Piaget's constructs. In their discussion of levels of spatial organization, they outline the four major stages or periods of spatial organization which correspond to the major periods in the development of intelligence. The knowledge of space as a geometric entity is the result of a series of developmental steps and they indicate that the child at the preschool level has a pre-operational concept of space with a topological understanding of spatial relations on an egocentric orientation system for large-scale geographical spaces. 'Topological properties are simple qualitative relations like *proximity* and *separation*, and *open* and *closed* which remain invariant under continuous deformations excluding tears and overlaps' (Hart and Moore, 1973, p. 270). Therefore, it is likely that the preschool child would use spacing behaviour in response to spatial and social density conditions and that a rudimentary concept of personal space would exist at the age of three.

Sense of Self-Identity

The development of a rudimentary concept of spatial organization in the preschool child is paralleled by the development of a sense of self-identity. The child between the ages of 2 and 5 becomes increasingly aware of himself/herself as an individual and, through social interactions, develops an awareness of the individuality of others.

Ames (1952) investigated the child's developing sense of self as implied in the child's verbalizations in a nursery school situation. She maintains that the child's sense of self-identity develops in relation to mother and then in relation to his/her peers. Ames' study indicated that the child at the 3-year-old level was in the process of moving away from the child—teacher relations toward child—child relations; and, while doing so, the 3-year-old's play appeared to be at the level of parallel play. Children at 3½ years of age entered into predominantly child—child relationships and as they established themselves as persons in their own right they began to treat their contemporaries as individuals with particular characteristics and were better able to adapt to the needs of others. At 4 years of age, the child was engaged largely in interpersonal interactions which were self-initiated. The children played in a co-operative manner and were responsive to the approaches of other children.

The development of a sense of self-identity is dependent upon the understanding of where the self begins and ends. Once this sense of self-identity has been established, the need to be able to control access to the self appears. Altman (1975) has postulated that the regulation of interpersonal interactions and self/other boundaries may be achieved through the mechanisms of personal space and territorial behaviour. Personal space and territorial behaviour separate to define limits and boundaries of the self and the space which one occupies.

Personal Space

Altman has defined the essential and general properties of personal space which is basically the compilation of the existing definitions provided by theorists such as Hall, Sommer, Little, and Dosey and Meisels. According to Altman (1975, p. 53):

> Personal space is an invisible boundary or separation between the self and others; it is literally attached to the self. Regulation of personal space is a dynamic process that permits differential access to the self as situations change; when someone crosses a personal space boundary, anxiety or stress or even flight may result.

Hall (1966), Sommer (1969), Little (1965), and Dosey and Meisels (1969) have individual yet overlapping views of the concept of personal space. Hall's analysis seems to be the most descriptive in that he presents his theory of personal space in terms of series of concentric circles around the body which represent four zones, each reserved for a particular quality of interpersonal communication. He maintains that people reserve specific zones of personal space for particular settings and social relationships. The intimate distance zone (0—18 inches) is reserved for loved ones and intrusion into this zone by others tends to cause discomfort and in some cases alarm; the personal distance zone (1½—4 feet) is the space most customarily used by people engaged in conversation; the social distance zone (4—12 feet) is typically used in business and general social interaction; and the public distance zone (12—25 feet) is the distance used for formal functions, e.g., lectures, performances. Hall maintains that the type of behaviour permitted within each zone is a function of ethnicity and culture and that each zone permits a type of interpersonal communication. He has specified four variables determining the distance maintained in an interaction: culture, status, personality, and the feelings of the interactants toward each other.

Sommer (1969) deals with personal space in terms of intrusion. He states that personal space refers to an area with invisible boundaries surrounding a person's body into which intruders may not come, and maintains that it is not necessarily spherical in shape nor does it extend equally in all directions. Sommer, like Hall, stresses that cultural differences determine the differences in personal distance.

Little (1965) defined personal space as the area immediately surrounding the individual in which the majority of his interaction with others takes place. Dosey and Meisels (1969) have interpreted personal space as a buffer zone which serves as a protection against perceived threats.

All of these theories have stimulated research wherein the factors explored are those which affect or are affected by personal space including the following: (1) individual factors (e.g., age, sex, personality factors, and cultural differences); (2) interpersonal factors (e.g., different types of social bonds, impact of positive and negative feelings, dominance); and (3) situational factors (e.g., the impact of the setting on regulation of personal space boundaries) (Altman, 1975).

The experiments which are most salient to this paper are those which point to the existence of a concept of personal space at the preschool level (McGrew, 1970) and those which help to chart the growth and development of the concept of personal space in preschool children. McGrew found that by the age of 3 or 4 years children are adept at adjusting their spacing behaviour to different spatial and social density conditions. Almost all of the studies on personal space in preschool children point to the substantial changes which take place between the ages of three and five. Lomranz *et al.* (1975) found that there are significant differences in the size of personal space between 3-year-olds and 5-year-olds with little difference occurring between 5- and 7-year-olds. The study indicated that 3-year-olds have a smaller personal space than 5- and 7-year-olds. These findings might account for the more frequent infringement of the 3-year-old on the personal space of older children in a day-care environment organized along the lines of 'family' age grouping.

The studies conducted by Melson (1976, 1977) and Post and Hetherington (1974) point to a developmental difference in personal space between 3-year-olds, 4- to 5-year-olds, and 6-year-olds. Melson (1976) found that when the sex of peer figures and the affect attributed to them were varied, 3-year-olds made distance judgements based on affect but failed to use affect cues in structuring personal space, whereas 4- to 6-year-olds readily perceived and used distance to communicate the affective quality of peer relations. Subsequently, Melson (1977) found that older preschoolers (4- to 5-year-olds) placed greater distance between an opposite-sex stimulus pair than between a same-sex pair, suggesting the use of distance to discriminate same-versus-other sex pair relations.

Post and Hetherington (1974) found that 4-year-old boys and girls used proximity in judging liking. They used these cues less effectively than the 6-year-olds and it was postulated that for the 4-year-olds the use of these cues may depend partly upon how salient the cue is in the immediate social context. Perhaps the egocentric nature of the young preschooler and the size of his/her own personal space would account for his/her innocent invasions of other children's personal space.

Territorial Behaviour

Another mechanism for the regulation of privacy is territorial behaviour. Research into territoriality began with the exploration of this innate behaviour in animals (Nice, 1941) and progressed from there to the heated debates of the mid-1960s when it was proposed that man possessed an innate territorial response (Ardrey, 1966; Lorenz, 1966).

Definitions of human territoriality widely accepted in this field of research have been proposed by Sommer (1966), Pastalan (1970), Lyman and Scott (1967), Proshansky *et al.* (1970), Edney (1976), and Altman (1975). These definitions deal with the possession or control of a delimited space that a person or group uses as an exclusive preserve. Proshansky *et al.* have suggested that as territory involves possession, 'objects' and 'thoughts' should be considered territory in much the same way that space is.

Territories can be primary, secondary or public and defence of these territories may occur when the boundaries are encroached upon (Altman, 1975). Primary territories are those which are owned and used exclusively by individuals or groups; are clearly identified as theirs by others; are controlled on a relatively permanent basis; and are central to the day-to-day life of the individual (Altman, 1975). The home itself may be viewed as a primary territory, and the rooms within the home over which an individual has exclusive use may be seen as a primary territory as well. Secondary territories are not as exclusive nor are they subject to the same amount and type of control as are primary territories. This concept of secondary territory corresponds to Lyman and Scott's (1967) interactional territory, an area where a social gathering may occur, and Brower's (1965) community territory, as in private clubs. Child-care/day-care centres may be seen as secondary territories that operate in a quasi-exclusive manner in that only those registered may enter the room and take part in the activities, but the composition of the population may change as children leave and others are added to the roster. In this situation, the children do not have exclusive use of and control over space and equipment, all of which must be shared; as possessions are not well defined, there is more conflict in this secondary territory than in primary territories. Public territories are defined as being temporary in nature in that the area becomes the territory of the current occupant but anyone has access to the area. In this type of territory, users must follow some social rules and norms. These public territories have also been labelled free territories (Brower, 1965) and jurisdictions (Roos, 1968). Territorial behaviour is related to and influenced by (1) the need or motives of the individual or group, (2) the size and location of the geographical space, (3) the population density, (4) the composition of the population — sex, age and cultural ethnicity, (5) the types of territorial markers which have been erected, and (6) the response of outsiders to these markers (their ability to 'read' these markers accurately). If possessions are viewed as territory then the number of objects and the availability of these objects will affect territorial behaviour. When any of these territories are invaded or encroached upon, defensive reactions are called into play. These reactions may take the form of turf defence, insulation or linguistic collusion (Lyman and Scott, 1967).

The studies of children and territorial behaviour indicate that territoriality is a part of the preschool child's repertoire of behaviour patterns. Paluck and Esser (1971a) indicate that territorial behaviour was prevalent in retarded 5-year-old boys who, having been removed from their original group, tried to reclaim their old territories when they were returned to the group. In a second study, Paluck and Esser (1971b) observed and recorded the means whereby 5-year-olds established and aggressively defended their territories.

The development of the child's ability to control a territory is presented in the text *No Trespassing* (Bakker and Bakker-Rabdau, 1973). If a child is to grow up to be able to hold his/her own in the territorial competition of the adult world, then he/she must be provided with graduated learning experiences in the acquisition and maintenance of territory. The acquisition of territorial skills is a graduated process and co-ordination between the child's developing skills and the amount of territory in which he/she is allowed to operate is of vital importance to maturation. Problems are created when a child's territory is allowed to expand before he/she has acquired the skills necessary to cope with increased territory. In situations where the child has no restrictions on his/her territorial expansion, the child may fail to learn that other individuals have definite territories and are willing to defend them and he/she will continually trespass across others' boundaries. Bakker and Bakker-Rabdau (1973) postulate that the lack of restriction upon territory leads to a general lack of development of acquisition skills and, as a general lack of mastery exists, the child will be impaired in the development of a personal identity. Therefore, the development of territorial behaviour and sense of self-identity are inextricably linked with one another.

Invasion, Intrusion and Encroachment

The functional importance of personal space and territoriality becomes evident when personal space and territory are intruded, invaded or encroached upon. Invasion involves bypassing boundaries and interrupting someone or taking over a territory on either a temporary or an enduring basis (Altman, 1975). Intrusion is an ecological placement of the body near another person (Goffman, 1971). Intrusions can occur by means of eye gazes, intrusive looks, interference with what someone else is doing and certain kinds of questioning (Altman, 1975). Encroachment involves unwarranted crossing of a self or a group boundary.

In situations of invasion, intrusion or encroachment, the coping mechanisms of the human are called into play. Research indicates that adults respond to a variety of personal space and territorial invasions by anxiety, non-verbal behaviour (such as shifts in angles or orientation), and flight depending upon the age of the intruder and the severity of the intrusion (McDowell, 1972; McBride *et al.*, 1965; Fry and Willis, 1971). Preschoolers (age 3 to 5) who respond to an intrusion of their personal space and territory do so with less subtle, more aggressive verbal and non-verbal behaviour than that employed by adults (Jacobs, 1977).

Adults are usually successful in warding off potential invasions by using a set of signals which other adults of the same cultural background can read. In addition, adults employ a variety of markers which indicate territorial possession and are mindful even of the most innocuous of markers.

Research indicates that preschoolers are less sensitive to territorial and boundary markers than are adults (Jacobs, 1977). While preschoolers of 4 and 5 years of age have been observed during free play setting up elaborate territorial markers by using blocks and portable structures and by rearranging chairs, the younger preschoolers have been observed invading and encroaching upon the territory of the older children. The young preschoolers are more egocentric and less mature in the development of their concept of personal space and tend to be incapable of reading privacy signals. Therefore they are more prone to encroachments and innocent invasions of the older preschooler's (5-year-old's) personal space and territory.

The research cited in this paper indicates that personal space and territorial behaviour are part of the repertoire of behaviours of preschoolers. In so far as personal space and territoriality operate as mechanisms in the control of self/other boundaries and interpersonal interactions, both may be viewed as regulators of privacy.

Privacy

Privacy has been defined in a variety of ways which include the control of information about the self (Edney, 1976), the maximization of freedom of choice and control (Proshansky *et al.*, 1970), and the control of interactions between the self and others (Westin, 1970). The one aspect of privacy which is crucial to the interpretation of privacy in a positive manner is that it is a 'dialectic-process' (Westin, 1970; Altman, 1975). Westin states that the individual is constantly engaged in a personal adjustment process whereby a balance between the desire for disclosure and the desire for privacy is maintained. Altman maintains that humans seek interaction and restriction of interaction in accordance with their momentary needs. When desired levels of privacy are not attained the individual will experience discomfort and will act to remedy the imbalance of privacy. Privacy as discussed here should not be considered as a habitual overriding behavioural style. It may involve only momentary withdrawal by individuals or small social units from main and larger groups. Viewed in terms of the relation of the individual to social participation, privacy is the voluntary and temporary withdrawal of a person from the general society through physical or psychological means, in a state of either solitude or small-group intimacy.

In a study conducted by Laufer *et al.* (1974), privacy was defined in terms of a series of analytic dimensions:

self/ego
interaction
life-cycle
biographical history

control
ecological-cultural
task orientation
ritual privacy
phenomenological.

The results of this study indicate that children as young as 5 years of age know what privacy is, and in some fashion can define their concept of privacy. The self/ego dimension, which involves the growth of autonomy through social interaction, and the interaction dimension, which deals with the balance between privacy and interaction for effective functioning of the individual, are most relevant to the issue of privacy in the day-care environment. Territorial behaviour operates in the control of access to specific spaces. If one has complete control over these spaces, then freedom of choice is maximized and the individual's interests reign supreme within that space. As personal space operates in the control of self/other boundaries it permits the individual to control access to the self. Territorial behaviour and personal space which regulate privacy are instrumental in the development of personal autonomy and self-identity in that they regulate control over space and self/other boundaries. The ability to control the environment strongly influences the individual's sense of self-identity and autonomy.

The Functions of Individual Privacy in the Young Child's Development

Privacy is seen as performing the following functions for adults:
(1) personal autonomy; (2) emotional release; and (3) self-evaluation (Westin, 1970). In the child's development, privacy aids in the development of (1) personal autonomy; (2) information processing; (3) emotional release; (4) self-evaluation; and (5) self-identity.

Personal Autonomy

Private moments offer the child the opportunity to come to terms with his/her own thoughts and feelings. Westin (1970) states that the development of individuality and independence of thought requires private time for sheltered experimentation and testing of ideas without fear of ridicule. Children may practise a new skill in private, until they have mastered it; then, they reappear and triumphantly display their accomplishment for public viewing. Singer (1973) has found that privacy fosters make-believe play as the child in a privacy situation is more likely to try out new roles and explore possibilities if given time away from other people, other types of distracting stimulation, and criticism of role portrayal.

Information Processing

Children, too, require time to process the information which is constantly passed on to them throughout the day. Without time to be alone with their thoughts, they cannot assimilate what they have learned, nor can they evaluate the information and accommodate to the new ideas which have been presented to them. They require private moments in which to reflect upon, to test, and to organize new information.

Emotional Release

Children, like adults, are required to conform to standards of behaviour that are higher than they can maintain at all times, although these standards are widely shared by the society in which they live. Non-compliance with these social norms usually leads to pressure and remonstrations from adults and a loss of self-esteem (Westin, 1970). Privacy affords the child time in which the standards of behaviour are relaxed and the pressures of social rules are dropped. For instance, the act of sharing is one of the social norms with which day-care children must comply. Eight hours of sharing can be a rather arduous task for a young child, but recognition of the child's territorial behaviour as a need to possess an object or space for a short period of time will ease the pressure felt by the child.

The day-care environment provides constant emotional stimulation from which children require periodic respites throughout the day. Children often require time and a private place in which to release their emotions without being admonished or ridiculed. They need a place to release a flood of tears, to suck a thumb, or to express anger. Private places plus recognized 'time out' for venting feelings meet this need.

Self-Evaluation

Privacy meets the needs of the individual to integrate his experiences into a meaningful pattern and to exert his individuality on events (Westin, 1970). Children require a private time in which to assess the outcome of their social interactions and to take inventory of their behaviour. A child who has been involved in a social encounter which leaves one child crying and the other one racing from the scene in search of a private retreat, requires a quiet, private place where he/she can work things through without interruption or interference. The effectiveness of these private periods is not dependent on the length of time spent in privacy. Moments of privacy provide the child with a sufficient amount of aloneness in which he/she may gather his/her thoughts, deal with his/her emotions, and relax from the rigours of societal norms and expectations.

Self-identity

Self-identity involves the person or group's cognitive psychological and emotional definition and understanding of themselves as beings (Altman, 1975). As the child interacts with peer groups, he/she becomes aware of individual differences. The opportunity to interact and then to withdraw from social interaction affords the child the opportunity to consider the outcome of interactions, to process information and to deal with emotional situations. Through this dialectic process of communication and momentary withdrawal, the child is afforded the time and space in which to develop an awareness of capabilities, interests, attitudes, strengths and weaknesses — as well as the ability to control access to the self and one's territory which enhances the child's self-esteem and self-identity through the mechanisms of personal space and territoriality.

The child develops a sense of control when territorial markers are respected and the verbal and/or non-verbal indication of a personal space intrusion is responded to by the intruder.

Privacy in the Day-care Environment

An observational study conducted at the Concordia University Child Care Center during the morning and afternoon free-play period examined the relationship between activity areas and the duration and frequency of privacy behaviour as measured by personal space and territoriality. The four areas observed were: the sand and block area; the table games and reading area; the play dough and housekeeping area; and the runway where a large appliance box was located.

The results of the study indicate that the frequency and duration of verbal territorial behaviour were significantly higher in the runway than in all other areas. The children tended to establish themselves in the box and defend themselves from invasions. As territorial markers and signs of occupation, they closed the windows and doors of the box (house). One child was observed standing inside the box with his arms extended through the windows, as he maneouvred a chair into position in front of the door to the box. Verbal defence of this territory was in the form of aggressive threats and gutteral imitations of gunshots.

The frequency of non-verbal territorial behaviour was significantly higher in the runway and games area than in the other two areas. In both of these areas, it was possible to establish a temporary territory and use a variety of markers to indicate the extent of the area which was occupied, but due to the limited size of these areas encroachment was not uncommon. The focal point of the runway was the appliance box into which only three children could fit comfortably; and because the demand for this particular space was high and the capacity was low, there was an increase in territorial behaviour. The focal point of the games area was a table upon which the more complex puzzles and fine-motor games were placed and were not to be removed. The unique quality of these games placed them in high demand and an increase in territorial behaviour occurred.

In both of these areas, although territories were quickly established, the markers were not always read correctly by the younger preschoolers; as a result, the territorial defenders resorted to pushing invaders away from their closely confined territory.

Privacy-seeking behaviour occurred more frequently during the unstructured play period when the children were free to wander from one interest area to another and were able to establish themselves in the areas which they found most appealing at the time. As privacy is an important aspect in the development of the young child, the provision of safe and interesting spaces for private moments in the day-care environment is vital.

Places for Privacy

Within the day-care centre, good play spaces maximize the freedom of choice for the child (Kritchevsky *et al.*, 1969). In these spaces, a child can restructure and manipulate the environment to suit his/her individual momentary needs. Successful structuring and use of an enclosure will enhance the child's sense of autonomy.

During the course of a day in a day-care centre, children do seem to seek out places to pause, such as enclosures where they may relax for a few moments away from the stimulation of the group. The enclosure of these places need not be absolute — a sense of privacy rather than physical isolation is desired (Moore, 1966). These spaces must be easy for the teacher to supervise, yet enclosed enough to provide the environmental sense of aloneness which the child is seeking.

Provisions should be made for gathering spots for intimate groups. These children tend to congregate in sheltered spaces such as stairs and nooks-and-crannies so that they can have a sense of privacy for their games, fantasies and discussions. The planning of safe, definitive, comfortable places takes the strain off heavy traffic areas such as stairs.

It is essential to provide pathways through activity areas so that territories are not unnecessarily encroached upon and aggressive defence of territory becomes an exceptional occurrence.

As the areas within the centre belong to all of the children, it is helpful to provide each child with a place for his/her own possessions. Plastic tubs with name labels are quite helpful; but if space permits, large open cubbies are even better.

Activity areas which attract small cohesive groups should not be located near the entrance to the centre as the child who arrives later than the others is treated as an invader upon entering the classroom — a most unpleasant way to start the day.

Placement of cots for the nap period requires careful consideration. In most North American homes, the one private place is the bedroom, even if it is shared. Furthermore, strict territorial arrangements are established in shared bedrooms. Therefore, in order to retain some consistency between home and school and to provide the day-care child with a modicum of privacy during the day, the sleeping arrangements must provide a sense of enclosure and privacy.

In keeping with Bakker and Bakker-Rabdau's (1973) theory of gradually enlarging the young child's territory as he/she indicates an expertise in dealing with a small space, it would be wise to locate the youngest group in a smaller room as a home room and introduce them gradually into the age-integrated large playroom.

The dressing-up/housekeeping area should provide a sufficient sense of privacy for active involvement in role playing and characterization without fear of criticism.

Highly structured play areas should be interspersed with loosely structured ones, as high structure does not offer the same opportunity for freedom of choice and privacy as loose structure does. These areas with loose organizations (e.g., the runway and the box (house)) should be located away from the mainstream of activity, so that innocent invasions are infrequent and aggressive territorial behaviour does not prevail.

Conclusion

Privacy aids in the development of self-identity and related concepts by defining the limits and boundaries of the self. As the development of self-identity is central to human existence (Altman, 1975), the provision for private time and space for children at the preschool level is of utmost importance. Personal space and territorial behaviour are mechanisms which function to regulate desired levels of privacy, and it has been shown that young children in situations such as free play in the day-care centre display both of these behavioural mechanisms in age-related degrees of sophistication.

Preschoolers who spend the majority of their time in their home environment tend to have sufficient opportunity to satisfy their privacy needs, as parents do not constantly monitor the child's activities or whereabouts; whereas the young child in the day-care centre is usually confronted with continuous interpersonal interactions and his/her activities and whereabouts are closely watched by the teacher, thereby greatly reducing the child's opportunity for privacy. In order to ensure that the day-care child has adequate time and space for safe emotional release, for self-evaluation, and above all for the development of a sense of self-identity and autonomy, provisions for privacy must be incorporated into the design of the day-care environment. Frequent aggressive responses to intrusions of privacy were in evidence during the observational research conducted at the Concordia University Child Care Center. Further research has been designed to examine the aggression displayed in response to an invasion of privacy versus the aggressive behaviour otherwise manifested during the unstructured play periods in the day-care centre. This research is designed to determine whether specific types of aggression can be associated with these invasions.

References

Altman, I. 1975. *The Environment and Social Behavior*. Belmont, Calif.: Wadsworth.
——, and J. F. Wohlwill. 1976. *Human Behavior and Environment*. New York: Plenum.
Ames, A. H. 1952. 'The sense of self of nursery school children as manifested by their verbal behavior', *The Journal of Genetic Psychology*, 81, pp. 193–232.
Ardrey, R. 1966. *The Territorial Imperative*. New York: Atheneum.
Bakker, C. and M. K. Bakker-Rabdau. 1973. *No Tresspassing! Explorations in Human Territoriality*. San Francisco: Chandler and Sharp.
Bates, A. 1964. 'Privacy – a useful concept?' *Social Forces*, 42, p. 432.
Brower, S. N. 1965. 'Territoriality, the exterior spaces, the signs we learn to read', *Landscape*, 15, pp. 9–12.
Chapin, F. S. 1951. 'Some housing factors related to mental hygiene', *Journal of Social Issues*, 7, pp. 164–71.
Dosey, M. A. and M. Meisels. 1969. 'Personal space and self-protection', *Journal of Personality and Social Psychology*, 11, pp. 93–7.
Edney, J. 1976. 'Human territories: comment on functional properties', *Environment and Behavior*, 8, 1, pp. 31–47.
Felipe, N. and R. Sommer. 1966. 'Invasions of personal space', *Social Problems*, 14, pp. 206–14.

Freeman, F. N. 1916. 'Geography: extension of experience through imagination', in *The Philosophy of Common Branches*. Boston: Houghton Mifflin.

Fry, A. M. and F. N. Willis. 1971. 'Invasion of personal space as a function of the age of the invader', *Psychological Record*, 2, 3, pp. 385–9.

Goffman, E. 1971. *Relations in Public*. New York: Basic Books.

Hall, E. T. 1966. *The Hidden Dimension*. New York: Doubleday.

Hart, R. and G. Moore. 1973. 'The development of spatial cognition: a review', in R. M. Downs and D. Stea (eds), *Image and Environment: Cognitive Mapping and Spatial Behavior*. Chicago: Aldine.

Jacobs, E. 1977. 'Privacy seeking in the day care environment'. Paper presented at the National Association for the Education of Young Children Conference, Chicago, November.

Kritchevsky, S. and E. Prescott, with L. Walling. 1969. *Planning Environments for Young Children: Physical Space*. Washington, DC: NAEYC.

Laufer, R. S., H. M. Proshansky and M. Wolfe. 1974. 'Some analytic dimensions of privacy', in R. Kuller (ed.), *Architectural Psychology*. Stroudsberg, Penn.: Dowden, Hutchinson and Ross.

———, and M. Wolfe. 1977. 'Privacy as a concept and a social issue: a multidimensional development theory', *Social Forces*.

Little, K. B. 1965. 'Personal space', *Journal of Experimental Social Psychology*, 1, pp. 237–47.

Lomranz, J., A. Shapira, N. Choresh and Y. Gilat. 1975. 'Children's personal space as a function of age and sex', *Developmental Psychology*, 2, pp. 541–5.

Lorenz, K. 1966. *On Aggression*. New York: Harcourt Brace Jovanovich.

Lyman, S. M. and M. B. Scott. 1967. 'Territoriality: a neglected sociological dimension', *Social Problems*, 15, pp. 235–49.

McBride G., M. G. King and J. W. James. 1956. 'Social proximity effects on galvanic skin responses in the adult human', *Journal of Psychology*, 61, pp. 153–7.

McDowell, K. V. 1972. 'Violations of personal space', *Canadian Journal of Behavioural Science*, 4, 3, pp. 210–17.

McGrew, P. L. 1970. 'Social and spatial density effects on spacing behavior in preschool children', *Journal of Child Psychology and Psychiatry*, 11, pp. 197–205.

Melson, G. 1976. 'Determinants of personal space in young children: perception of distance cues', *Perceptual and Motor Skills*, 43 pp. 107–14.

———, 1977. 'Sex differences in proxemic behavior and personal space schemata', *Sex Roles*.

Moore, R. 1966. 'An experiment in playground design'. Unpublished master's thesis, Department of City and Regional Planning, Massachusetts Institute of Technology, Cambridge.

Nice, M. M. 1941. 'The role of territory in bird life', *American Midland Naturalist*, 26, pp. 441–87.

Osmon, F. L. 1971. *Patterns for Designing Children's Centers*. New York: Educational Facilities Laboratories, Inc.

Paluck, R. J. and A. H. Esser. 1971a. 'Controlled experimental modification of aggressive behavioral condition of severely retarded boys', *American Journal of Mental Deficiency*, 76, 1, pp. 23–9.

———, and A. H. Esser. 1971b. 'Territorial behavior as an indicator of changes in clinical behavior condition of severely retarded boys', *American Journal of Mental Deficiency*, 76, 3, pp. 284–90.

Pastalan, L. A. 1970a. 'Privacy as a behavioral concept', *Social Forces*, 45, p. 2.

———, 1970b. 'Privacy as an expression of human territoriality', in L. A. Pastalan and D. H. Carson (eds), *Spatial Behavior of Older People*. Ann Arbor: University of Michigan Press.

134   *The Privacy Behaviour of Preschool Children*

Pennock, J. R. and J. W. Chapman. 1971. *Privacy*. New York: Atherton Press.

Post, B. and E. M. Hetherington. 1974. 'Sex differences in the use of proximity and eye contact in judgments of affiliation in preschool children.'

Proshansky, H. 1974. 'Theoretical issues in environmental psychology', *School Review*, August, 82, p. 4.

——, W. Ittleson and L. Rivlin. 1970. *Environmental Psychology*. New York: Holt, Rinehart and Winston. 2nd edn.

Roos, P. D. 1968. 'Jurisdiction: an ecological concept', *Human Relations*, pp. 75–84.

Schwartz, B. 1968. 'The social psychology of privacy', *American Journal of Sociology*, 73, pp. 741–52.

Simmel, A. 1971. 'Privacy is not an isolated freedom', in J. R. Pannock and J. W. Chapman (eds), *Privacy*. New York: Atherton.

Singer, J. L. 1973. *The Child's World of Make-Believe: Experimental Studies of Imaginative Play*. New York: Academic Press.

Sommer, R. 1966. 'Man's Proximate Environment', *Journal of Social Issues*, 22, pp. 59–70.

——, 1969. *Personal Space*. Englewood Cliffs, NJ: Prentice-Hall.

Stea, D. 1965. 'Territoriality, the interior aspect: space, territory, and human movements', *Landscape*, Autumn.

Westin, A. F. 1970. *Privacy and Freedom*. London: The Bodley Head Ltd.

Wolfe, M. and R. Laufer. 1974. 'The concept of privacy in childhood and adolescence', in S. Margulis (ed.), *Privacy*. Proceedings of the Fifth Environmental Design Research Association Conference. Stroudsburg, Penn.: Dowden Hutchison and Ross.

8 ELEMENTARY SCHOOL CHILDREN'S PLAY BEHAVIOUR DURING SCHOOL RECESS PERIODS

Shani Beth-Halachmy[1]

Introduction

Several times a day, nine months a year, the school bell rings, signalling the beginning of recess. Hundreds of school children pour out of their classrooms running, jumping, shouting and singing. During the next fifteen minutes, the play-yard vibrates with children. They play jump-rope and jacks, climb bars, watch, hide, find, talk, play tag. It ends as it began — with the ring of the bell. The children migrate back to their classrooms. Some return with much enthusiasm and excitement. A few walk slowly, reluctantly; a couple of children still breathe rapidly, perspiring; others walk toward their rooms still playing.

The school play-yard, where most school age children spend their free time, provides a unique playing environment, different from any other play setting such as neighbourhood streets and playgrounds, or youth centres. School recess activities must be carried out within the school boundaries. In addition, there are temporal constraints on the children's activities. They may play in the yard only during several specified short periods of time per day. Within these periods, children have the opportunity to choose and pursue their play activities relatively freely. Their actions are closely supervised by adults whose job is to ensure that the children behave according to the school rules and regulations; however, these play-yard supervisors do not usually direct the play activities or structure them.

It is during these periods of unstructured play that children learn to join others and co-operate while taking part in group activities. This paper explores the social dimension of children's unstructured play, as one aspect of children's play behaviour.

Many studies of children's social behaviour suggest that it follows a developmental pattern. For example, as children grow and develop, they tend to enlarge their social sphere by increasing the size of their social group (Barker and Wright, 1954; Moore and Wochiler, 1974). Interpersonal distance during play is decreased (Blurton Jones, 1972; Meisels and Guardo, 1969) while the frequency of interpersonal contact during play is increased (Smith and Connolly, 1972).

135

The development of social behaviour, however, is not uniform between sexes. Although there are few sex differences in social behaviour at the very young age (Blurton Jones, 1972; Clark *et al.*, 1969), these differences increase as children grow older. For example, seven-year-old girls play in small groups with one or two best friends, while boys of the same age play with large groups of children (Waldorp and Halverson, 1973). Six- to eight-year-old girls stand closer to their peers than boys do (Aiello and Jones, 1971), but the distance they place themselves from another person is more likely to be a function of how well they know that person than it is among boys (Maccoby and Jacklin, 1974).

The evidence previously presented illustrates the existence of age and sex differences in social play behaviour. Many questions, however, remain unanswered. What brought these differences about? One explanation that has not been explored in any depth is that sex differences and perhaps even age differences in social play behaviour are a function of culturally determined play activities and games. The study reported in this chapter is a first effort to examine social play variables and types of activities at the same time.

The questions addressed were:

1. Are there sex and age differences in the extent of elementary school childrens' social interaction during free-play periods.

2. If sex and age differences in the extent of social interaction exist, are these differences related to the kinds of activities pursued by elementary school children during free-play periods.

Method

Sixty-five children (35 boys and 30 girls) from predominantly Caucasian, middle-class families attending school in a suburban Northern California college town participated in the study. Thirty-three subjects (17 boys and 16 girls) were from the primary grades (first through third) and 32 subjects (18 boys and 14 girls) from the intermediate grades (fourth through sixth).

The school in which the study was conducted is comprised of several one-storey buildings which are roomy and aesthetically attractive. Between the buildings there are several grass areas and a large asphalt area surrounding them. The school yard also includes a large grass area and several pieces of play apparatus. While some pieces of the play apparatus are of traditional style, others are non-traditional wooden structures. The children, therefore, have a large and pleasant outdoor area in which they can freely run around, play and explore.

A child was selected for the study at random as he/she left the room for recess. An observer followed the child and recorded his/her behaviour until the termination of the recess or for ten minutes, whichever came first. Observations were recorded on a standard record form. Every 30 seconds, the observer looked at the child, then recorded the specific activity the child was engaged in and the number of children involved in that activity.[2]

The implicit assumption in this study, as in many other studies where observers are present, is that the effect of observers on children's behaviour during recess was minimal. To minimize their effect on children's behaviour, observers reacted as little as possible to the approaches made to them by the children. They moved about discreetly, maintaining a minimum distance of 30 feet from the observed child. As in previous research, conducted with preschool-age children, the majority of the children ceased to respond to passive observers within a few observation periods (Connolly and Smith, 1972). It is, therefore, the author's opinion that the presence of observers on the playground did not cause disruption to the usual environment.

The total number of other children with whom each child interacted was used as the measure of social interaction. In order to obtain a clear understanding of the patterns of social interaction in elementary school children, the following five dependent variables were used in a 2 x 2 (sex and age) analysis of variance (ANOVA) design:

1. average number of children each child interacted with during any one observation;
2. percentage of the time a child played alone;
3. percentage of the time a child played with one other child;
4. percentage of the time a child played with two to five children; and
5. percentage of the time a child played with six or more children.

Children's activities were recorded when they actively participated in a game. The following three dependent variables were used in a 2 x 2 (sex and age) analysis of variance (ANOVA) design:

1. percentage of the time a child played some kind of a ball game (basketball, baseball, bouncing ball, dodgeball, kickball, etc.);
2. percentage of the time a child played some kind of an active game that did not require the use of a ball (bean bag throw, tag, pogo stick, etc.); and

3. percentage of the time a child played some kind of a passive game (cards, jacks, etc.).

Results and Discussion

All children spent the greatest amount of time (38.9 per cent) interacting in relatively small groups of 2 to 5 children. Over all, children spent the least amount of time alone (9.6 per cent), and a relatively large amount of time (30.6 per cent) with large groups of six or more children.

On the average, boys played with 6.4 children at one time, whereas girls played with 3.7 children. Significant sex differences, however, appeared only during the intermediate years (grades 4—6).[3] Primary-grade boys interacted with an average of 4.4 other children at one time, and primary-grade girls interacted with an average of 4.6 other children. Intermediate girls decreased their number of children associates to 2.6 at one time. Intermediate-grade boys interacted with the larger number of 8.3 children at one time. Table 8.1 displays the means for each

Table 8.1: Mean Number of Children Interacted with and Percentage of Time Utilized for Social Interaction

Group	Mean Percentage of Time (and Standard Deviation)				
	Spent alone	Spent with one child	Spent with 2—5 children	Spent with 6 or more children	No. of children interacted with
Primary Grades					
Boys	19.0[a] (35.8)[b]	13.0 (19.4)	38.5 (36.0)	29.5 (37.8)	4.4 (3.3)
Girls	6.2 (12.3)	7.8 (10.7)	53.2 (40.7)	29.1 (39.5)	4.6 (3.5)
Intermediate Grades					
Boys	10.9 (17.9)	16.6 (29.1)	13.1 (20.2)	50.8 (44.5)	8.3 (7.0)
Girls	0.4 (1.3)	35.4 (43.3)	56.1 (41.1)	7.9 (20.9)	2.6 (1.5)
Total	9.6 (22.1)	17.6 (28.7)	38.9 (38.3)	30.6 (39.6)	5.1 (4.8)

[a] Mean.
[b] Standard deviation.

Figure 8.1: Average Total Number of Children Played With

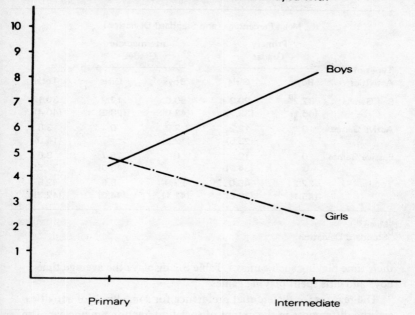

social participation variable. Figure 8.1 presents the average number of boys and girls of primary and intermediate grades played with.

Over all, boys spent more time alone than girls[4] and more time with large groups of six or more children.[5] This was true for both primary and intermediate boys. An interaction also occurred on this variable between age and sex, with intermediate boys devoting more time with large groups of children and girls devoting very little time to such large groups.[6] Significant age differences also existed in the amount of time spent with one child.[7] This age difference can be attributed to the large amount of time intermediate girls spent interacting with one other child.

There were also sex and age differences in the kinds of activities boys and girls pursued. It is only the intermediate-level children who exhibit these differences. The activity patterns for boys and girls in the primary grades is similar. Both boys and girls in the primary grades spent about 30 per cent of their time pursuing various active and ball games. This pattern changed in the intermediate-grade children. Intermediate boys spent a larger amount of their time (approximately 53 per cent) playing various active games while intermediate girls spent only 13 per cent of

Table 8.2: Percentage of Time Spent Pursuing Various Games

| Types of Activities | Mean Percentage (and Standard Deviation) | | | | |
| | Primary Grades | | Intermediate Grades | | |
	Boys	Girls	Boys	Girls	Total
Ball Games	32.2[a] (45.1)[b]	20.3 (33.7)	50.0 (43.0)	12.9 (28.3)	30.1 (40.4)
Active Games	0	12.2 (23.5)	2.9 (12.5)	0	3.8 (14.0)
Passive Games	0	12.5 (34.2)	0	25.7 (43.0)	8.6 (27.5)
Total	32.2 (45.1)	45.0 (39.6)	52.9 (41.1)	38.6 (44.0)	42.5 (42.2)

[a]Mean.
[b]Standard Deviation.

their time playing such games.[8] Table 8.2 displays the average time boys and girls spent playing games.

The reasons for differential preference for some kinds of activities and the differences in the extent of social interaction are unclear. The predominant involvement of older elementary school boys in certain kinds of activities may be due to awakening of biological motivators to engage in competitive physical activities requiring a large amount of physical strength and energy. Sex differences in activity patterns and social interaction may, however, also be due to adoption of sex roles defined for boys and girls by their cultures. It may also be due to an interaction between biological determinants of behaviour and environmental influences.

Whereas there are few sex differences in social behaviour and activity preferences during the early ages, more differences are noted in later childhood years. Similarly, within-group variability in primary boys was similar to within-group variability in primary girls. Both groups displayed varied choices regarding their preferences for the types of social interactions. Their behaviour was not yet stereotyped according to their sex identification. Within-group variability of the intermediate boys was, however, different from within-group variability of the intermediate girls.[9] Environmental influences on the social behaviour of the intermediate groups are evident through the stereotypical behaviour of the intermediate girls. Almost all girls displayed the same kind of social behaviour; namely, there were few individual differences among intermediate girls regarding the number of other children[10] with whom they interacted. This was not evident for the intermediate boys. A more varied pattern of social behaviour, with greater individual differences,[11] was the case for this group. It is the intermediate girls who are most subjected to environmental influences which possibly restrict their willingness to explore various behavioural patterns to fit their individual needs, abilities and personalities.

Conclusion

Sex differences in children's play behaviour during free-play periods appear primarily in the intermediate grades. The play behaviour of boys and girls during the primary grades is homogeneous. It is only during the intermediate years that boys and girls begin to represent two distinct groups in regard to their social behaviour and their activity choices. During these years, boys spend much time playing active games, particularly ball games, which are usually played in large groups, e.g., dodgeball, basketball, etc. The predominant involvement of the intermediate-age boys in such games is related to the extent of their social interaction. Intermediate-age girls, on the other hand, tended to socialize with a small number of other children. They were not as involved in playing large group ball games as boys were. They spent their free time walking around the play-yard, sitting and talking, playing jacks, or playing cards — activities more often pursued in small groups.

In summary, the strong demonstration that there are positive relationships between the extent of social interaction and the activity pattern in upper-grade children indicate that these two variables should not be studied independently. Instead, the investigation of children's play behaviour necessitates simultaneous study of all related variables using multivariate techniques.

Notes

1. The author extends sincere gratitude to Dr Jonathan Sandoval for his help in all phases of this research, and particularly in reading and editing this chapter. Also thanks to Robert Chayer for making this research possible.
2. In total, there were 1,180 observations, relatively evenly split among the 4 groups of children. Periodically, inter-observer reliability was tested by having two observers focus on one child simultaneously. The over-all level of agreement for each pair of observers averaged 90 per cent.
3. $F(1, 61) = 7.07$, $p \leqslant 0.01$.
4. $F(1, 61) = 4.79$, $p \leqslant 0.01$.

5. F(1, 61) = 5.13, p ≤ 0.026.
6. F(1, 61) = 5.19, p ≤ 0.025.
7. F(1, 61) = 4.57, p ≤ 0.035.
8. F(1, 61) = 4.48, p ≤ 0.036.
9. F max = 10.09, p ≤ 0.002.
10. Mean = 2.6, standard deviation = 1.5.
11. Mean = 8.3, standard deviation = 7.0.

References

Aiello, J. R. and S. E. Jones. 1971. 'Field study of the proxemic behavior of young school children in three subcultural groups', *Journal of Personality and Social Psychology*, 19, pp. 351–6.

Barker, R. and F. H. Wright. 1954. *Midwest and Its Children*. New York: Row, Patterson.

Blurton Jones, N. 1972. 'Categories of child–child interaction', in N. Blurton Jones (ed.), *Ethological Studies of Child Behavior*. Cambridge: Cambridge University Press.

Clark, A. H., S. M. Wyon and M. P. M. Richards. 1969. 'Free play in nursery school children', *Journal of Child Psychology and Psychiatry*, 10, pp. 205–16.

Conolly, K. and P. K. Smith. 1972. 'Reaction of pre-school children to a strange observer', in N. Blurton Jones (ed.), *Ethological Studies of Child Behavior*. Cambridge: Cambridge University Press.

Maccoby, E. E. and C. N. Jacklin. 1974. *The Psychology of Sex Differences*. Stanford: Stanford University Press.

Meisels, M. and C. J. Guardo. 1969. 'Development of personal space schemata', *Child Development*, 40, pp. 1167–78.

Moore, R. C. and A. Wochiler. 1974. 'An assessment of a "redeveloped" school yard based on drawings made by child users', in D. H. Carson (ed.), *Man-Environment Interaction: Evaluation and Application* (vol. 3). Stroudsberg, Penn.: Dowden, Hutchinson and Ross.

Smith, P. K. and K. Connolly. 1972. 'Patterns of play and social interaction in pre-school children', in N. Blurton Jones (ed.), *Ethological Studies of Child Behavior*. Cambridge: Cambridge University Press.

Waldorp, M. F. and C. F. Halverson, Jr. 1973. 'Intensive and extensive peer behavior: longitudinal and cross-sectional analysis'. Unpublished manuscript, Child Research Branch, National Institute of Mental Health, Washington, DC.

Part Three

LEADERSHIP TRAINING

9 A PROGRAMME FOR TRAINING PLAY LEADERS

Nancy L. G. Ovens

Introduction

Over the last 17 years the School of Community Studies at Moray House College, Edinburgh has developed a programme for the professional training of social workers, and youth and community workers. This paper explains the programmes offered and how they have developed through remaining responsive to the community at large. One of the largest training schools in Great Britain, it is known as an innovative agency for training in the field of human relationships. The courses are designed to give the maximum opportunity for generic training. The students enter both courses at a three-year course entry-point or a two-year entry-point. (See Figure 9.1.)

The three-year student has academic entry qualifications suitable for professional or university entrance. In the first year, students undertake a pre-professional training programme in which the core subjects are Psychology, Sociology and Social Policy, with practical work assignment to Service Provision, e.g., housing departments, public health, etc. The students are divided into tutorial groups which are not professionally based, but which comprise both student course groups.

The two-year student is a mature student with life experience or experience in the professional field in an untrained capacity. These students sometimes have little or no academic qualifications; therefore, there is a rigorous selection procedure to ensure that they are capable of undertaking an academic training.

The three-year and the two-year students join for all the basic programmes, and are divided into generic groups for the workshop programmes of Principles and Practice. The professional group meets with the home tutor who will work with a group of ten students for the next two years — both in the group and with the individual student. In this year the emphasis is placed on the need to learn about self and the relationship of self to others, hence the commonality of the training process for all the students. At the same time, the students have their first experience in a field-work practice setting.

When the students move into the third year, most of the academic learning is based on a credit system in which each student individually creates his/her own course from a range of modules covering a wide

Figure 9.1: Professional Training Courses in the School of Community Studies

Youth and Community Work	Social Work
First Year	
Pre-professional	3-year student with academic entry.
Sociology	
Psychology	
Social Policy	+ Attachment to Service Provision
Second Year	
Entry point for 2-year course student mature and/or experienced.	*Generic for base subjects*
	Sociology
	Psychology
	Social Policy
	Principles and Practice + field-work practice in professional field setting
Third Year	
	Based on tutorial groups with professional tutor
	Modular based course — course credits + field work practice

Figure 9.2: SESTA: South East Scotland Training Association

Training Association composed of representatives from

Lothian Regional Authority	serviced by one
Borders Regional Authority	Senior Lecturer and
Voluntary agencies within the above two regions	administrative
Moray House College of Education	staffing.

This association provides (1) In-service courses for professionals
(2) Training for part-time and voluntary workers

spectrum of topics. Some may be grouped as professional studies, others as academic subjects; students are required to complete a certain number from each area. The remainder would be chosen from various electives.

The South East Scotland Training Association

Moray House College of Education, along with other colleges of education in Scotland, offers in-service courses to professional workers in the field — teachers, social workers, youth and community workers — who are qualified workers from any institution working in the proximity of the college. There is a training association serviced by a senior lecturer of the School of Community Studies, which provides in-service courses for youth and community workers and social workers. This association also provides training opportunities for part-time and voluntary workers. Some courses for these workers may be on a regular weekly basis for a period of some months, or may be for as little as a day or a weekend. This training association is known as SESTA — the South East Scotland Training Association. (See Figure 9.2.) The executive committee of this association is composed of representatives of the statutory regional authorities and the local voluntary organizations. SESTA originally came into being to provide a basic training for members of the community who were interested in working as volunteers or as part-time workers in any community service provision. The common element in training is one of providing a basic understanding of working with people, the history of the service to the community, simple knowledge of group work skills and other allied learning. Structuring the courses in this way created valuable communication links and utilized resources for training economically. Using the resources of the College of Education also has widened the opportunities for all concerned. Through this system, courses are now offered to the community at large, covering a wide variety of learning topics, as well as the basic course. Some of these courses are seen as Stage I and II courses, allowing members of the community to develop considerable expertise in one particular aspect of working in the community, e.g., group work, counselling, community decision making.

Play and Play Leadership

Throughout the years during which the School of Community Studies developed, the Director of the School, Brian J. Ashley, has retained his interest in the International Playgrounds Association. Part of that interest was expressed in the initial planning of the courses when Play Leadership training was included in the training programme. Ashley was a member of the original UNESCO group which was responsible for the initiating of IPA. Moray House College of Education has been a member since its inception. For the past five years, the author has been responsible for the courses on Play and Play Leadership and liaison with IPA.

Every student in the second year takes a course called 'Perspectives' on Play. (See Figure 9.1 again.) This course includes theories of play, planning for play, and the settings for play. In the final year optional courses are offered such as Adult Involvement in Children's Play which is designed to look at the roles adults play in the provision of children's play. The two sub-sections of this programme could be seen as, first, the indirect involvement of adults through the types of provision for play, and, second, the intervention of adults in play through such functions as leadership in adventure playgrounds, hospital groups, special needs groups, etc. The other course is one which is geared to the individual interest of a student and requires the student to programme, in consultation with the programme director, a project which will meet the student's learning needs within the allocated time.

Throughout the planning and setting up of these courses, there was close consultation through programme-planning groups with field practitioners. As far as possible, practitioners were involved through presentations, either coming into the classroom to work with the students or taking the students out to the field setting. Increasingly therefore, there was community participation in these programmes as the needs for involvement extended. It was also possible to be flexible enough to be able to adapt the programmes to permit the maximum involvement of guest speakers whenever this was possible and appropriate. One of the most exciting days which took place in this way was a seminar with Robin Moore when the course members met with him and also a wide variety of community organizations and members of communities were invited to join to learn of the Washington Environmental Yard at Berkeley.

It became increasingly obvious that the courses which were designed in this way were of interest to people and were meeting the needs of people engaged in a voluntary commitment to a community-based group, and also to professional workers for whom knowledge of play might not have been a course component in their previous professional training. While courses could be offered through SESTA to these interested individuals, one of the major advantages to both the students and the community members would be lost, that is the dynamics of the interaction between the various interest bases and the opportunities for direct information exchange. It seemed as if negotiating formal agreement to the combining of the student-based course with an in-service course and a SESTA-based course would be the next logical step to take. Agreement was sought through the procedures of the college for the courses on play to be made available to others who were interested in attending and participating in these courses. Since this request was not combined with any other consequent change (e.g., more finance), there was no objection to the proposal. The next development followed rapidly when some of the newcomers to the courses asked if the assessment component could be part of the course offered to them, in the same way as presently being undertaken as a requirement by the students. This, also, within the course, was agreed.

Several years later, through SESTA, certain of the student-based courses are being pursued by non-professional individuals within the community as a means of continuing education and extending their capacity as voluntary or part-time workers. In the total of the professional student programme there is now a First Year Sociology course available to others; in the Second Year, a group of people have been undertaking the Principles and Practice workshops; and in the Final Year a number of modules are now available on this basis.

Some of the issues which are now emerging from this experimental approach are of interest in considering the future use of resources to meet the needs of professional training and to meet the complementary needs of the field to train voluntary and part-time workers. (See Figure 9.3.) SESTA's role in this is one of developing and facilitating courses and there is now clearly a need to look at the profile of a new full-time student who, over a period of time, is building a number of modules of professional or SESTA courses into a significant and assessed statement of competence.

What recognized qualification will emerge for this person? A system

Figure 9.3: A Programme Model

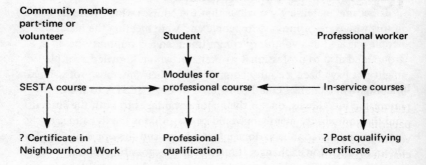

of in-service training, over an extended period of time, is now beginning to emerge as a viable alternative on paper, if not yet in practice. What issues are raised for the institution? The most significant issue in this theoretical possibility would most probably be the financial one. Is it right or acceptable that there is no charge, or only a nominal charge, for a non-professional person to participate in the acquisition of a course credit for which the full-time student has contributed through the payment of course fees?

Another issue might become the extended time which a non-professional student would need to undertake a course of study and, perhaps more significantly, the relationship between the academic or theoretical study area and the practice area.

Some of these issues are now being approached by the executive of SESTA in discussion of a proposed Certificate Course in Neighbourhood Work. If it is decided to implement these proposals, it will be interesting to hear whether some of these issues might be clarified at least. Since the discussion is *sub judice* at present, it is only possible to conjecture, but it is to be hoped that the progress of involvement between the field and the institution will continue to develop, that the influence of the community on the training and education processes will become more significant, and that the resources of the institution will continue to be made available to the community in the fullest ways.

10 LEADERSHIP TRAINING FOR WORK WITH THE SEVERELY HANDICAPPED

Joyce Knowles

Introduction

It is necessary to present some of my background in order to put this paper into its proper context. I am employed by The Spastics Society, a voluntary organization in England and Wales which is one of the biggest charities concerned with the welfare of handicapped people. Its services range from preventive medicine and research through a series of provisions for children, schools, employment services, workshops, and residential care of older handicapped people. Whereas its services are mainly directly available to cerebral palsied children and adults, the implications of its publicity and political activities spread over a wide field of disabilities. In particular, of recent years its great concern has been for those cerebral palsied and other handicapped people of relatively low intellectual abilities who have been placed in hospitals for the severely subnormal.

My role is to organize training services within The Spastics Society. To this end, a college — the Castle Priory College — was established in 1964 and acts as the hub of its staff services. Among the groups involved over the past years have been professional nurses, auxiliaries, volunteers, and others concerned with the leisure activities of handicapped people. It is with this type of personnel that this paper will deal.

The question might arise as to why such a need has manifested itself now when there have been severely handicapped people in institutions for the past hundred years. The answer is that the original role of the hospital was concerned with nursing care (i.e., the meeting of physical needs) and the secondary role was the custodial one of taking care of people who were likely to be in a dependency state for the whole of their lives. It is relatively recently that concern for the quality of life and the way in which people spend hours of enforced leisure has led to interest in the needs of mentally handicapped people of all ages. This paper discounts working with children — partly because I believe it is now a much more widely accepted fact that children must play, but also because it is usually less acceptable to view the needs of adults in this area. Also in the United Kingdom there have been changes in attitudes towards children in institutions, as witnessed by fewer admissions, the dependence for their long-term care being much more on family grouping in the community. The battle is not yet won, but the time is approaching when handicapped children will be offered greater play facilities alongside non-handicapped children. However, many disabled and multiply handicapped adults — among them those who have known no childhood — are still, and are likely to continue to be, living in institutions for the remainder of their lives.

Why 'Play'?

Why talk of 'play'? The answer lies in the basic fact that elementary play in the earliest developmental stages (in which, alas, are many hospital residents) is a fundamental emotional and social stage, the basis for physical well-being and the foundation for intellectual growth. Therefore, many patients are in those developmental states in which, in childhood, one would regard play as necessary and desirable. It is only in the incongruity of physical size and chronological age that it becomes less acceptable. Without investigating in great depth the causes of their retardation, it is true to say that in some cases the environment itself has been a depressing factor. Many of the residents have rarely played, and this lack of play opportunities in childhood may have been a contributing agent in the retardation cycle. It is true that toys and games may be sent to hospitals, especially at Christmas time, in quite large quantities, but their suitability for adults is questionable. Often because of the visual incongruity of 'adults' playing with children's toys they may never reach the patients who need them most.

What Is Play?

What is play for such severely handicapped people? Is it an alternative to work? It is first necessary to consider why some of the more acceptable alternatives to work are not available for the residents of such large institutions.

Many residents with communication difficulties or poor hearing are unable to spend a great deal of time in the ordinary social relationships that those in the community would enjoy in their leisure periods. Some have difficult speech articulation and poor vocabulary, partly through lack of environmental stimuli and also because in some cases there is difficulty in interpreting spoken language. With some of the residents, the concentration required to carry on a conversation for long is lacking and the problems involving short memory span make conversation almost impossible. Many who have lived in institutions for a long time in fact also lack communication skills through lack of usage rather than lack of ability. This may result in a behaviour problem in addition to the original difficulty in communication.

For most people, leisure has a component of pleasure in it; this comes from the relaxation and freedom from workday responsibilities, and the using of alternative faculties. Many of these handicapped people, however, have very little to do anyway and no workday responsibilities. The situation demands little from them and, as their abilities are very limited, the idea of employing compensatory skills or using alternative skills, when one has so few on which to draw, is very remote. Poor motor function and the lack of communication skill noted above do not allow them to participate in many kinds of sport or social activity. Even if they are able to attend workshop situations in the day, very often the 'work' which is produced is not of a high quality. In some occupational therapy units, the creative work would be similar to that of a child in a 'play' situation. Therefore, in order to make the leisure time different, one would have to look a long way to find skills in addition to those used in the day in therapy or workshop.

The organized 'play' of the institution often revolves around visits to the cinema or trips in the bus to the seaside or to a restaurant or, for those who can co-operate, to a dance floor. These journeys, though interesting and relevant for many, are not always suitable, however, for the multiply handicapped; indeed, the nature of their disability may well preclude their company. Therefore, the very individuals who most need the stimulus of an extra-mural activity are left behind and the cycle of deprivation starts once more.

The Components of Play

These are, therefore, some of the reasons why more ordinary adult leisure pursuits are neither realistic, nor realized, for many hospital residents. To enumerate all the components of play would take a whole paper in itself, but to take just a few and relate them to severely handicapped adults would be sufficiently appropriate to offer a primary thesis.

Movement and Co-ordination

First, there is the physical value of play to stimulate movements and to aid co-ordination — aspects of development possible for many, but often stereotyped to fit in with concepts of physical maturity. It was Dalcroze who warned of the folly of imposing adult standards on children's movement. So often mentally handicapped adults can be seen only moving in accepted patterns of walking or standing or shuffling, partly perhaps in fear of movement due to lack of personal confidence, but also because of lack of opportunity and experience to use movement freely. The hyperactive patient who runs around the hospital is restrained from so doing; therefore, the example shows that free running is a 'bad' thing and other patients grow up with limitations set on their patterns of running and jumping and on exercising the freedom which so enhances body image and movement potential. This is not to suggest that there can possibly be such a completely disorganized approach to care that freedom is possible at any time, anywhere, but it is important that areas and times are found where unconventional movement may take place. Examples include using the floor, and simple apparatus such as that found in children's adventure playgrounds — tyres, barrels, pipes, ropes — all important stimuli to movement and concept development.

Movement in water, an early 'recreational' medium for so many children, is often denied to the non-swimmer adult. Bath is not a 'play area' for adults; water play on the campus is frowned upon, yet trailing feet or fingers in water as a most basic stimulus is so simple to provide. Initiating movement from the rhythms of music or from the relationship with another person are other areas of development. In Britain, the Sesame groups are promoting such schemes with very severely handicapped patients in hospital surroundings, and it is an extremely useful initial way of involving volunteers in a close personal relationship. The One to One movement in New York is another group which makes this kind of activity a possibility.

It is always blatantly obvious how many non-handicapped adults grasp at any chance of movement expression, particularly on holidays or in leisure periods. There is also a phenomenon that the farther away from home people are, the more unconventional their behaviour, sometimes almost becoming conventional by the uniformity of the phenomenon. (For example, the Englishman on the Costa Brava is a very different animal from the one at Brighton!) Fathers roll down slopes with their children, bury them in sand, contort in a variety of acrobatics — all excusable because they are with their children in holiday or leisure circumstances. These opportunities are denied to handicapped and retarded people because there are no children present to be the excuse; the image to be preserved for the general public is one of propriety and sobriety.

Elementary sports are possible with many disabled and/or retarded adults, provided the rules are made to suit the comprehension of the participators and the selection of entrants, and that the adaptation of skills required gives a chance of success to all participators. Part of normal development is play in children's games of selection and competition, a necessary prerequisite of social and normal growth, yet it is often omitted from the life pattern of so many institutionalized patients.

Play has an extremely important role in the promotion of concepts of body schema and function, space and causality, and in the establishment of basic ideas of laterality, direction, shape, size and weight. Why, then, are individuals lacking or retarded in the development of such concepts denied play for so much of the day? Why are they expected to sit or lie relatively immobile?

Creative Activity

The second basic need stems from the desire to create something personal and individual. Much has been written about the depersonalization of individuals in institutions and the limiting of any form of personal creativity. It is sufficient to note that, in the training of many occupational therapists nowadays, more importance is placed on early skills in developing free expression, such as in finger painting, paper tearing, even in scribbling. Occupational therapists are in short supply, however, and the staff responsible for leisure and social activities do not always have included in their preliminary training the necessary rationale for such aspects in a care situation, or are not given ideas on how to carry them out.

This is an area on which much emphasis is placed at Castle Priory College. It is often criticized as being expensive, but perhaps an awareness of where to get scrap material and how to use it is one of the most basic assets. Egg boxes, yogurt cartons and factory waste of all kinds are useful.

Another area to develop creativity is found in music — a clean and acceptable form of recreation! Alas, most wards and day-rooms feed unrestricted and unselected sound to the patients. The contribution of the individual is negligible and often there is no personal choice. A limited reaction of spontaneous head nodding or foot tapping becomes the only response. The areas of 'created' music are far less explored, yet responses to music by movement and products of sound are part of developmental play and games. It is suggested that musical activity should be extended into percussion and string, by the use of home-made instruments, many of them made, or assisted in manufacture, by the retarded residents themselves using scrap material again — a cheap range of sounds is soon available. Making music together is a corporate activity and, for some, one of the few occasions on which interdependence is essential and meaningful.

Movement which leads into drama is useful in an educational-type situation linked closely with day-to-day events. Mongoloid patients (Downs Syndrome) particularly have very good abilities to mime and copy, and the various examples of social behaviour which can be taught in a 'play'-type situation are almost unlimited. Learning domestic skills using real-size equipment but in a play-type simulated situation can be extremely useful and offer the controlled release of energy.

Fresh Air and Exercise

Use can also be made of environmental studies and outdoor activities. Whereas most institutions have progressed beyond the two-by-two walk as the only exposure to fresh air, in some cases they have not moved far beyond this. In the United Kingdom especially, many larger establishments are located in the countryside, a fact which cuts them off from many of the social activities of the urban community, but which does offer opportunities for a variety of open-air activities. The joy of gardening as a play activity — another creative area sometimes frowned upon as unclean or hazardous — gives great interest and increases the knowledge of how things develop, and of colour, shape, size and sequence.

Another important opportunity is found in days out in the open air. Experience with taking groups of institutionalized adolescent mentally retarded people camping has demonstrated all kinds of latent talents of wood collection, stoking, cooking — all the things which children love but for which, for many of these adults, this was the first opportunity. Observation of birds and small animals, explained and aided by adults or volunteers, gives a great deal of interest and a basis for future development.

Sense Training

Games involving sense training of discrimination — involving listening, touching, smelling, finding things, and all the feelings, sequences, directions and body images found in a simple game of hide-and-seek — are 'new' situations for some residents.

Staff experienced in play activities will immediately be able to think of other useful areas and the reasons why they would be valuable.

Staff Training

The title of this paper referred to training personnel, while the exposition thus far has developed only a rationale. This is because for many staff several aspects of the concept of 'play' present problems: they are not convinced that handicapped adults should play, are uncertain which areas of play are appropriate, and lack the confidence that within themselves is a wealth of musical, artistic and dramatic potential.

Who are the trainers? The fact that play therapists and occupational therapists could be eminently suitable is really only of academic interest as there are far too few to be involved in leisure activities in institutions on anything like a large scale. In England, there is no such person as the 'leisure therapist' and no special training for such a role as is possible in some countries. Therefore, those most involved in the leisure care of handicapped people in residential situations are nursing staff (either qualified or auxiliary), a few teachers from further education establishments, former physical training instructors, and volunteers of variety of ages, abilities and experiences. Enthusiasm is also a variable, not so much for lack of interest, but, in some cases, because the confines of the institution seem to close up and inhibit experimentation and change of routine. Therefore, a cross-disciplinary programme seems to help in a widening of interests and the promotion of a greater desire to experiment. It is in this latter field particularly that Castle Priory College feels it plays the most important part. Therefore, the College's courses are practical, full of action, using its own facilities and those of the immediate environment. Cost limits prevent the more exotic situations being explored, but over the years the staff have learned to adapt, to scrounge, to use waste materials, and to devise a range of equipment possible for handicapped people.

What is the curriculum of such courses at Castle Priory College? Apart from instruction as to why play is necessary and desirable in an enlarged discussion as formulated above, the function is to allow the 'trainers' to find their own interests. Expert guidance is offered in ideas on art, music, etc. Under such tuition it is possible for people to use media they have rarely used, to participate in activities never done since their own school days, to 'let their hair down' in dramatic situations, and personally to live the freedom and spontaneity which play situations can evoke. It is believed that the College's house, grounds and relatively relaxed way of life contribute to the possibilities of the students becoming absorbed in their experiences; for this reason, the College is as uninstitutional as it is possible to be in a group-living situation. 'Nowhere is there a place quite like Castle Priory for those working with handicapped people' is an exaggerated claim, but it is one which is often repeated by students on all types of courses. Because this is the College's *raison d'être* professional barriers can be broken down, boundaries can be crossed in terms of what one may or may not attempt with disabled people, and fun can be had in so doing — which is perhaps the most important thing. It is firmly believed that those who work with the most difficult retarded and disabled patients need more than the skills themselves. They need a belief that all is not impossible, for it may be more difficult to go on than to give up, and even the most elementary amendment to the lives of some of the residents is so much better than sitting around. Of course, attempts are also being made to break down the institutions themselves, but progress is slow and another generation of people cannot wait — their lives need enrichment wherever possible and it is strongly believed that in play and recreational activities will be found the key to much of this improvement.

Many may argue that this is in fact 'teaching', but if one accepts that the basis of education is in play and that in normal developmental conditions play commences well before a preschool level and is 'taught' by 'untrained' mothers, why then is it so illogical that those retarded people (whose development in some aspects may well be at the preschool level) should spend much of their days in play activity of some kind, encouraged and led by staff who with enthusiasm and confidence and with the rudiments of special training are not necessarily possessed of high academic qualifications? It is in promoting this enthusiasm, in giving opportunities for gaining this confidence, and in promoting the idea that the spirit of childhood rarely dies in any of us, that the College's training courses have their greatest value; and the flow of personnel of all kinds who continue to come to the courses is testimony to the need to supply this form of training.

References

Ash, B, A. Winn and K. Hutchinson. 1971. *Discovering with Young Children*. London: Elek.

Baxter, C. 1974. *A Framework for Music Making*.

Campaign for the Mentally Handicapped. 1972. *Our Life*. Conference Report. London.

——. 1973. *Listen.* Conference Report. London.
Council for Children's Welfare. *No Childhood.* Occasional Papers on Child Welfare, no. 3. London.
Jeavons, T. 1974. *Art and Cerebral Palsy.* London: The Spastics Society.
Johnson, R. and J. Knowles. 1977. 'Recreation and Leisure Pursuits for the Long-Stay Multiple Handicapped Resident', *Apex*, 5, 3, pp. 24–5.
Laban, Rudolf. *Modern Educational Dance.* London: Macdonald and Evans.
Lear, R. 1974. *Do It Yourself.* London: Toy Libraries Association.
Marzollo, J. and J. Lloyd. 1977. *Learning through Play.* London: Penguin.
Mayhew, M. and C. Mayhew. 1970. *Fun with Art.* London: James Galt and Co.
Oswin, M. 1971. *The Empty Hours.* London: Penguin.
Solly, K. 1977. *A Philosophy of Leisure in Relation to the Mentally Retarded.* London: National Society for Mentally Handicapped Children.
Tilley, P. 1975. *Art in the Education of Subnormal Children.* London: Pitman.
Toy Libraries Association. *Play for Mentally Handicapped Adults.* London.

11 GAMES FOR GROWTH — A LEADING QUESTION

Lanie Melamed

Introduction

The intention of this paper is to explore the social values of game playing and to consider the implications this has for the games leader. The past few years have seen an expanding interest in children's games on the part of psychologists, psychiatrists, behavioural scientists, folklorists, and therapists. Games have moved from the playground to the university! The research has been fruitful and important; game playing is being analyzed for its potential in social, emotional, physical and intellectual learning, from the study of the 'It' role in children's games to teaching the concepts of territory, safety and risk. Because the scope of the topic is so vast, this paper will focus on one aspect of game playing: the impact that games have on individuals for learning about themselves and others.

As a practitioner, the author has used games in working with children and adults in a variety of settings: playgrounds, summer camps, schools, classrooms, hospitals and leadership-training institutes. It is argued that games have a great deal of potential to help people re-create themselves and to transform individuals into groups and sometimes into communities. The opportunities which games provide for spontaneity, release and laughter are valuable in themselves and all too rare in our work-filled lives. Games are great equalizers. Through games, children and adults are enabled to overcome personal, ethnic, language, generational or racial barriers between and among different groups of people. Most importantly, games are fun!

While games are traditionally thought of as the business of children and are usually relegated to the street or playground, they have great value for adults as well. Older people are often denied satisfying and wholesome play opportunities, particularly in physically and socially disadvantaged communities where leisure activities are costly or are not readily available. The social values gained from positive play experiences are different only in degree for children and adults. Because most of the following remarks are intended to apply to both children and adults the words 'individual' and 'people' will more frequently be used.

In contrast to passive amusement, the play referred to in this paper focuses on doing, sensing and solving — processes which engage people

160

toward discovery and re-creation. For this reason, the games described here are 'low organization' games or those which require no special skills and can be played by all ages. Because they require no previous training, people can start where they are and become immediately involved. Participation and involvement are the key elements. No formal definition of the word 'game' is attempted since any definition will have an arbitrary and elusive quality. For the purposes of this paper, a game is an activity which participants enter freely; which has fixed limits of time, rules and boundaries; to which there is usually a stated goal; and in which some tension or opposition exists between different forces.

Games and Cultures

Games are more complex than many imagine. Most young people treat them as passing fads, something which their own group invented or learned from the 'kid down the block'. At a recent workshop, teenagers from many countries were amazed to find that they all knew 'Cat's Cradle'. 'How could this game my sister taught me have travelled to playgrounds in Japan, Egypt, Pakistan and Canada?' The sense of connectedness to others is overwhelming at times like these.

As reflections of universal concerns, games often express basic human attitudes toward life and death, the real and the supernatural, authority and power, courtship, trades and life work. A society's world view is reinforced by its games, validating the skills and traits which that culture sees as important. Games in the Inuit culture stress co-operation as a mode of winning; without this trait Inuit life would have disappeared long ago. Developing strategy and competition are the skills which the Western world relies on for success. It is no surprise that these traits are present in games which in turn form a part of the acculturation process for children.

What most people do not realize is that games are seldom created anew, but like other folk customs are the result of additions and alterations by successive generations. Modern times have changed their form, but not their essence. The game 'Footsies' is a good example. This recent craze in North America (and marketed throughout the world to make its owner rich) has been a popular game in the Middle East for centuries. Today, a plastic hoop and ball has replaced the string and stone of olden days. Hiding, chasing, guessing and counting-out games are universal. Because of their common roots, many popular games are familiar to generations of young and old in widely scattered parts of the world.[1]

Games for Growing

The simple and most obvious value of games is enjoyment and the sharing of social experiences with others. For most people this is sufficient. As workers in human relations settings, recreation practitioners must look deeper. What is the potential of games for helping people to learn about themselves and others? How can this medium be best used to help children and adults gain the skills they need for more healthful and satisfying living? From the viewpoint of games as micro-systems, all human behaviour is possible and probable in game playing. To be aware of the opportunities is to begin to use them more skilfully. For the individual, game playing can, among other things:

1. encourage and foster physical, intellectual, attitudinal and social development;
2. teach a variety of physical and intellectual skills;
3. help people learn to deal with aggression and to resolve conflict;
4. provide opportunities to act on feelings rather than keeping them bottled up inside;
5. teach co-operation and responsibility, and help people to accept the consequences of their actions;
6. help build self-confidence, improve self-image and encourage risk taking;
7. encourage the testing of reality (where the results are not for keeps);
8. help people deal with acceptance and rejection;
9. encourage creativity;
10. provide opportunities for leadership.

For the group as a whole, game playing may:

1. help participants learn how to function as part of a group;
2. learn the value of working and sharing with others;
3. teach skills for living with conflict and ambiguity;
4. help members learn how to lose with dignity;
5. provide practice in leading and following, and in learning how to relate to authority;
6. provide opportunities for making decisions and solving problems;
7. demonstrate the power of the group through participation and co-operation;

8. increase tolerance toward diverse personalities and help people learn to value difference.

While these values emphasize the positive, Sutton-Smith (1972, p. 339) points out that other socially useful skills are also being learned:

> . . . in games children learn all those necessary arts of trickery, deception, harassment, divination and foul play that their teachers won't teach them but that are most important in successful human interrelationships in marriage, business and war.

Inter-group values are also significant. The appreciation of cultures and groups other than one's own often results from playing the games of other countries. For example, in a recent training programme, a Canadian businessman was forced to re-evaluate his assumptions about the intelligence of native Africans after learning to play the game 'Awari' (Count and Capture). The game, which involves a series of complicated strategies planned well in advance of each move, took a week for him to learn. Sharing game playing where there are barriers to verbal and social interaction can be a painless way to make connections with people from contrasting cultures and life-styles.

A Leading Question

The single most important factor in facilitating the learning which comes from interacting with others through playing games is the group leader.

'How-to' books abound which discuss the leader's style, personality attributes, what to do before, during and after the games session. Issues which can be considered basic can be summed up under three broad categories:

1. understanding the needs of both individuals and groups, and a genuine interest in working with people;
2. an awareness and appreciation of the play materials used to enhance the quality of the play experience; and
3. an awareness of oneself, as a leader, what one does and why, and a concern for feedback and self-improvement.

Succinctly, it is the self, the group and the activities (or means) which when blended together create the *gestalt* of a good play experience. The development of individuals as skilled leaders is a lifelong endeavour, in which momentary pauses of self-satisfaction give way to more exposed areas of inadequacy and desire for growth. The process of becoming more aware, more skilled and more creative can develop through formal education, but comes mainly through experience. Learning from experience, however, implies spending the time to reflect, analyze and criticize one's efforts.

It is useful to take the time to anticipate the needs of the group before meeting them, to assure choosing games which are relevant. The resources in the group should be used for goal setting and decision making and in developing leadership whenever possible. In short, the games session should help children and adults to achieve goals which are important to them.

A personal file of games with comments on how they were played and how they were received by different groups can be a helpful aid in improving leadership skills. The more extensive the leader's repertoire, the more relevant his/her programmes can be. Constant evaluation should increase successes and turn mistakes into important opportunities for learning.

Knowing which play materials to choose to help people experience themselves in new ways and which to use for the various stages of a group's development is less frequently discussed in leadership manuals. The remaining portion of this paper will attempt to explore some of these issues.

Valuing the Potential of Each Game

Each game can be valued for its unique qualities. Various games:

1. help one to feel more comfortable in the group, by involving the person in a group action in which he/she does not have to be 'it' or volunteer;

2. ease one's entry into the group by allowing the person to bump into and touch others through the mad scramble for a scarce chair;

3. enable one to use his/her creativity by pantomiming a word or drawing a symbol;

4. give one a feeling of belonging by being on a team in which he/she plays a contributing role toward reaching the goal;

5. help one to determine one's own level of risk-taking by allowing the person to decide to run across the room for an extra chair or to slide into the one nearby;

6. help one to lose oneself in the group and behave more spontaneously by providing situations where perfection is not expected and where *everyone* misses some of the time.

Understanding the special dynamics of each game helps the leader to select the right one for the right moment; which ones are easy to move into and require little pressure to participate; and those which are highly organized, active and involving. There is truly a 'right' game (or several 'right' games) for the right moment. The ability to combine the right game with the right moment comes from experience, accompanied by awareness and understanding of the social interaction patterns in game playing.

The manner in which people play tells a lot about them too. It can relate information to others of which they are not aware or with whom they hesitate to share. It can show how they face problems, take risks, solve problems, strategize, step forward or hold back, or work as part of a group. People who do not perform well in physical or verbal games get their chance to excel in dramatic or pencil-and-paper games. The game experience also provides insights into the way people are seen by others.

Because the behavioural dynamics involved in game playing are so rich, the same game played twice is never the same. Once the group leader is aware of this, he/she can be constantly stimulated by the potential to learn more about people through this medium. In clinical environments, nurses, social workers and recreation workers may well learn as much from playing with their constituents, as from taking detailed social histories.

Opportunities for the personal and interpersonal learning which emerge during game playing can come at the end of each session, during breaks or meetings, or in periodic group evaluations. With children as well as adults, the leader can initiate a discussion about how it felt to be on the winning (losing) team, how Joe felt when Mary hid the ball, when the game was at its best, and alternative ways for the settlement of a conflict. Helping people become more aware of themselves and their interactions is an essential leadership function.

Challenges in Problem Solving

An essential component of good games often overlooked by most leaders is the opportunity for problem solving. There are a hundred-and-one ingenious methods for working out a game's different solutions, many of which are unpredictable.

A game which does not offer problems to be solved (preferably in a variety of ways) is not worth playing. Finding a game's solutions presents both cognitive and sensory challenge for the players. Leaders who have had past experiences with a game may already know many of the ways to win. Lest they become too complacent, there are always surprises in store. Individuals are incredibly creative and often invent solutions which leaders, in their 'wisdom', were sure did not exist. When teaching a game it is important to teach the basic rules, but to avoid telling the players how to play. Much of the joy of the game depends on players having the opportunity to explore and discover alternative solutions for themselves. An understanding of this dimension is essential in maximizing the values in game playing. The following example will illustrate the difference between a game's basic structure and its problem-solving potential.

'Who Started the Motion' (sometimes called 'Chieftain') is a semi-active game in which group members work in unison with each other. Briefly described, the players are seated in a circle. One person is chosen to be 'it' and leaves the room while the rest of the group selects a leader. The leader starts a motion (e.g., clapping both hands on shoulders or knees) which is copied by the others. 'It' is called back into the room and asked to stand in the centre of the circle. The leader changes the motion frequently while the group continues to imitate each new motion. 'It' must discover who the leader is in three guesses. The following kinds of solutions may be enacted by the leader or the group. The leader may choose active noisy motions (foot stomping) or quiet ones (head scratching). Changes may be made dramatically, in quick succession, or varied only slightly, by changing one finger or the rhythm. The motions may be changed only when 'it's' back is turned. The players in the circle may decide to keep their eyes on secondary leaders instead of watching the selected leader. If this happens, 'it' must devise strategies other than watching, to pick up clues. 'It' tries to solve the problem by watching people's faces for non-verbal clues, checking to see who looks flustered or too blasé. 'It' can turn suddenly from side to side, or feign ignorance and stealthily creep up on the culprit. 'It' may make a false guess or two while 'casing' the situation for more clues. He/she may guess wildly and give up quickly, or prolong the game and his/her place in the centre of the stage. Each game calls for its own solutions. Valuing the learning to be gained through problem solving helps the players play better, and the leader to delight in their attempt.

Co-operation and Competition

Although competition is intrinsic to most games, the leader has the power to maximize or minimize it. Competition is found in many forms in games; it may be against a goal, another team, a previous score, or one's own previous record. It is a strong motivating force for individuals and groups, often enabling them to excel, to pull together and to work harder. Unfortunately, the values in competition have been perverted by commercial sports — both the little and big leagues — which penalize losers and idolize winners. When money is involved, the idea of playing for fun becomes harder to believe and encourage. As a play leader involved in the socializing effects of games, one needs to help people understand competition *and* teach co-operative skills for playing, working and living together.

Games which foster co-operation are being designed and researched by a handful of people. Many of these games do not fit the definition of games noted above and are more like pastimes or activities, largely because of the complete absence of competition. In the author's opinion, it is impossible or even undesirable to remove all tension or competition from games. Many of the non-competitive games the author has used with older children have not been interesting enough to sustain the group's attention for any period of time. Games are available which minimize competition. The real challenge is to help players gain from the challenge of competition, while helping the players learn to deal with it. It is impossible to be a winner all of the time, but one can learn to play a game well (even with excellence) and to enjoy that satisfaction whether one wins or loses.

Games — such as that old favourite 'dodgeball' — can become a veritable battleground for children, especially when one team monopolizes the ball and is chiefly interested in ways to 'get' the other team. One way to combat extreme hostility is through the selection of games which minimize team loyalties and which change team members at random. It is also possible to substitute inanimate targets for human ones, e.g., a wall, a bat or a tin can. Teams can be chosen randomly unless it is important to match ages, weight or skill. It is unwise to divide teams according to sex, race, religion, language or age if social cohesiveness is a goal.

In general, ending a game should be left to the discretion of the leader. When a game is going well it should be kept in motion; when it no longer evokes interest, it should be ended. Predetermining a winning score takes the flexibility out of programming and, worse than cutting off a game when the group is 'high', it may extend it until everybody is bored. Some children like to be 'it' in every game. This is not always desirable since many games will have reached their peak long before each person has had a turn. Moreover, when each child is promised a turn, those who have already been 'it' tend to become disruptive and uninterested. It is better to play the game until its logical finish.

Hopefully, there will be another time for a next turn.

Prizes, team wars and other high-pressure tactics to honour the winning team are not necessary. If the satisfaction is in the playing, then external rewards are not only redundant, but destructive of the values one is trying to build.

Encouraging Trust

By avoiding games which eliminate, humiliate or single people out for embarrassing roles, the leader will quickly win the trust and confidence of the group. Elimination games usually succeed in removing the more self-conscious players first, the ones who were not so sure they wanted to be there in the first place. Sometimes it is possible to remove or modify the element of elimination from a game and to substitute other goals. This is done in 'Ghost',[2] where the players are given five chances to continue in the game, or in 'Twenty-One Ball', where the group collectively tries to achieve twenty-one perfect throws, instead of eliminating the player who misses. 'Good' elimination games eliminate by chance rather than skill and are as much fun to watch as to play. In games like 'Last Couple Stoop', the eliminated players can have as much fun watching the strategies of their peers as in playing the game. Players who leave the circle can become judges in the remaining part of the game.

The use of stunts should be avoided. They have a tendency to make fun of people, put them on the spot, and create 'High and Low Power' groups. Since it depends on taking advantage of the uninitiated, once a stunt is learned it cannot be repeated — a waste of human potential on all counts!

A game must be explained carefully before asking for volunteers so that people will know what is expected of them. Some games require more or less risk-taking than others. In some cases, 'it' is in control and can direct the other players; in others 'it' is powerless and at the mercy of the other players (Gump and Sutton-Smith, 1971). It will be safer for people to volunteer if they know in advance what is expected of them. They can then decide whether or not they can cope with the role.

Putting It All Together

Attention to programme planning will also enhance the message that people can learn and grow through game playing.

Each game programme — whether it lasts one hour or three hours — should have a beginning, a middle and an end.

Team-building games and mixers should be chosen at the beginning

of the play session to encourage participation. If resistance to playing
is likely, games which are thought to be 'sure-fire' should be used first.
These are usually the games which have a minimum number of rules,
engage people quickly, include random movement and confusion (but
not too much), are usually accompanied by laughter, and are almost
sure to 'break the ice'. The middle of the programme should ease into
more challenging or complicated games, balancing those which are
active and inactive, require standing and sitting, are organized into
teams, circles or random groups, use balls or other equipment. Variety
and interest are important programme components.

Endings may be riotous or calm, depending on the special needs of
the group, the weather or the hour. More slowly paced games, which
require less energy and concentration, are well placed at the end to help
people settle down. Singing games or dramatic games provide pleasant
endings, as do games which physically bring people together in a group
before leaving. These add the feeling of reinforcement and togetherness,
a sense of 'we-ness and belonging' before people go their separate ways.

Conclusion

Changing attitudes from competitive to co-operative game playing will
not be easy, especially in a society which rewards winners and punishes
losers. Changes in the way people live and treat each other and the
environment must, however, begin to take place for Western society to
continue to exist. In a world in which everything is interrelated, the
quality of life must be improved for every person before it can be
improved for each person. The changes must take place on many levels.
Why not through games?

Notes

1. The current New Games movement in the United States is experimenting
with modifying the rules of familiar old games according to the 'here and now'
interests of the players. Rules and boundaries in games exist to be broken. It
remains to be seen whether or not these games will become rooted in the society,
or are simply a reaction on the part of some adults to too many societal structures.

2. See Harris (1966) for a description of these games.

References

Avedon, Elliott M. and Brian Sutton-Smith (eds). 1971. *The Study of Games.*
New York: Wiley and Sons.

Boyd, Neva. 1971. *Play and Game Theory in Group Work*. Chicago: Jane Adams
  Graduate School of Social Work, University of Illinois.
———. 1975. *A Handbook of Games*. New York: Dover Press.
Brewster, Paul. 1953. *American Non-Singing Games*. Norman, Oklahoma:
  University of Oklahoma Press.
Caplan, Frank and Theresa Caplan. 1974. *The Power of Play*. New York:
  Anchor Press/Doubleday.
DeKoven, Bernard. 1978. *The Well Played Game*. New York: Anchor Press/
  Doubleday.
Fluegelman, A. (ed.). 1976. *The New Games Book*. New York: Doubleday.
Gump, P. V. and B. Sutton-Smith. 1971. 'The "It" role in children's games', in
  E. Avedon and B. Sutton-Smith (eds), *The Study of Games*. New York:
  Wiley and Sons.
Harris, Frank. 1966. *Games*. Detroit: Eastern Cooperative Recreation School.
  (May be ordered from Harris, 14597 Warwick, Detroit, Mich., 48223.)
Herron, R. E. and B. Sutton-Smith (eds). 1971. *Child's Play: Collected Readings
  on the Biology, Ecology, Psychology and Sociology of Play*. New York:
  Wiley and Sons.
Huizinga, Johan. 1950. *Homo Ludens: A Study of the Play Element in Culture*.
  Boston: The Beacon Press. (Reprinted in paperback, 1964.)
Jacks, Lawrence Pearsall. 1932. *Education through Recreation*. London:
  University of London Press.
Melamed, Lanie. 1970. *Action and Interaction, Activity Methods for Group Work
  Practice*. Montreal: McGill University (mimeo).
Middleman, Ruth R. 1968. *The Non-Verbal Method in Working with Groups*.
  New York: Association Press.
Norris, Ruth. 1962. 'The human values in recreation', *Recreation*, November,
  pp. 442–3.
Orlick, Terry. 1977. *Winning through Cooperation*. Washington, DC: Hawkins
  and Associates.
Rohrbough, Lynn. n.d. *The Handy Games*. Delaware, Ohio: Cooperative
  Recreation Service.
Spolin, Viola. 1963. *Improvization for the Theatre*. Chicago: North-western
  University Press.
Sutton-Smith, Brian. 1972. *The Folkgames of Children*. Austin: University of
  Texas Press.
Watson, Betty. 1975. 'Games and socialization', in C. S. Greenblat and R. Duck
  (eds), *Gaming-Simulation – Rationale, Design and Application*. New York:
  Sage.

12 PUT MORE MUSIC INTO PLAY: A PLEA TO PLAY LEADERS

Shelley Gordon Garshowitz[1]

Introduction

Children respond enthusiastically to music from very early in life. Rhythmic rocking lulls a crying baby. Soft lullabies put a restless child to sleep. Rousing marches will inevitably elicit responsive movement from young children.[2] Music has universal appeal and has always been one of the principal components of children's play, enhancing the play experience. Melody, rhythm, movement and speech combine to involve the total child and add vitality to the play. Evidence can be found on the playground where children use music to jump rope, bounce balls, count out and play singing games.[3]

Why is it then that there is an ever-decreasing use of music in children's play activities? It is suggested that the answer can be traced to the fabric of the North American[4] life-style and the values it emphasizes. There is little in Western culture that encourages direct involvement in musical activity. Yes, people do listen to music on radio, records, tape recordings and television. A few people occasionally attend concerts. But how often does the average person gather with others to sing, dance or play musical games? Society has become, by and large, a consumer one the habits and tastes of which are fashioned by a handful of commercial enterprises. Art forms and recreation are selected, mass-produced, packaged and promoted by these entrepreneurs.

Records and tape recordings not only influence individual tastes, but also glorify the performer. Young people throng to concerts where a few musicians are the music makers, while thousands listen in awe-struck worship. Television, too, casts people as lowly spectators of a vast array of stars to entertain and to remind them that only the 'gifted' may make music happen. (At the same time, television robs children of free time in which they might explore and discover their own potential.)

At home and at school are further reminders that excellence of performance is the passport to the arts. How often are people told to stop singing because they are off-key, to stop dancing because their rhythm is not accurate? How many children have been excluded from school performances after auditions selected the few who were most skilled?

171

Technological development has further minimized the value of the individual. Preoccupation with high fidelity and stereophonic sound, reliance on electronically amplified instruments, and the ear-piercing noise of discos are de-humanizing — diminishing the contribution of the person and removing him/her from intimate and direct involvement. It is, therefore, not surprising that in December 1978 a Gallup Poll estimated that only 23 per cent of Canadians play a musical instrument. This is considerably lower than the 41 per cent who did so in 1947.[5]

In children's play, as well as in adult free-time activity, there is a heavy emphasis on sports with the concomitant winner—loser ethic. Here again, since to win is more important than to play, the most competent become the stars — the rest remain spectators.

Furthermore, crowded urban living, often in high-rise dwellings, robs children of space and freedom to play noisily and in groups. And musical play is a group activity that often requires space and always produces sound.

Play can be a powerful force in moulding human beings. While children on the playground can spend happy hours in self-directed play, they also benefit from, and indeed need, constructive intervention by a skilled adult. The play leader can stimulate interest in participation and in a greater use of the total self. New vistas can be opened by introducing children to activities they may not already have in their repertoire. More importantly, the play leader can choose these activities with concern about how they contribute to building strength in the individual and comfort within the group.

Musical play abounds with opportunities for personal growth and group building. For these to be realized, however, there must exist a climate of real play; that is, the activity must be happening because the participants are having fun with it. The satisfaction that comes from playing is both the means and the end. Neva L. Boyd (1971, p. 79), pioneer and educator in group leadership, recreation and social group work, put it this way: '. . . to play is to transport oneself psychologically into an imaginatively set up situation and to act consistently within it, simply for the intrinsic satisfaction one has in playing.'

The structure provided by songs, dances, singing games, or games done to music creates this imaginative situation in which true play can happen. These are activities that stimulate a person's energy, initiative, and the use of the total self. They provide opportunities to laugh and be joyful in the use of one's muscles, rhythms and feelings. Requiring no special skills, they are available to all who will play.

The leader facilitates the process by choosing appropriate and diverse material and by setting a climate of warmth, concern and respect so that each person can move at his/her own pace toward self-expression in interaction with others.

With such important benefits for the child, why is it that leaders often avoid music in play activities? Those who have studied music were taught to view it with such seriousness that they see it as an art form and not as play material. Leaders with no music training, on the other hand, are hampered by their awe and fear of the medium. They doubt their ability to use it effectively. This is understandable, for they too have been influenced by the 'star' system and have accepted the spectator role. Is there a way to overcome some of the inhibitions?

If one can think of music as an extension of natural processes, it may help to dispel some of the fear of this delightful pastime. It may be helpful to recognize that, without being aware of it, people do make music in some form all the time. There is rhythm in walking or running; there is melody in speech. When one calls to a friend across a distance, 'Hi, Nancy', or answers a telephone call 'Hello', two, three or more notes, different in pitch, are actually being sung. Body parts, such as heart and lungs, have rhythms of their own. With a little bit of effort, musical play can become available to most leaders on some level.

Play to music can happen in a variety of ways. This paper will focus on activities that the author has found to be well received and practical in a play setting. The qualities inherent in each type will be noted, as each has unique characteristics that make specific contributions toward generating fun, comfort and growth. Some guidelines for effective leadership will also be given.

Singing

In group singing (sometimes called sing-songs or singalongs), there is the possibility of involvement at different levels. This makes it an activity with broad appeal, one that can include people in a wide range of social and skill development, while enjoying a sense of community.

There are times when children need play that makes no demands. In singing sessions, there is the opportunity just to listen and still be a legitimate member of the group. Those who wish and are ready for more active involvement may contribute by improvising, doing solos, harmonizing, suggesting songs to sing and, of course, by just plain singing.

Songs have the power to blend with existing moods or to create new ones. They can transport the singers to far-away places and acquaint them with people and ways of life that are new to them. They can quiet an excited group or stimulate a complacent one. More valuable, perhaps, is the satisfaction that comes from blending one's voice with others to produce a pleasing sound.

In planning a song session, preference should be given to folk songs. Since these are born out of people's real experiences, they have an honesty to which youngsters respond and a clear rhythmic and melodic structure that they can handle. Yet this is good music: 'Its value as good music has been democratically determined by general agreement and group acceptance' (Seeger, 1948, p. 24).

It is preferable to start with songs that both the leader and the group know (e.g., 'Jingle Bells', 'Michael Row the Boat Ashore', 'Kumbaya') Concern about finding that first note can be shared with the group; they will help. Wordy songs should be avoided as they can be boring. When teaching new material, small units should be presented one at a time. The leader can hum, whistle, 'la, la, la' the tune; words can wait. Frequent repetition is in order as children like familiar songs.

If the leader provides the opportunity, children delight in contributing their own ideas. In a Scottish folk song, 'Achen Drum', they can decide what materials will be used to make the body parts of this man who lives on the moor.

And his arms are made of noodles, of noodles, of noodles. . .
and his name is Achen Drum.

Similarly, in 'Old MacDonald', they might divide into small groups, each choosing a farm animal and being responsible for the sounds it makes.

Movement is a natural adjunct to folk songs. They have a vitality that invites rhythmic activity. This can take the form of clapping, snapping, patching (hands on lap), stamping. In several combinations and with varied rhythms, they enrich the vocal sound.[6]

A singing programme should include quiet and lively songs, action songs and rounds. Each has its own value and a mixture will produce a well-balanced programme. One word of caution is appropriate: it is often assumed, and, it is suggested, mistakenly so, that children need to have silly songs or fine songs embellished by meaningless sounds and gestures in order to enjoy singing. While an occasional experience of this type can add a light note to the proceedings, it should only be occasional. Children are discriminating; they can appreciate songs that say something worthwhile and in a dignified way. By assuming otherwise, adults do them an injustice.

Play Party and Singing Games

Play party and singing games are game-like dances done to songs. Play party games (sometimes called 'play parties') offer a variety of dance patterns; an example is 'Betsy Liner', in which dancers in two facing lines are instructed to

> Bow down, Betsy Liner . . . right hand swing, Betsy Liner,
> won't you be my darling. (Garshowitz, 1978, p. 43)

Singing games include dramatic action; an example is 'Sur le Pont d'Avignon', a French game in which the players pantomine actions suggestive of various members of the community — gentlemen, ladies, soldiers, shoemakers (Millen, 1965, p. 162).

The songs, if not already familiar (e.g., 'Jingle Bells', 'Working on the Railroad'), are quickly learned because of the abundant repetition of words and melody. The dance patterns are uncomplicated (often indicated by the words of the song) and the foot work required is already part of the child's vocabulary — walk, run, skip, slide. Once learned, these dance games can be organized by children themselves. Needing no equipment, they can be enjoyed in any setting.

Since the emphasis is on the game, the shy singers will forget to worry about the quality of their singing, and the reluctant dancers — mostly boys — will join in gladly. The frequent change of partners combined with the ease of execution probably make these activities the most relaxed and informal form of musical recreation.

In introducing a play party or singing game, the first step is to get the players into the required formation. A short segment should be taught at a time — song and action simultaneously — with emphasis given to the action. The song can be improved on later. The leader should join in the game — unless this displaces a child — and may need to 'carry' the song until the children become more familiar with it.

Folk (and Square) Dancing[7]

It would be difficult to find a musical play form that can generate as much joy and sociability as folk dancing. This wholesome and vigorous activity has been described as '. . . rhythmic movement of ordinary people in traditionally accepted formations and patterns' (Farwell, n.d., p. 5), or again as '. . . a spontaneous expression of the gaiety of neighbors who like each other. . .' (Norris, 1962, p. 442). Here is an opportunity to loosen muscles and join hands with neighbours in a joyous and informal dance form which can be done by the average child.

Unlike singing, which allows for several levels of involvement, dancing demands equal commitment from all the members. (Indeed, it guarantees equality.) A square dance cannot be executed unless all eight dancers follow the caller's instructions. In the English Maypole Dance the ribbons carried by the participants will not become properly entwined unless all the dancers move in the prescribed patterns. A folk dance can be compared to a piece of weaving — bodies moving in and out in relation to each other. Only by co-operating can they produce the finished piece of work. Having made the commitment to partner or group, the dancer then throws himself/herself into the activity with a sense of ownership, responsibility and interdependence. The reward is a feeling of belonging, of being needed, of being a vital force in a dynamic social process.

Then there is the challenge and satisfaction of mastering one's body, of getting it to move in the proper rhythm and in the right direction. What a pleasure it is to be part of a circle as it works its way left and right, to the centre and back, hands clapping, feet stamping as in the Serbian 'Pleskavac' (Garshowitz, 1978, p. 75). What fun to be chasing a fox in the Israeli 'Hashual' or prancing like a horse in the Russian 'Troika' (Garshowitz, p. 75).

And yet, the peak of the dance experience is attained when the music, steps or patterns are especially beautiful. The exotic melodies and rhythms of many Balkan circle and line dances, the graceful movements of Japanese or Philippino dances, the fascinating patterns in English and Scottish group dances are but a few examples of a rich source of material that can transport the participants to an aesthetic, and even ecstatic, experience that is hard to match. It is this opportunity to create beauty that makes folk dancing an activity in which one can *feel* beautiful. In a society that defines beauty by very different criteria, this is a rare event indeed.

How fortunate it is that folk dancing is within reach of most people – it comes after all from ordinary folk. Elizabeth Burchenal (1938, p. v), a serious student and enthusiastic educator in this field, felt that

> More people can express themselves aesthetically through dancing than through any of the other arts. That is, a greater number of people can learn to dance than to sing, play, write poetry, paint pictures, or do anything else of an artistic character.

Dancing requires of the leader more preparation, imagination and care than do singing, play parties or singing games. To begin with he/she must acquire some comfort and familiarity with the medium. It is the leader's knowledge and enthusiasm that will help the group overcome some of its misgivings. There are children (namely boys) who classify dancing as 'sissy' stuff. This may be due to the fact that they rarely see men dancing. Some worry about partnering — they may have been forced to dance with 'the other' sex when they were not yet ready to do so with comfort. Some associate folk dancing with regimented physical education, which was often devoid of fun. Then there is also the normal fear of doing something new.

The leader can do much to counteract these inhibiting factors. Warm-ups to dancing can go a long way toward establishing more confidence and enthusiasm for what is to follow (Garshowitz, 1978, p. 71). If a session starts with a dance that requires only walking, and is done to music that is familiar and supportive (e.g. 'Green Sleeves', 'Chimes of Dunkirk' (Garshowitz, p. 80 and p. 74), the children will quickly discover that they can dance after all. If they are allowed to choose a partner, they stop worrying about the embarrassment they anticipated. Boys will not view folk dancing as 'for girls only' once they have done 'Yan Petit', a French boys' dance that involves vigorous calisthenic-type movements (Garshowitz, p. 81).

In a warm, accepting climate where 'how to' is emphasized and mistakes are good naturedly seen as steps to learning, where fun and camaraderie are the primary goals, folk dancing can become a truly joyous, exhilarating, social and very musical play activity.[8]

Games

Because games are such a common activity among children, adults sometimes fail to look critically at the nature of children's games. Games can do much good for people, but they can also do much harm to people. A game is good if it is inclusive (anyone who wants to can play), challenging (physically, mentally), builds personal satisfaction and group cohesion, and remains interesting with repeated playing. Too often, games are played that generate antagonism, emphasize competition, resort to scapegoating, or are an insult to the players' intelligence.

Folk games, much as folk songs and folk dances, are a good source to tap. Since they were created by communities who wanted to enjoy being together, they facilitate happy, friendly and co-operative interaction. Even when competition is involved, it still leaves the players as a unit. Winning or losing are secondary to the fun of playing. This is very different from team sports that emulate professional models, and in which, as Boyd (1971, p. 84) says: 'In striving for excellence, freedom and spontaneity are almost inevitably sacrificed. Interest tends to be centered in self and competition is over-emphasized.'

Games break down reservations and inhibitions quickly. They are a good way to start almost any programme. The leader is well prepared who (from a large collection) can select the game appropriate to the given situation: 'From a group leader's point of view, a repertoire of games is not only handy but essential' (Harris, 1976, p. 1).

Music adds a dimension to a game that makes it even more enjoyable. One must be careful, however, that it is not artificially superimposed. In order to feel 'right' it must be genuinely part of the game, it must be a necessary element. A good example is 'Magic Music' (Boyd, 1971, p. 85). In this game, the group determines a task to be performed by a player who has volunteered to go out of earshot while the decision was made. (The task might be: open a window, turn on a light, or shake someone's hand.) When the volunteer returns, he/she moves about guided by the singing of the group. (They had also chosen a song familiar to most, e.g., 'Frère Jacques', 'Jingle Bells'.) They sing louder when the 'it' is going in the right direction and softer when he/she is not. Thus the modulation in their singing guides the 'it' to performing the chosen task.

The leading of games deserves the same care as the choosing of material. Here are some important considerations. The game needs to be clearly explained and quickly started. The leader's job is to get the group into formation and to give the rules; the problem solving is the players' domain. A leader who participates in the game contributes to its success by sharing his/her enthusiasm and by acting as model. A good time to end is when enthusiasm runs high.[9]

Conclusion

Four categories of musical play have been recommended: singing, play parties and singing games, folk and square dancing, and games done to music. Any one of these can be built into a play programme. The leader is likely to draw more on some than on others, depending on familiarity and comfort with the medium. Significant benefits can be gained by dipping into all four types. In dozens of programmes in schools, libraries, camps, playgrounds, festivals, the author has combined all four.[10] It is suggested that the success of the ventures was due in large measure to the variety of offerings. A varied programme not only holds the group's interest, but is also likely to reach some part of the whole person. An individual is made of many parts — each needs an opportunity to function. Every person is potentially a singer, dancer and problem solver.

Both the leader and the players will be more at ease in some play forms than in others. The confident singer may have qualms about dancing. The dance enthusiast may have concerns about success with problem-solving elements of games. Each person approaches new situations with some degree of self-doubt. The confidence gained from doing something about which one feels good allows the person to approach new situations with more ease.[11]

By offering variety in programmes, the leader creates a climate in which people can bloom in new directions. By choosing activities that encourage friendly interaction he/she helps to build communities of people who enjoy being together. By putting more music into play he/she not only enriches the fun of playing but also lays the foundation for enjoyment of music as a free-time activity throughout one's lifetime. This confidence is expressed in a German round:

> Though all things shall perish from under the sky;
> music and joy shall live . . . never to die.
>
> (Garshowitz, 1978, p. 30)

Notes

1. Much of the material in this paper is condensed from Garshowitz (1978), which may be obtained from the Ontario Ministry of Culture and Recreation, 77 Bloor Street West, Toronto, Ontario, Canada M7A 2R9.

2. All of the above also holds true for adults.

3. For two fine collections of these activities see *Sally Go Round the Sun* by Edith Fowke (1969) and *Circle Round the Zero* by Maureen Kenney (1975).

4. Specifically, Canada and the United States.

5. *Toronto Star*, 22 January 1979.

6. Rhythmic activities such as warm-ups or accompaniment to singing can be found in Garshowitz (1978, p. 3).

7. Square dancing is just one type of folk dancing. It was developed in North America by European immigrants. Because it is familiar, it has gained more acceptance than its international cousins.

8. Additional guidelines for leaders can be found in Melamed (1977).

9. For additional information on games leadership, see Harris (1976).

10. This also holds true for programmes with adults or mixed age groupings.

11. These principles form part of the philosophy of the Eastern Cooperative Recreation School in the north-eastern United States (c/o Ed Moyer, R.D. 1, Millmont, Pennsylvania, USA) and the Recreation Workshops Cooperative, Toronto, Canada (c/o Seymour Kantor, 14 Botfield Avenue, Islington, Ontario, Canada). They are adult workshops for people interested in recreation as a valuable and important activity for furthering human development and human relations.

References

Boyd, Neva L. 1971. *Play and Game Theory in Group Work*. Chicago: Jane
　　Adams Graduate School of Social Work, University of Illinois.
—— 1973. *Handbook of Recreational Games*. New York: Dover Publications
　　(also Toronto: General Publication).
Burchenal, Elizabeth. 1938. *Folk-Dances and Singing Games*. New York:
　　G. Schirmer.
Farwell, Jane. n.d. *Folk Dances for Fun*. Delaware, Ohio: Cooperative
　　Recreation Services.
Fowke, Edith. 1969. *Sally Go Round the Sun*. Toronto: McClelland and Stewart.
Garshowitz, Shelley G. 1978. *Play to Music*. Toronto: Ontario Ministry of
　　Culture and Recreation.
Harris, Frank W. 1976. *Games*. Detroit: Eastern Cooperative Recreation School.
　　(Obtainable from the author, PO Box 571, New Millford, New York 10959.)
Kenney, Maureen. 1975. *Circle Round the Zero*. St Louis, Missouri:
　　Magnamusic-Baton.
Melamed, Lanie. 1977. *All Join Hands*. (Obtainable from the author, 494
　　Victoria Ave., Montreal, Quebec.)
Millen, Nina. 1965. *Children's Games from Many Lands*. New York: Friendship
　　Press.
Norris, Ruth. 1962. 'The human values in recreation', *Recreation*, November.
Seeger, Ruth Crawford. 1948. *American Folk Songs for Children*. Garden City,
　　NY: Doubleday.

13 DRAMATIC PLAY IN EARLY CHILDHOOD

Dorothy Jane Needles

Introduction

For centuries it has been known that man, like all animals, learns through play. He learns the essential skills of physical co-ordination, walking, running, reaching, throwing, catching and so on, by repeating the motions time and time again. He practises these skills in make-believe situations, in various locations, alone or with his fellows. Thus, such games as tag and hide-and-seek serve an important purpose in his development.

In today's society, these physical skills are not as important for his survival. As adults, few people depend on speed and endurance to obtain enough food, or to protect their homes. As a result, modern man relegates physical skills to the area of 'sport', something one does with one's leisure time. His moral and religious pressures tend to make clear distinctions between work (which is facing life with grim reality) and play (which is relaxing and enjoyable and therefore somewhat suspect).

To an adult, such attitudes may or may not have detrimental effects — that is not the concern of this paper. Rather, the concern is with children and, in particular, with small children. While the above-mentioned skills may seem to be of less importance today, in actual fact children who do not have a chance to develop them will be distinctly handicapped in approaching the world around them. Children need a large percentage of time to spend exploring the physical world, not only to enhance muscle development, but because it is by using one's body in relationship to one's surroundings that one makes order and sense of the universe. Play is the way children communicate their ideas to themselves, and is thus of tremendous importance towards their over-all intellectual development.

Types of Play

Unfortunately, the pattern of life in urban centres precludes the two essentials of play: space and time. There are few safe areas for children to use in their play, either outside, with private property rights and heavy traffic interfering heavily with freedom, or inside, where cramped living quarters allow no space to linger with a project, nor any privacy in which to try out ideas. With few safe spaces available, children

181

cannot be allowed blocks of time to use as they wish. More and more, children are required to relinquish their freedom and be structured into adult-type concepts of leisure activities, such as hobby instruction (piano, ballet, skating), organized competitive sport (Little Leagues), or passive intake (television and movies).

This means that play, the kind of activity which is of the children's own choosing and where they themselves are in charge, is given less and less priority. The time available to 'learn for themselves' is decimated, and their play is reduced to the point where only one or two types of activities are recognized as being important. One of these is organized sports, with the attendant instruction. Another is the so-called 'playing with friends', which is an open-ended, peer-pressure oriented style of play. Yet it must be remembered that all kinds of play are important to a child's development.

There is the sensory-pleasure type of play, in which children handle materials, touching, smelling, tasting, seeing, hearing, purely for the pleasure gained. They stroke the stuffed animal, sift the sand through their fingers, manipulate the paint on paper, run a stick along a fence, or just stand and stare at a landscape. These are examples of sensory pleasure, and without this kind of experience, where children give themselves pleasure through their own actions, they may grow up lacking the essential ingredient of curiosity, which is the basis of all learning.

There is the gross-motor skill type of play. In this kind of play, skills are practised, using muscles in constantly more demanding ways. Climbing trees, riding a bicycle, balancing on top of a wall, are all gross-motor activities. Children test themselves, challenge themselves and compete with themselves. Through all these experiences, they learn to respect themselves as persons. A positive self-image, developed through this kind of play, makes later learning tasks far easier.

There is also the cognitive skill type of play, in which children learn about concepts such as shape, size, colour, texture and the changing nature of the world around them. Through construction toys, water, sand, jig-saw puzzles, objects to sort and classify, weighing, measuring, and many other types of materials, children teach themselves about relationships, conservation of number, how things can change yet be the same, how things can be two different things at the same time. It is this kind of learning that has brought man from the primitive world of the nomads to the space age.

There are many different ways to categorize play but, however it is done, there is one supremely important kind of play that interrelates with all the others: dramatic play.

Dramatic Play

Dramatic play is the type of play in which children transform themselves and/or their surroundings into something other than what they are. Through interaction with the materials at hand, children put themselves into a world where they are in command, where what they decide should happen does happen. This can be done while using any of the other categories of play mentioned above.

The child rides a tricycle. 'Look at me, I'm Batman', he shouts, whizzing by.

He sifts the sand through his fingers over and over again. 'It's snowing', he chants softly. 'It's snowing, it covers the house, and Mummy. And my rubbers. It's snowing. Look, it's snowing.'

She builds a structure from Lego. 'This is my house. And here's my car. I'm going to crash. CRASH!! I knocked the house over. It's dead. Here's my house. It's the jail. Here's the tower. No windows. The bad man's in there.'

Sometimes the situation is independent of any apparent immediate materials or occupation. Children move about, lost in a world of their own choosing. They can be Superman, Wonder Woman, or another of the countless folk heroes encountered on television or in picture books. A child may be a chef, making cakes, and serving them to unlimited hosts of friends. They can fly, tunnel, climb, fight off monsters, or simply lie still 'being dead'. This is pure dramatic play and can involve other people or just oneself. It can go on for hours or a few moments. From a learning stand-point, it can be considered to embrace all the other classifications and, as such, it rates high in importance.

It is through dramatic play that children learn to organize their thinking. They can test out ideas with no one interfering, or saying that such-and-such is 'impossible', or 'wouldn't work'. They can find out for themselves how logical or illogical they are being. They can make inner predictions concerning social behaviour and test these predictions in play situations with their peers. They can practise 'being' in countless different ways, playing different roles and experiencing the emotions and reactions that each entails.

When two-year-old children pick up a toy car and run it along the floor, making the sound of a truck, they are consolidating their experiences of what noises trucks make as they pass their house. They are 'at cause' over the trucks, in a way they can never be in real life. Because of this mastery of the situation, they relax about trucks in

general and free themselves to learn more about them. They find out
for themselves from their own actions that wheels move when they
push, that this truck can go faster or slower, and that it can be made
to swerve around corners like the real one. They are playing, and
through this play they are learning to symbolize, to be the cause of
things happening, and to predict, while gaining the satisfaction that
using these skills can bring.

A four-year-old is playing with a friend. Listen to the conversation
that ensues:

> You should be Mummy, and I'm your little girl.
> I'm Mummy, and you should be bad.
> I'm running away, and you should catch me. (running, catching,
>   spanking)
> No! You should put me to bed. 'Cause I'm bad.
> I'm Daddy coming home, You're a bad girl.
> No, you should be Daddy, and you're taking me out. Hi, Daddy, I
>   want an ice-cream cone. . .[1]

There are several points of interest here. For one thing, neither of
these two children had ever been spanked, yet, to make the play
dramatically satisfying, they chose this kind of conflict. Were they
perhaps acting out secret fears of situations where parents did act this
way, where children did 'bad' things, and were suitably punished? At
one time, professionals might have jumped to these conclusions, but
there are other possibilities. Perhaps they were testing their prediction
skills: 'I act this way, and such-and-such a thing happens.' Perhaps it
was a variation on the primitive catch-me-if-you-can situation. Perhaps
they were simply reiterating a familiar role-playing that gives pleasure
from its predictability, like an old pair of shoes.

The children accepted each other and shared the same symbols with
no problem. It was a safe environment and minor variations on the
theme could be tried, accepted or discarded with minimum risk to the
continuance of the play. This seems to be an essential ingredient for
dramatic play at this level. Another point to notice is how the play runs
on and on, with no tight plot sequence, and frequent changes of
character and situation. This kind of play will fill up any amount of
time and only ceases (if not interrupted) when one or other of the
participants loses interest.

You're a bad girl, and I'm going to spank you.
Let's play on the swing.
No, you should cry, and say you're sorry.
OK. (She runs to the swing.) I'm swinging. Push me.
I want to swing.

Obviously, both children are ready for a change. The transition is made smoothly, and presently another form of dramatic play may begin, involving the swing.

Two years later, the child's dramatic play should be becoming more sophisticated. Six-year-old children often rely on environments, using blocks, boxes, dining-room chairs — in fact, anything handy to make the space-ship, the airplane, or the bus. Through practice, the ability to symbolize has grown and now children may find it easy to accept any makeshift environment as the setting for play. The peer group and other outside pressures have, however, begun to influence their play and their attitudes towards it. While a three-year-old child will happily play fireman in the bathtub, in church, or in the doctor's waiting-room, older children seem to require more security before they can let themselves go. The outside world, with its approval and disapproval, is constantly ready to encroach. Perhaps this is why they concern themselves with environments.

Planning and making the setting serve a social purpose as well. By now, they can sometimes operate successfully in a group as large as five or six. Working on the building gives a chance for the individuals within the group to 'size each other up', to establish certain pecking orders, and eventually to give a shape to the play.

Six-year-old children are more sustained in their dramatic play and they enjoy making use of available materials as they find the need for them. The stick represents the sword; the block of wood is the stolen money. Directions thrown to playmates are more specific, come faster and seem to require more active compliance.

Come on, we've got to run.
No, this way!
You've shot me.
Go on, shoot.
You missed!

Often it seems as though the loudest voice directs the play, but close examination may reveal that the members of the group are only marginally aware of the central story line. Each child is fulfilling his/her own needs and picks up the suggestions thrown out by others only when his/her own inventiveness fails.

However sophisticated the use of symbolism, six-year-old children are only rarely able to prestructure a story and produce what adults consider 'a play'. They can think up beginnings. ('I'm an engine driver — You're a bad girl.') They can project middles. ('You should be Daddy come home, and you should get mad. I'm a bus driver and there's going to be a crash-up.') Endings, however, are beyond them. The play ends when interest flags, or when it is interrupted. Ask children to repeat their play and it will be radically changed, almost unrecognizable. They cannot play from another's point of view. They cannot separate themselves from their own immediacy; when they enter into their play, it carries them away. If an adult takes over and 'directs' the play, the children will usually be capable of learning what is required. But this product is a far cry from the open-ended kind of play which is their natural medium. Even when children of this age make up plays and demand an audience, the play is almost always non-existent. The children may set up chairs for the audience, mark out the stage, make tickets and arrange for their sale and collection, but when it comes to the play itself, it will almost certainly turn out completely lacking in structure. What is happening is that the children are play-acting putting on a play. The open-ended part of the dramatic play, the seating of the audience, the sequence of selling and collecting tickets, even the announcement of the different acts, cast, and so on, these are all unstructured and can be handled. The formal structure of the entertainment itself is beyond them and what is produced is a rambling, repetitive hodge-podge, which quickly wears out the patience of the audience.

Adults will often try to help the children to structure what they are doing, not realizing that the children are simply not ready for formal structure. This is not the time to send a child to drama classes 'because he is always acting'. It is not the time to pressure children into assembly or concert presentations, even when the teacher is convinced that the performances represent the children's own ideas. Perhaps the ideas are the children's, but the structure is adult-oriented. Until children reach what Piaget has termed the 'concrete operational' stage, they will not be able to prestructure an idea into a story, with a beginning, a middle and an end. They need enough time to work on their own with materials and ideas so that they can internalize the concept of a story. When they have achieved this, they will be able to conceive the story as being something apart from themselves. The story will be a vehicle for their play, in which they can participate if they wish, but also something they can disassociate from, as well.

The Role of the Adult

The role of the adult in children's play will be, for the most part, an exterior one. At times it can be as director, announcing meal-times or bed, setting rules and limits for safety, or dealing with emergencies. It can also be as a resource, providing ideas or materials as they are needed or requested. There can also be another role that the adult may be required to play, that of a model.

There are many children who do not show the growth in play skills that might be expected. Children who live in cramped areas with no safe play space will often use little symbolism in their play. Children whose time is filled with passive activities such as television watching and manipulating undemanding highly structured toys show the same lack of development. Symbolic play does not seem to develop if the child is never exposed to unstructured materials, such as blocks of wood, fabric, empty boxes, sand, water and junk materials of all kinds. The age of cheap plastic toys means that many children never have to improvise; this in turn means that they do not develop an ability to project fantasies in their minds. The result is that their reactions to any stimulus are apt to be purely physical. These children can be seen in such places as subways, waiting-rooms, or any place where they are confined for any length of time. They are not so much hyperactive, as incapable of thinking about anything, for any period of time. Their level of fantasy play is extremely low and this is closely allied to the crucial ability to symbolize. These children are at great risk when they begin school, since so much of what they will be called upon to learn, such as reading and writing, depends almost entirely on their ability to symbolize. As James Britton points out, 'Reading is the most symbolic of all communication.'

Children of this type find it difficult to wait their turn, since any waiting requires the individual to fill a blank within their minds. If children cannot symbolize, they cannot truly 'think' about anything. They have to resort to physical activity. When their group is made up of members all as unskilled as they are, the result will naturally be aggressive, even destructive. Too often, when groups of children of this type attempt to play, the structure degenerates into fights and name calling, with no one gaining much in the way of satisfaction.

Adults who are skilled, watchful and patient can help. They can assume this third role of model. They are not directors, who tell the children what to do, nor resources, who supply materials as needed; they are active participants in the play. Older siblings or, more commonly, skilful peers can take on this role of model, but if no one in the group shows the required ability, the adult is quite justified in moving in. The playground leader, the parent, the teacher, the visiting uncle — any of these people can play with a group to advantage. There are, of course, pitfalls in this approach which must be avoided. Adults must become part of the group to the extent that they accept the limitations put on any of its members. This means they cannot assert authority to further their own aims at the expense of other people's ideas. This would be assuming the role of director. Any child in the group who did this would be immediately ostracized. Another pitfall to avoid is playing with an eye to being watched by one's own peers. Examples of this are seen at picnics or pool parties, where the generations are brought together. Too often an adult will join the children, not with the idea of playing with them, but rather to show off to his/her own contemporaries. Comments will be made, designed to fly over the heads of the children, to make the adults laugh. This is making mock of the children's efforts to play and can do nothing but harm to their self-esteem and their respect for the adult. To act as model, one must be willing to accept the children at their own level, to play on an equal footing with sincerity and enthusiasm. Last, but not least, an adult must be willing to withdraw, as soon as his presence seems to be redundant, allowing the children to carry on alone.

The distinction between directing and modelling play cannot be too clearly drawn. As director, the adult stands outside the activity, defining limits, telling what should be done, evaluating, even policing the area. There are times when this role is necessary. As model, however, the adult must be involved in the play, to the exclusion of all other considerations, for this is the way children themselves play. Because of higher skills, the adult's participation may take the group far beyond its own capabilities. New techniques are thrown in or new ideas for exploration may be introduced. The adult, however, must be willing to abdicate the leadership and to allow the children to continue on their own, even if they seem to be floundering. If the adult remains involved too long, the children will lose their initiative and rely too much on the adult's ideas.

Given enough safe space, uninterrupted periods of time, sufficiently challenging ideas and materials, and someone to act as model, imaginative dramatic play should be evident in what the children do.

Its importance must not be forgotten. Dramatic play is a crucial ingredient in the consolidation of thinking skills.

Note

1. Actual record of two four-year-old children at play.

Part Four

SPECIAL GROUPS

14 PLAY FOR CHILDREN IN HOSPITAL AND THE PLAY SPECIALIST'S ROLE

Jan Kubli

Introduction

During the past fifteen years there has been a growing awareness of the emotional welfare of children in hospital. Many paediatric wards now have open visiting hours and provide facilities for parents to be resident with their sick child. Some nursing staff on children's wards have come out of uniform. Hospital play schemes are being run by trained play specialists. Meeting children's emotional needs, as well as their physical needs, is being seen as a necessity in the total care of hospitalized children.

Children coming into hospital enter a foreign world. They experience events, perhaps painful, that they may not understand. They may be separated from their parents and be cared for by strangers. These children may feel that their whole world has collapsed.

> Young children have very strong feelings of love and hate towards those they care most about, and on whom they are most dependent. The hostile feelings a child may have toward his parents who have seemingly deserted him, and towards the hospital staff who may cause him to suffer pain, as well as alleviate it, must have an outlet. (Harvey and Hales-Tooke, 1972, p. 27)

Hospitalized children need a chance to work through their fears and anxieties. They can be helped to cope with their situation by play.

The hospital play specialist is an important member of the paediatric team. Jolly (1969, p. 487) notes that 'the main role of the play specialist is to help the child through play to understand and cope with all the strange things that happen to him in hospital'. The play specialist sets up an environment in which children can play. Play can be organized on the ward, as well as in isolation cubicles, or in a playroom. Ideally, the playroom should be connected to the ward, so that the children can roam freely from the playroom to their beds.

The play specialist provides a variety of activities each day. Messy play (e.g., sand, water and painting) should not be excluded. Children in hospital should have exposure to all types of play, in order to continue normal growth and development.

Children of all ages enter hospital and it is possible that the play specialist may work with infants, as well as adolescents. There are not many play situations in which staff work with such a wide age range; therefore, flexibility is an essential quality in a play specialist. This is also essential because of the quick turnover of children on a hospital ward. Relationships must be made easily with the children admitted to the ward and their parents.

In an environment in which nurses and other members of staff change because of shifts, holidays and ward changes, the play specialist can be an important factor in providing security for the child.

The Roles of Volunteers and of the Medical Staff

The play staff can represent one of the more consistent facets of the children's hospital experience. The children can rely on the staff members to be there five days a week between the hours of nine and five. This is not, however, satisfactory coverage of children's needs, as children do need play provision at weekends and in the evening. At present, finances are not available in the United Kingdom to employ a sufficient number of play staff for total coverage.

Volunteers are often utilized at times when the play staff are off duty, to supplement their work. A hospital play scheme run totally by volunteers, however, runs the risk of the children being exposed to a number of strange faces at a time when continuity of staff is important to their emotional welfare. The play specialist is the one person who is not called away from the children to perform other duties on the ward.

Playing with the children is a vital part of the nurses' duties on a children's ward, and play staff should encourage them to join in the play activities. The nurses, however, have to get on with their nursing duties and are not always able to spend long periods of time with the children. It has been suggested, for economic reasons, that nursing staff could provide play for children in hospital as part of their duties. Nurses, however, are trained to nurse the sick, not to run play schemes. Nurses also do not feel qualified to provide the quality of play that a trained play specialist can provide.

Play Staff Involvement in Other Tasks

Just as it is important for the nurses to play with the children, play staff should be involved with the more painful tasks that must take place on the ward. The play specialist who holds a child while having a blood test can help the child cope with the procedure, by talking with the child about his/her feelings, and offer comfort when it is all over.

Children should not be distracted from what is going to happen, but helped to understand and accept it. Doctors and nurses should also be encouraged to carry out examinations and tests in the playroom. Removing children from their play can cause more distress than the procedure itself. Children feel more relaxed in the playroom than behind the closed doors of the treatment room.

Another important aspect of helping children cope with the unpleasant and frightening procedures that take place in hospital is to provide the child with opportunities to play with hospital equipment. The hospital play box should contain real syringes, charts, stethoscopes, bandages, IV drips, and proper uniforms cut down to the sizes of the children. This equipment should be readily available to the children. Through hospital play, the children become familiar with these items and begin to work through some of their fears and gain a better understanding of their treatment.

Through play, children can be prepared for operations and treatment. This preparation play or 'play prep.' is more structured than the spontaneous play mentioned previously. The play specialist must have an understanding of the particular child's operation, so that she can explain it to him/her. 'Play prep.' is best done when the nurses, play staff and parents combine their skills. The nurse has the medical knowledge; the play specialist can put that knowledge into terms the child can understand; and the parents know their child best. Preparing the child is a difficult task, because the staff have to judge just how much the child can manage to take in. Too much detail may prove too frightening for the child.

There are various books available concerning the emotional preparation of children coming into hospital. These take the form of text books for professionals, reference books for parents, and story books for children. It is helpful to begin the preparation with a story. Children can then relate themselves to the character in the book, and gain a better understanding of what is going to happen to them. With help from the play specialist, the children can now use items in the hospital box in their play. By dressing up in surgical gowns and familiarizing themselves with the equipment, they learn about their future treatment. They can anaesthetize the teddy bear with a mask, or give it an injection. This type of play is therapeutic in helping the children work through their fears about their operation.

With so many stresses placed on children in hospital, it is understandable that they may regress from their normal stage of development. Their ability to concentrate decreases and they may choose activities at a much lower level than their capabilities warrant. The children are reassuring themselves that their bodies are still working, and must be allowed to go at their own pace. The play specialist, of course, would make sure new challenges are always available and encourage the children to try them.

Play Materials

The play specialist often has to adapt play materials to provide for the child's individual needs. For example, children in traction have their own special needs and can pose a specific problem for the staff. Active children confined to bed by traction get frustrated by the restriction of being tied to their bed. Children with fractured femurs may be in traction for eight weeks. This can be an eternity to a child. After the first week when the pain and trauma decrease, the children are basically well. They become frustrated and their behaviour may become aggressive and demanding. Children in traction also have worries concerning their rehabilitation. These children must have outlets for their built-up aggressions.

It is the play staff's responsibility to channel the children's energy in a more positive way. Attaching a punch ball to the traction frame is a good method of burning up energy. Tossing bean bags at a suitable target is another method. The play specialist must devise ways to extend the children's play space. Bed tables and trays are useful for this. A baby bath on a tray can be used for water and sand play. Large sheets of plastic can be used to cover the bed, so messy play can continue. It is important to move the children in bed and to give them a change of scenery; when weather permits, they should be moved to the outside play area if one is available. Play staff should make sure that bed-ridden children are included in group activities. By setting up activities around children confined to bed, mobile children are encouraged to their bedside.

Children nursed in an isolation cubicle, for reasons of infection, are of great concern to the hospital play specialist. Not only are they children placed in a strange environment, but also they are in solitary confinement. The play staff and other members of the paediatric team must give isolated children as much attention as possible. They rely completely on others to make contact. The play specialist must make sure that suitable play materials are available in the children's cubicles, so that they can occupy themselves when the specialist cannot be there.

Isolation reduces possible occupations, as the children cannot join in activities with other children on the ward. For reasons of infection, toys taken into the children's cubicles must remain there until their discharge. All play articles must then be sterilized along with the cubicle. Careful thought is used in providing play equipment for isolated children. They must be able to withstand sterilization, and be out of use to other children on the ward for the length of the children's stay.

The staff must be alert to the needs of isolated children. They should try to reduce their loneliness by helping them make contact with children on the wards. There are ways of breaking down the barriers of isolation. Battery-operated telephones allow the children to communicate with others on the ward; by providing writing tablets on each side of the glass, they can be encouraged to interact with other children in isolation.

Special attention and time must be spent on children in isolation. They must be reassured that their isolation is not a form of punishment. These children need the opportunity to play through and talk about their feelings towards their isolation. Appropriate play materials and company will help them deal with this particular stressful situation.

Play in Other Parts of the Hospital

There are areas in hospital other than the paediatric wards that should have organized play schemes. The paediatric out-patients' clinic is one of them. A child's first impression of hospital may be in an out-patients' clinic. By providing a play scheme, with a play specialist to run it, the clinic becomes a more welcoming place.

Play helps to relieve the anxiety that children may be feeling during the long wait to see the doctor. Play between parent and children reduces the tension that parents often feel about the visit to the clinic. If possible, the same play specialist should be responsible for a certain clinic each week. She/he is then able to build relationships with the children, their parents and the staff working in the clinic. The play specialist sets up activities in the waiting area of the clinic. These activities should be simple and quick to complete, as the children may be called in to see the doctor at any time. Painting, drawing and play-dough are quite successful. Toys such as cars, small dolls and jig-saw puzzles are useful and the children can take them into the examining room with them.

The play specialist working in an out-patients' clinic is able to meet children who may have a future hospital admission, and the children then recognize a familiar face when they arrive on the ward. This can be an important factor in the children's adjustment to hospital.

In the clinic, the play specialist can recommend that the parents take the children to visit the ward prior to admission. It is best if she/he can take them herself/himself and introduce the children to other members of staff and show them the playroom. The play specialist working in the clinic also sees children who have previously been on the ward, thus helping to provide continuity to the children's experience of hospital.

The medical staff often use the play specialist's knowledge of child development in the clinic. Doctors may request information on a child's development or perhaps details on the relationship between the child and his/her parents. These important observations can be essential to a doctor who only sees the child for a short time in the examining room. The play specialist would then write any relevant information in the hospital notes.

The Play Staff and the Parents

Although they are called play specialists, their role does not stop at providing play for children. The play staff work closely with parents. Parents often ask questions of the play staff, rather than the nursing or medical staff. Parents may feel they are more approachable, or do not want to bother the doctors and nurses.

The play specialist must have some basic medical knowledge and be able to talk with ease about the child's illness with the child and his/her parents. Of course, if she did not feel confident to answer the question, she would then inform the doctor or nurse about the parents' worries. The days can be extremely long for resident parents. They too are away from home in a strange place and it can be reassuring to have another adult to chat with. Parents often like to help the play specialist and feel they are useful.

As mentioned previously, children in hospital sometimes regress or have changes in behaviour. Parents may become disturbed when children become aggressive or unruly on the ward. The play staff can assure them this is a normal response to being in hospital, and it may continue when they return home.

Conclusion

Play provisions have grown in Britain since the first play scheme started in a London hospital in 1963. In 1976, a government report, 'The Expert Group Report on Play for Children in Hospital', recommended that a trained play specialist should be employed to organize play for all children in hospital; however, with the present economic situation, this has not been implemented on a large scale.

Organizations such as the National Association for the Welfare of

Children in Hospital (NAWCH), which has worked so hard to establish open visiting hours on children's wards, have also contributed in the area of play. Not only are they responsible for much of the written material on the subject, but they have also set up their own play schemes on children's wards.

With the expansion of play for children in hospitals, the play specialists themselves wished to form a national association. The National Association of Hospital Play Staff (NAHPS) was formed in October 1976. It is the organization's aim to establish the profession of play staff in hospital, with common policy on questions of status, training and salaries. It also intends to collect and distribute information on play for children in hospital, as well as promote international collaboration.

There is still a considerable amount of work to be done in the area of play for children in hospital. A number of hospital administrators and medical staff still need to be convinced of its value. It is difficult to measure children's feelings about their stay in hospital. Fortunately, many paediatric teams are recognizing the valuable contribution hospital play specialists can make and are requesting their help in the care of the whole child. This, coupled with the support from professional organizations such as NAHPS and NAWCH, could assist in the implementation of the recommendations of the 'Expert Group' and help put it into practice. All children in hospital will then be allowed to continue to grow and learn through play.

References

Harvey, S. and A. Hales-Tooke. 1972. *Play in Hospital*. London: Faber and Faber.
Jolly, H. 1969. 'Play is work', *Lancet*, II, p. 487.
——. 1978. 'The work of the play specialists in Charing Cross Hospital', *Journal of Association of the Care of Children in Hospital*, II, 2, p. 6.
Latimer, E. 1978. 'Play is everybody's business in the children's ward', *Nursing Mirror*, II, 11, p. 147.
Tizard, B. and D. Harvey. 1977. *Biology of Play*. London: William Heinemann Medical Books Ltd.

15 PLAY NEEDS OF IMMIGRANT CHILDREN

Mavis Burke

Introduction

> The child shall have full opportunity for play and recreation, which
> should be directed to the same purposes as education; society and
> the public authorities shall endeavour to promote the enjoyment of
> this right. . .[1]

Immigration is not, in itself, a new phenomenon for Canada, but the
past two decades have been remarkable for the total increase in and the
high proportion of young people arriving here as immigrants.
Immigration statistics indicate that in the Province of Ontario, for
example, a substantial number of immigrants during the period
1969—76 were aged eighteen and under. (See Tables 15.1 and 15.2.)

Meeting the needs of immigrant children has become a major
preoccupation of educational and social agencies, but the diagnosis of
play needs as perceived by immigrant families from different cultural
backgrounds is often at variance with the norms of the host society.
Attitudes to play and to recreation in general are often diametrically
opposed to accepted practices. This paper analyzes some aspects of the
problem, reflects the experiences of children from their own
perspective, and examines the extent to which new trends in
recreational provision can promote the learning and socialization needs
of immigrant children.

Profile

Most newcomers to Canada have tended to settle in urban centres;
recent shifts to suburban areas have widened the scope of the 'inner-
city' concept rather than serving as a dispersal agent.[2]

The profile of the immigrant child under consideration is as urban
dweller, inner city arrivant, deprived of accustomed life-style, and
having to adjust to displacement in terms of physical, social and
emotional environment. Socio-economic background in the home
culture may have varied from middle- to lower-income levels, with
resulting differences in home environment. Family structure may differ
appreciably from one culture to another, but the inner city necessity
tends to exert a common influence and response from disparate groups

200

Table 15.1: Immigration to Canada and Ontario of Children under 18 years of Age, 1966–76

Calendar Year	Ontario	Canada
1966	32,251	56,045
1967	30,919	58,309
1968	24,266	46,273
1969	21,240	40,130
1970	19,651	35,804
1971	16,176	30,745
1972	17,005	32,142
1973	25,596	45,774
1974	35,306	62,161
1975	31,565	58,918
1976	21,996	44,539
Total	275,971	510,840

Source: Ontario Ministry of Education, 1976, p. 25.

Table 15.2: Immigration to Ontario of Children Aged 18 and Under, 1969–76

Age Group	1969	1970	1971	1972	1973	1974	1975	1976	Total
0–4	7,490	6,793	5,322	5,546	7,860	10,230	8,437	5,416	57,094
5–9	6,833	6,152	4,999	5,320	8,179	11,776	10,386	7,177	60,822
10–14	4,362	4,078	3,556	3,757	5,860	8,684	8,450	6,147	44,894
15–18	4,460	4,125	3,476	3,663	5,731	6,558	5,958	4,574	38,545
Total	23,145	21,148	17,353	18,286	27,630	37,248	33,231	23,314	201,355

Source: Ontario Ministry of Education, 1976, p. 26.

experiencing similar life situations as new arrivals in the metropolis.

Implications of Parental Attitudes to Play

Parental perceptions of immigrant children's needs inevitably relate first to practical considerations of diet, clothing, and the outward signs of good health in coping with the new climate. The urge to be protective extends to psychological fears for the child's safety among a new peer group unknown to the family, as well as the physical hazards of the city environment. The newcomer family is faced with a crisis of survival and is forced to adopt a task-oriented regimen. New responsibilities are placed on all family members, with little time to choose the pace for developing new skills. A tight work schedule may control all family movement, particularly in cases where both parents are employed. Children may also have to become wage earners.

My Job

I'm ten years old and work seven days a week, six days in Kensington Market. I'm a salesman. My boss tells me the lowest price I can give my customers for each thing we sell. Then I give my customers a higher price but make them a discount. I never give a thing away for the lowest price. Sometimes my boss gets mad because he leaves me in charge of some things and the girls sell them for the wrong prices, so I get in trouble. That's what gets me mad. It's a good job, but the money is bad.

On Sunday I deliver newspapers. I just started last week. It's a fun job. Fifty-two papers I deliver, two to my friend's house. (McClard and Wall, 1978, p. 77)

In this context, children's real needs may, understandably, be misjudged. For many incoming groups, play has never been consciously recognized as a valuable learning experience. From an early age, children in many cultures are expected to demonstrate academic skills such as proficiency in reading and number work, while play experience is relegated to the sphere of time-wasting activity. Parental response to requests for play opportunities in the new setting may therefore be negative. However, it must be remembered that in the home culture such opportunities could be expected to be present in the natural process of daily life. Even in Canada, as one writer noted:

Children did not need a 'special' place for playing in the years of yesterday. They had woods, fields, backyards and safe pathways in which to adventure. They grew up in the midst of their elders in their shops. . . . As the adult worked at his trade, the child was able to contemplate, imitate and assimilate simply through play.

Today, the rural areas continue to be wealthy in this abundance of ideal, natural places in which children can play. However, in the city of today . . . the trend to greater urbanization has created the new problem of providing special playgrounds for children. (Fjeldsted, 1978, p. 16)

Immigrant parents are often wary of these artificial but uncontrolled environments. They may not have recognized the extent or the

significance of children's improvization in making play objects from
dried fruit, seeds, tree bark, old boxes and cans, bits of paper, etc. They
may therefore find it equally difficult to assign part of a scant income
to toy buying for replacement activities.

The element of socialization through play remains a constant source
of anxiety to parents of immigrant children. Restrictions about forming
friendships are a frequent source of conflict between parents and
children in Canadian multiracial and multicultural settings. Friends are
sometimes viewed as a potential source of negative influence rather than
a necessary extension to life experience, even though adult family
members in newcomer family units usually have no time to participate
in children's play activities. Parents may not perceive the depth of the
emotional needs involved in this process.

> My grandfather lived in Hong Kong. He is ninety-eight years old.
> He is good. Sometimes he took me to the playground to play. I like
> my grandfather but my father said, 'We will go to Canada', so I came
> to Canada. I can't ever play with him. (McClard and Wall 1978, p. 23)

In many cultures, opposition to recreational activity is much greater
for girls than for boys. Sex-role stereotyping tends to make sharp
distinctions in relation to acceptable forms of physical activity for
females. Adult adjustments to new demands are rarely reflected in the
upbringing of their children who have to make their own personal
transitions.

> In Portugal only the men are supposed to work and the women are
> supposed to stay home and take care of the house. But here in
> Canada mostly all of the women and men have to work to support
> their family. . . .
> My mother works . . . at an office building and she cleans offices.
> But she doesn't get as much as the men who work with her do. I
> think something should be done about it because women are humans
> too. (McClard and Wall, 1978, p. 70)

Schools are finding it difficult to break through the stereotypes set
for children by immigrant families. Freedom to choose play activities
has not resulted in major new directions but reinforced trends
maintained in the home from early childhood. In such cases the modern
educator, encouraging girls to hammer and boys to sew, is running
counter to the values of the home and must risk creating further

conflicts in the life of the immigrant child. Directed play can help to show the learner that there is equal capability to perform a variety of activities and that these can be enjoyed by any learner.

Assessment: Needs of Immigrant Children

How can one assess objectively the needs of immigrant children and the extent to which they can be met by play? What are the critical factors to be taken into account for physical and emotional well-being in the initial period of adjustment?

The newcomer needs the opportunity to develop a sense of location and a sense of self. It has been noted (daCosta, 1976) that immigrant children may experience a keen sense of loss and mourning and may require time and opportunity to relive the immediate past, to maintain a temporary connection through attachment to a toy or loved object from the former environment. Imaginative association may take the form of individual role playing, reflective activity, or re-creation of past experience through art, writing, imaginary conversations, etc.

A sense of continuity may be encouraged through opportunities for familiar activities. Unstructured materials may suggest these and may also develop new skills, serving as a bridge between the old and the new. Creative capacity and natural curiosity should also be called upon for the task of building confidence and a sense of achievement.

In association with these needs, the socialization of the immigrant child emerges as the most acute initial problem. It seems likely that adjustment to the physical environment will take place in time, if there is the security of the caring adult and welcoming peer group. Play opportunities should provide for both kinds of co-operative relationship. Interaction with peers is a significant learning activity for the newcomer. Immigrant children develop communication skills through body language and may rely entirely on non-verbal behaviour if they do not understand the language of the host country. The experience can be traumatic but provides a necessary relationship, as well as an exercise in informal immersion learning, which for children is the most effective method of achieving oral language facility. Associative play gives language context and meaning.

Speaking English

When I came to Canada,
I didn't know how
to speak
English.

> When I went to school,
> I saw so many kids
> that I never
> had seen
> before.
> I felt like a mouse
> being surrounded by cats.
> Now that I know
> a little English,
> I don't feel
> like that
> no more.
> (McClard and Wall, 1978, p. 60)

Even in situations where there is some degree of language comprehension, the play needs of the immigrant child are inextricably interwoven with the total experience of displacement and the nostalgia of the need to remember.

> Cicely followed Mei Ling to the concrete playground. It was cold. She stood with her coat tightly bundled around her, watching the others laugh and play. She thought of the warm sun, the beach in St. Anne's Bay, of Winsome and her friends at school. They spoke as she did. They understood everything she said. She wished she were back home in Jamaica.
>   For the rest of the morning, Cicely didn't feel like speaking to anyone. . .
>   When she reached the apartment, Cicely unlocked the door with the key her mother had given her. In Jamaica, the door was always open and there was always someone at home. Feeling very lonely, she went to get her conch shell. She put the shell to her ear and listened to the roar of the ocean waves washing over a far away beach. 'Well, I know you are my friend', she said. 'You understand what I say.' (Singer, 1976, p. 19)

The child is also dependent on a helping relationship with adult family members to provide guidance and support through the mass of new experiences which assault the sense of the newcomer. The adult serves as a point of reference and can give direction to the disoriented youngster by sharing in recreational activities of different kinds.

Urban Play Environments

Indoor

Apartment living in the urban setting often restricts the immigrant child's opportunities for meaningful play activities. In addition to problems of electrical wiring, carpeted floors and other child play hazards, indoor areas may have little free floor space and no possible extensions. For example, corridors are usually out of bounds, and recent incidents in Ontario have shown that both window areas and balconies may be unsafe for children. Using television as baby-sitter cannot replace the need for movement, for creative expression and associative learning. A sense of space is important for development.

Outdoor Playgrounds

It seems equally doubtful that the now traditional structured playground of slides and fixed climbing equipment will meet some of the significant play needs of the immigrant child. There is certainly no reminder of previous home play areas or materials, little opportunity to exercise creative abilities or develop imaginative associations, and no need for co-operative activity and communicative skills.

From the perspective of play needs of immigrant children, the 'adventure' playground concept seems likely to come much closer to meeting newcomer needs. Comparisons of the 'traditional' versus the 'adventure' playground indicate that the free-play concept with experienced play leaders provides the kinds of opportunities necessary to restore the confidence of immigrant children (Fjeldsted, 1978). In support of the introduction of this concept, Adventure Education Concept Inc., a charitable, non-profit organization operating out of Harbourfront, Toronto, identifies the child benefits as mental, social, environmental and physical. These advantages can be summarized as shown in Figure 15.1.

Relating to inner-city needs, Adventure Education Concept puts forward the view that 'the freedom to manipulate one's own space and then create one's own environment is a valuable and needed constructive release for society's child today'.[3] This point has been further developed (Passantino, 1975) by commentators who observe that many destructive acts classified as vandalism actually possess elements of play, and suggest that adventure playgrounds could serve to defuse such activities by absorbing energies creatively and relieving the boredom and frustrations of inner-city adolescents.

Figure 15.1: The Benefits of Adventure Playgrounds

Mental	Social	Environmental	Physical
Mental stimulation	Associative play	Experiencing nature	Testing strength
Imaginative activity	Meeting point		Developing co-ordination
Manipulating materials	Interracial mix	Understanding natural elements	Exercising motor skills
Decision making	Group interaction	Using natural environment	Physical energy release
Project completion	Sharing	Discovering dangers of elements	Exploring capabilities
Sense of pride	Communicative skill development		Using tools

. . . my neighbourhood was lots of trouble — like getting in trouble all the time, fighting, climbing on roofs, on peoples' property. . . . I hurt my hand when I punched the windows out of a house no one was living in. (McClard and Wall, 1978, p. 39)

Another important element for immigrant children in the adventure playground concept is maintenance of the natural terrain or its re-creation with trees and vegetation. The natural qualities of the outdoor environment can provide reassurance as well as challenge. Working in the earth and with growing things or having an opportunity to care for pets may provide the kind of link which will take newcomers out of themselves in identifying with familiar kinds of everyday activities. It is not only the young child who needs the experience of sand box, white mice and aquarium. These needs have to be interpreted for older children in a less confined and structured learning situation, providing outlets for self-expression which may also demonstrate capabilities which many immigrant children already possess.

The role of the adult in being 'present' to the immigrant child may be a more critical factor in play than has often been recognized. Parents from some cultural backgrounds may have no difficulty in seeing the need for playground activity and may send the child out to play in order to encourage independence and self-reliance. The indications, however, are that newcomers, regardless of cultural orientation, need to have access to experienced play leaders or concerned adults to assist in the process of socialization with peers through recreational activities. It is arguable that even the traditional playground requires the presence of someone who will show appreciation of the demonstrations of agility encouraged by play apparatus. Without the caring adult, 'free play' often dissolves into boring repetitions without the need to keep attempting to achieve more challenging tasks.

In multiracial societies where visible differences, as well as linguistic and other cultural modes, may be a source of conflict or misunderstanding, there is an urgent need for a helping hand to resolve conflicts as they arise. Recent reports on race relations in the city of Toronto, for example, stress the fact that the playground is often the context in which discrimination is displayed. It has been noted that because of racial problems in schools most South Asian children go home from school instead of playing in the school playground (Ubale, 1977). On the other hand, there have been complaints about students from the black community congregating on school property after school because there is nothing purposeful for them to do at home (Toronto Board of Education, 1978), the suggestion being that after-four programmes be operated by the school board and the Department of Parks and Recreation.

The play leader has an important function to perform in these situations, but will need specialized training in coping with this added dimension in meeting the play needs of immigrant children if 'full opportunity for play and recreation' is to be promoted as directed in the United Nations Declaration of the Rights of the Child.

Notes

1. United Nations General Assembly, Declaration of the Rights of the Child, 1959.
2. The Canada Immigration Act, April 1978, is designed to change this pattern of settlement by assigning prospective immigrants to non-metropolitan areas.
3. Brochure, Adventure Playgrounds Ltd, Toronto.

References

Adventure Playgrounds Ltd Brochure. PO Box 7006, Adelaide Station, Toronto M5C 2K7.
Anderson, W. W. and R. W. Grant. 1975. *The New Newcomers.* Toronto: York University.
daCosta, G. A. 1976. 'Counselling and the black child', *Black Students in Urban Canada: Special Issue of T.E.S.L. Talk.* Toronto: Ontario Ministry of Culture and Recreation, January.

Fjeldsted, Brenda. 1978. 'Standard versus adventure playgrounds', *The Journal of the Canadian Association for Young Children*, May, pp. 16–32.

McClard, Judy and Naomi Wall (eds). 1978. *Come with Us: Children Speak for Themselves.* Toronto: Canadian Women's Educational Press.

Ontario Ministry of Education. 1976. *Education Statistics – Ontario, 1976.* Toronto: Ontario Ministry of Education.

Passantino, Erika D. 1975. 'Adventure playgrounds for learning and socialization', *Phi Delta Kappan*, January, pp. 329–33.

Singer, Yvonne. 1976. *Little-Miss-Yes-Miss.* Toronto: Kids Can Press.

Toronto Board of Education. 1978. *Draft Report of the Sub-Committee on Race Relations.* Toronto: Toronto Board of Education.

Ubale, Bhausaheb. 1977. *Equal Opportunity and Public Policy: A Report on Concerns of the South Asian Canadian Community Regarding Their Place in the Canadian Mosaic.* Submitted to the Attorney General of Ontario by the South Asian Canadian Community, October, Toronto.

Wolfgang, Aaron (ed.). 1975. *Education of Immigrant Students: Issues and Answers.* Toronto: Ontario Institute for Studies in Education.

16 PLAY INTERACTION DIFFERENCES BETWEEN NORMAL CHILD/MOTHER AND RETARDED CHILD/MOTHER DYADS

Colin Pryor, Walter Filipowich and Mayah Sevink

Introduction

The play behaviour between a mother and her child is generally recognized as being critical to the development of the child's skills and capabilities. It appears that it is through the interaction inherent in play that children gain cognitive and affective competence.

Previous studies have indicated that in play the retarded child has particular difficulty in achieving an effective and reinforcing interaction pattern (Jones, 1977; Mogford, 1973; Tilton and Ottinger, 1964; and Weiner, Ottinger and Tilton, 1969). By definition, he/she is less able than his/her normal peers to affect his/her environment. The child's lack of responsiveness, damaging in itself, has further effect in that it makes difficult the parent's role as an effective playmate. In a sense, the child's lack of output creates a vacuum where normal parental comment and dialogue becomes dysfunctional.

Despite intuitive clinical judgement as to the problems faced by parents in interacting with their retarded children, little investigation has been directed toward an analysis of what a play interaction involves for children beyond infancy. The majority of studies focus on more controlled and ultimately more static variables:

> Empirical studies which have dealt with play as a social behavior have examined the role of age, sex and ethnic identity in determining the choice of play activities or partner or have treated setting as an independent variable affecting physical or psychological features of play. (Garvey, 1974, p. 163)

The characterization and analysis of interaction between infants and their mothers has been described in some detail by a number of authors (e.g., Jones, 1977; Pawlby, 1975; Richards and Bernal, 1972; Stern, 1974; and Trevarthen, 1975).

In an initial attempt to develop a methodologically sound and clinically viable analysis technique, Gaussen (1976) proposed a mixture of ethological principles and a systems approach. He submitted that interaction might be viewed in terms of: inputs, behaviours which in some manner cue action in a co-player respondent; outputs, the respondent's response; and feedback, information transmitted to the respondent concerning his performance with respect to the input. Within such an analysis, outputs can be further categorized as matching the input, partially matching the input, or mis-matching the input. Input can be transmitted by either member of the interaction dyad (or pair).

It is the purpose of this paper to investigate the nature of play interaction and, further, to quantify the varying play interaction patterns which are both common and different between mothers and their retarded children and mothers and their normal children in a play situation. In order to quantify the play interaction patterns in both groups, a transcript of distinct behavioural units was coded from videotaped play sessions. These behavioural units were further categorized into input, output and feedback responses and in the final step of the analysis coded into match, mis-match or partial-match categories to assess the relationship of inputs to outputs within the two groups. Data were also obtained on toy selection, duration of play with specific toys, and language used by mothers and children during play interaction.

Method

Subjects

Five mothers with normal children volunteered in response to an advertisement in the local newspaper to take part in the study. The normal children ranged in age from 3 to 4 years. The mothers' ages ranged from 20 to 31 years. Four of the normal children had one younger sibling (mean age = 1.25 years).

The mothers of the retarded children were contacted through a local nursery school for the mentally retarded. As far as possible, families were selected which matched the families with normal children on variables of age of mother, age of child, age or presence of a sibling, and socio-economic class. The retarded children had been referred to the nursery by a variety of professionals in the area.

No normative data were available on the retarded children, but all exhibited developmental delays of such severity as to have them placed at a nursery school for the retarded. Four of the retarded children demonstrated delays in all developmental areas. One child exhibited behaviours during the play sessions which indicated that he may have been functioning at the appropriate level in some areas, but was evidently still exhibiting deficits to the degree that the professionals involved maintained his placement at the nursery. The children selected had no critical physical deficits that could interfere with toy play in a significant manner.

The retarded children ranged in age from 3 to 7 years with mothers ranging in age from 21 to 39 years. Three of the retarded sample had one younger sibling (mean age = 1.7 years), and one child (aged 4 years) had an older sibling aged 7 years.

No effort was made to specify diagnosis for the mentally retarded as the emphasis was not on the nature of the child's retardation, but on the effect of his intellectual capabilities within the interaction that occurred between himself and his mother.

It should be stressed that investigations pursued in this study were not primarily intended to be normative; rather, the work represents an extensive and detailed assessment of that population of interactive behaviours which occurred within mother/child pairs. Correlations between individual pairs may thus be viewed as being replicated measures in a series of individual data studies (Kogan and Tyler, 1973). While every attempt was made to produce some degree of comparability between pairs (the handicapped mother/child population and normal mother/child population), it was decided that the lack of precise matching and the limited number of families observed did not detract significantly from the findings presented.

Apparatus

The videotape sessions were conducted in a room 4.5 x 5m (13.5 x 15 feet). On one wall of the room was a two-way mirror which was covered during videotaping. On the same wall as the mirror and mounted five feet above the floor in the corner of the room was a Shibedan studio camera. The camera was operated manually from an observation room, and the operator was not visible to the subjects in the playroom. The camera was linked to a Sony 3600 ½ inch video recorder.

Eight toys were available for the mother and child to use in their play. The toys were arranged in a semi-circle facing the camera. Toy position was randomized across the mother and child's three visits. Toys remained constant. The toy selection covered as wide a range of play opportunities as possible. The toys used were a tricycle, a Fisher-Price garage, a shape poster, a Lego car construction set (large, easily fitted pieces), a tea set, a doll, a hammer peg board and a nut-and-bolt threading toy.

Procedure

All mothers were initially visited in the home and a 'screening' interview given (Pryor, 1978). It was explained to the mothers that the investigators were interested both in how mothers and children played and the differences between retarded and normal children's play. No reference was made to the research interest in the interaction patterns between themselves and their child. All 10 mothers brought their children to the play centre on three separate occasions over a period of three weeks.

Mother and child were left to play in the observation room for 20 minutes after the experimenter delivered the following verbal instruction:

> We are looking at some of the ways in which mothers play with their children. We would like you to play with . . . . as you would at home.

The first play session was an orientation session to allow the mother/child pairs to adapt to a new environment. The video equipment was run and the camera tracked the interaction, but this initial videotape was not included in the analysis.

Analysis of Videotape

Random four-minute blocks were selected from the videotapes recorded across play sessions two and three. Responses occurring within the four minutes of interaction recorded on each tape were transcribed onto standardized recording sheets. (See Figure 16.1.) The recording sheet served two purposes. It allowed the rater to code what a behaviour by an adult or child was directed toward, e.g., in the adult/object category,

Figure 16.1: Coding Sheet

Child/ Adult	Adult/ Child	Adult/ Object	Child/ Object	Adult Non- specific	Child Non- specific
'Mommy give'					
	'You want another biscuit'				
			Holds out plate		
		Puts biscuit on plate			
			Takes biscuit off plate		

Figure 16.2: Criteria for Coding

| INPUT | | OUTPUT |

A behaviour which transmits information by means of either the verbal mode, the non-verbal mode, or through both modes simultaneously and *operationalizes* the response required of the receiver

A behaviour that occurs in the verbal mode, the non-verbal mode, or through both modes simultaneously and follows the reception of input information

FEEDBACK

A response which is cued by observation of output and transmits information to the output performer directly related to the output observed but *not* carrying new input information

the behaviour was directed toward an object. It also coded the sequence in which behaviours occurred by ordering behaviours on a vertical scale.[1]

For each transcript, the sequence of interaction behaviours was coded into input, output and feedback categories. The criteria for coding into each category were defined as shown in Figure 16.2.

Within the coding of each transcript, raters coded behaviour sequences into I, O or F categories. If, in the rater's judgement, a behaviour could not be coded exclusively into one category, a dual rating was assigned. Consequently, a behaviour could be coded as both an output for one sequence and an input for the next.[2]

The sample transcript (Figure 16.3) illustrates the recording technique. Each entry represents one observed behavioural event with verbal behaviour identified by italics. Figure 16.3 represents 10 seconds of interaction. In this sample, the inputs, outputs and feedback coded were as shown in Figure 16.4.

Raters scored in pairs, each rater within a pair scoring an identical transcript. Three of the six raters used were independent from the research team and were paired with team members. The independent raters were rotated between team members following the coding of two transcripts. The first transcript was considered a training transcript and not used for analysis. The second transcript covered a four-minute time block and was used for analysis.

Figure 16.3: Sample 10-Second Scored Interaction

Child/Adult	Adult/Child	Adult/Object	Child/Object	Adult Non-specific	Child Non-specific
	'There, putting things together toys' Input	Looks at box containing Lego toys Input			
			Child looks at Lego box, picks box up and holds on lap, looks in box Output (Match)		
	'Let me show you' Input	Opens box and points inside Input			
	'Look at that' Input		Looks away from box toward hammer set Output (Mis-match)		
	'See . . . drop the box' Input	Tips box contents onto floor Input			
			Picks up some pieces, drops one Output (Match)		
	'Oh, you dropped one' Feedback				
	'Now this man can sit on top of the box and stay there' Input	Picks up man and box, places in front of child Input	Holding pieces and looks at box with man on it Output (Match)		
	'Do you want to make a man sit?' Input				
'No' Output (Match)					Crawls to far side of room Input
			Picks up hammer set Input		
'Mommy bang' Input	'Mommy bang' Output (Match)				
		Picks up hammer, bangs peg Output (Match)			
		Rubs hammer on floor then bangs floor Output (Partial Match)			

Figure 16.4: Sample Coding

	Input	Output	Feedback
Mother	9	1	1
Child	3	5	0

Figure 16.5: Definitions of Match, Mis-match, and Partial Match

Match	The receiver perceives information (input) and responds appropriately: output = input
Mis-match	The receiver of input does not respond appropriately: output ≠ input
Partial match	The receiver's output is partially appropriate (output does not completely fulfil input requirements).

In assessing initial rater agreement within transcripts coded, raters independently scored identical transcripts. In computing rater agreement, agreement was credited where input/output/feedback coding coincided for identical behavioural units. Omission of categorization or conflicting categorization was scored as disagreement.[3] Following reliability assessment, rater pairs forced disagreements into one of the three categories to determine one final analysis of each transcript. These data were used in analysis.

In the next step of the analysis, outputs were further coded into match, mis-match and partial match categories as defined in Figure 16.5.

The same procedure was followed by the six raters to code outputs into match, mis-match and partial match categories and to assess rater agreement.[4]

In addition to the analysis described above, the language used by mother and child within the scored transcripts was analyzed using an adaptation from Murphy and Messer's (1977) scale for language analysis. Categories scored in the analysis were: toy labelling, questions, commands, descriptive comments, toy description, and interactive and relational comments.[5]

Topographical information quantifying the number, specific toy used, and duration of play with each toy was scored directly from both 20-minute videotapes for each group by an independent rater.

Results[6]

Comparison between samples across all interaction categories yielded the following results: normal children provided significantly more inputs[7] and significantly more outputs[8] to their mothers than did handicapped children, with no significant difference noted in feedback responses. Retarded children differed significantly in that their rate of output to objects[9] exceeded that for normal children. The ratings were comparable with respect to inputs and feedback to objects.

Mothers of retarded children provided significantly more input[10] and feedback[11] to their children than did mothers of normal children, though ratings of outputs delivered to the child did not differ between groups. In addition, mothers of retarded children directed more inputs to objects[12] than did those in the normal sample with similar ratings obtained for output and feedback to objects.

At the level of match, partial match and mis-match, normal children more often matched mothers than did handicapped children,[13] though there were no significant differences between groups in rates of partial match or mis-match. Retarded children more often partially matched[15] at an object level with both groups matching at similar rates.

While rates of match by the mother to the child did not differ between groups, mothers of retarded children were more often observed either partially to match[16] or to mis-match[17] their child's input. A similar trend was noted at the object level in that the rate of mis-match by the mother to the object was higher[18] for mothers with retarded children than for those with normal children.

Transcripts were further analyzed to yield information regarding the language used by mothers and children during play interaction. While the verbal behaviour of children in both groups did not differ significantly on the dimensions of labelling and toy description, normal children asked significantly more questions,[19] gave significantly more commands,[20] and made significantly more descriptive[21] and interactive[22] comments than did retarded children.

Across all categories, mothers differed only in that those with handicapped children gave marginally more commands.[23]

Both 20-minute videotapes were analyzed for all subjects to yield the following topographical data. There were no differences between groups in either the over-all number of toys played with or in changes in toy use throughout the session. Normal children, however, significantly more often introduced a toy into the play situation[24] than did handicapped children. Conversely, mothers of handicapped children more often introduced toys than did mothers of normal children.[25] Rates of finishing with toys were comparable with respect to mothers in both samples; they differed significantly for children, however, in that handicapped children more often finished with a toy than did normal children.[26]

Summary

This study used a new method of analyzing parent/child interaction. The advantage of the method was that it enabled the quantification of differences in interaction style between mothers with handicapped and normal children. In addition to the interaction analysis, language style, toy choice and the frequency and duration of toy use were examined. It is recognized that the size of population sampled was small and, therefore, that normative statements have limited validity. There would appear, however, to be some noteworthy differences between mother/child dyads which warrant further investigation.

The mothers of the handicapped children appeared more likely to input their child both directly and through the use of objects. They issued more commands and gave more feedback than the mothers with normal children. Despite their high profile within the play situation, the mothers of the handicapped were significantly more unsuccessful than the mothers of normal children in responding appropriately to their children's productions. Some explanation for this pattern may be found in the handicapped children's behaviour, which was less rich in output than their normal counterparts. They presented within the interactions analyzed as 'object-centred' players who, even when dealing with objects, did significantly less well than their normal peers, achieving significantly more mis-matches and partial matches to their mothers' inputs. In contrast to being object-centred, normal children were more people-centred. They described their play situations to their parents, stated what they wanted, questioned when they required information, and made more interactive statements. They insured that play was a two-way phenomenon. If play is conceptualized as a process of turn taking in which both parties modify the environment (Mogford, 1973; Newson, 1974; Pawlby, 1975), then the parents of the handicapped face special difficulties, for they find themselves negotiating with a partner who is less able to operate effectively within this paradigm and whose contribution to the interaction is likely to be non-verbal and unsuccessful. It would appear from this study that parents respond to their children's inabilities by assuming a directive, task-centred approach to play. They further comment on their child's play performance, describing his/her actions for him/her in the absence of the child's own comment. It is not surprising that, within the role of being both players at once, the parent sometimes overlooked the child's production.

The problem faced by handicapped child/mother dyads may further be conceptualized as one of operationalization. The handicapped children in this sample appeared ill equipped, both to understand the parents' operational direction (input) and to generate their own. By default, the children entered a vicious spiral of movement through play materials and movement away from interaction with their mothers. Parents, in turn, sensing their inability to guide or understand their youngster, resorted to that form of interaction which requires no verbal response from the child, but rather an action response in terms of the object — the verbal command. Of course, the other verbal characteristic adopted by the parents of the handicapped — feedback — demands no response from the child, and it may be guessed that they knew from experience that replies to questions would not be forthcoming.

In summary, it would appear that the mothers of the handicapped assumed a more dominant role in play with their children. They provided more input, introduced more toys, used more verbal direction and offered more verbal comment. The mothers' behaviour stood in contrast to the performance of the children they played with, who appeared less verbal than their normal counterparts and less able to understand the demands made upon them. From their level of performance, it may be assumed that their abilities were ill fitted to the interaction in which they found themselves. Thus, while the parental interaction patterns may have been born of the desire to help their children, the result was antithetical to the authors' concept of play, that is, the encouragement of individuals to develop their own exploration of the world and to meet new experiences within their own capabilities and understanding. Play cannot occur by command in task-centred training sessions. While structure may be important in the facilitation of play exploration it is not synonymous with direction and control. It is the role of psychologists involved in the business of play to help parents reconcile their handicapped child's need for structure and the equally important need for autonomy. It would seem from the experience in the play centre described above that alternative models for interaction and play structuring are necessary if the task-centred, highly verbal styles of play interaction which parents often assume or are told is the right way are to be avoided.

A beginning to a different way of approaching children's play is suggested in the data presented here and by others. Retarded children by definition do not have the same qualities and abilities as their normal peers. As such, their developmental needs may be better served by the parent or professional seeking parallel play activities, activities which allow and encourage the child to contribute. Indeed, if the handicapped child is to develop the richness and quality of responses which present research ascribes to the normal child, then it is essential that he/she assume a greater measure of autonomy.

Notes

1. Inter-rater reliability was computed on the initial coding of behaviours occurring within each category. Over-all reliabilities across raters within each category were: child/adult, 80.5 per cent; adult/child, 90.5 per cent; adult/object, 84 per cent; and child/object, 95.5 per cent. Over-all reliability across all categories was 87.6 per cent.
2. Dual coding was a rare occurrence and accounted for less than 1 per cent of total behaviours coded.
3. Observer agreement for the categories defined was: input, 89.9 per cent; output, 86.9 per cent; and feedback, 78.6 per cent. Over-all rater agreement across the three categories was 85.2 per cent.
4. Observer agreement at this level was: match, 92.8 per cent; mis-match, 84.2 per cent; and partial match, 84.4 per cent. Reliability across all three categories was 87.1 per cent.
5. Reliability across rater pairs was 90.9 per cent.
6. Data were subjected to analysis using the Mann–Whitney U Test due to the small number of subjects in each group. Since this statistic deals only with the relative magnitude of the measures in the two groups and requires no assumptions either about their stability in repeated sampling or about the normalcy of their distribution, it was appropriate for analysis of the data reported here.
7. $(U = 22.5, p < 0.05)$.
8. $(U = 25, p < 0.01)$.
9. $(U = 6, p < 0.10)$.
10. $(U = 6, p < 0.10)$.
11. $(U = 4.5, p < 0.05)$.
12. $(U = 5, p < 0.10)$.
13. $(U = 25, p < 0.01)$.
14. $(U = 24, p < 0.01)$.
15. $(U = 23.5, p < 0.05)$.
16. $(U = 22.5, p < 1.05)$.
17. $(U = 22.5, p < 0.05)$.
18. $(U = 19, p < 0.10)$.
19. $(U = 22.5, p < 0.05)$.
20. $(U = 19, p < 0.10)$.
21. $(U = 25, p < 0.01)$.
22. $(U = 22, p < 0.05)$.
23. $(U = 5.5, p < 0.10)$.
24. $(U = 14, p < 0.001)$.
25. $(U = 4.5, p < 0.05)$.
26. $(U = 11, p < 0.001)$.

References

Blurton Jones, N. 1972. *Ethological studies of child behaviour*. Cambridge: University Press.

Garvey, C. 1974. 'Some properties of social play', *Merrill-Palmer Quarterly*, 20, pp. 163–80.

Gaussen, T. H. 1976. 'The interactional approach and the educational psychologist: theory and practice with special reference to preschool handicapped children and their parents'. Unpublished master's thesis, University of Exeter.

Jones, O. H. 1977. 'Mother-child communication with pre-linguistic Down's Syndrome and normal infants', in H. R. Schaffer (ed.), *Studies in Mother-Infant Interaction*. London: Academic Press.

Kogan K. L. and N. Tyler. 1973. 'Mother-child interaction in young physically handicapped children', *American Journal of Mental Deficiency*, 77, 5, pp. 492–7.

Mogford, K. 1973. *Play and Handicap*. Nottingham, England: Development Research Unit, Nottingham University.

Murphy, C. M. and P. J. Messer. 1977. 'Mothers, infants and pointing', in H. R. Schaffer (ed.), *Studies in Mother-Infant Interaction*. London: Academic Press.

Newson, J. 1974. 'Towards a theory of infant understanding', *Bulletin of the British Psychological Society*, 27, pp. 251–7.

——. and S. J. Pawlby. 1975. 'On imitation'. Paper presented at an inter-university colloquium at Nottingham University, England.

Pawlby, S. J. 1975. 'Imitative interaction', in H. R. Schaffer (ed.), *Studies in Mother-Infant Interaction*. London: Academic Press.

Pryor, C. 1978. 'A parent referenced child assessment questionnaire'. Unpublished paper, Sudbury and District Association for the Mentally Retarded, Sudbury, Canada.

Richards, M. P. and J. F. Bernal. 1972. 'An observational study of mother-infant interaction', in N. Blurton Jones (ed.), *Ethological studies of child behaviour*. Cambridge: University Press.

Stern, D. M. 1974. 'Mother and infant at play: the dyadic interaction', in M. Lewis and L. A. Rosenblum (eds), *The Effect of the Infant on Its Caregiver*. New York: Wiley.

Tilton, J. R. and D. R. Ottinger. 1964. 'Comparison of the toy play behavior of autistic, retarded, and normal children', *Psychological Reports*, 15, pp. 967–75.

Trevarthen, C. 1975. 'Early attempts at speech', in R. Lewin (ed.), *Child alive*. London: Temple Smith.

Weiner, B. J., D. R. Ottinger and J. R. Tilton. 1969. 'Comparison of the toy-play behavior of autistic, retarded and normal children: a re-analysis', *Psychological Reports*, 25, pp. 223–7.

17 DESIGN GUIDELINES FOR HANDICAPPED CHILDREN'S PLAY ENVIRONMENTS

Leland G. Shaw

Preface

At the 7th World Congress of the International Playground Association a session entitled 'Developmental Approaches to the Design of Play Environments for Handicapped Children' was presented by Professor Gary T. Moore, School of Architecture and Urban Planning, University of Wisconsin-Milwaukee and this author. Each participant delineated a set of design guidelines they believe can be used to improve the quality of play environments for handicapped children. Moore has labelled his team's guidelines 'design principles'. The author has chosen the term 'primary design criteria'. Many of these guidelines are similar in content and because they evolved out of different processes their applicability to a wide range of situations is suggested.

This paper is not a summary of that workshop, but rather one that explains the author's primary design criteria. These criteria are part of a fourteen-step design process. Specifically the discussion will centre on the two steps in this design process in which the design criteria have their initial and most significant impact on the formation of a play environment.

The design principles discussed by Moore are explained in detail in Moore *et al*. (1979). This paper includes only a brief summary of their project. Basic similarities and differences between their behaviourally based design principles and the author's design criteria have been noted.

Introduction

Since 1968 the author has been involved with researching, designing and building various types of play environments for both handicapped and 'normal' children. The information in this paper is a result of these experiences. The facilities that were designed are all located in the State of Florida and are all attached to existing institutions such as schools, hospitals and training centres.[1] These projects address different groups of handicapped children including physically handicapped, mentally retarded (profound and trainable) and psychotic. Many populations included children with multiple handicaps. Because of their geographic locations (Florida), all sites enjoy the potential of open-air play 12 months a year. The climate much of the year can be categorized from warm humid to hot wet.

Because the primary design criteria are an integral part of a design process the author uses when executing a project, one must understand how they relate to the whole. This design process assumes that the designer's services have already been solicited by the client. The fourteen steps are:

1. Awareness: the objective analysis by the design team of the tangible and intangible aspects of the future users of the proposed facility and the existing physical environment in which the facility will be located.

2. The feedback to these future users of the awareness results and idea brainstorming with those users.

3. The formulation of the design concept.

4. The explanation of the concept to the future user group and a reassessment of concept.

5. The design development: evolution of the concept into a recognizable physical solution.

6. The explanation of the physical solution to the future user group and a reassessment of it.

7. The design refinement: the fine-tuning of the physical solution.

8. The explanation of the refined physical solution and the reassessment of it by the design team with the future user group.

9. The development of construction documents by the design team (working drawings and specifications).

10. The pre-construction process, including the bidding procedure, and the education of the builder.

11. The construction of the facility.

12. The post-construction analysis of the built facility.

13. The execution of the necessary modifications to the facility based upon the post-construction analysis.

14. The incorporation of the results of the post-construction analyses into the design process of the design team.

The primary design criteria are first used for reference in Step 3, but they are more important in Step 5. This paper will deal in depth with these two steps: 'concept formulation' and 'design development'. They are the key steps in translating the designer's ideas into physical form and, therefore, have a most significant effect on the final organization of the play environment.

The list of steps in the design process isolates each step used by the author, but it is the importance of the whole process that should be underscored. Perhaps one should think of the entire process as constituting the criteria for design. The process is a methodology, one that aids the designer in creating built environments that express the needs of the users and the ideas of the designer. Each step is one rung on a ladder that ends with built form. Consequently each step builds upon the knowledge gained, synthesized and communicated in the previous steps. Conversely, this outline represents a symbolic attempt to organize the whole and does not do justice to the parts. Each step is a complex procedure in itself. For example Step 1, awareness, is involved with understanding the primary users: the children. It also deals with the secondary users: the staff. Additionally it includes the awareness analysis of administration (local and remote), the institutional structure, the organizational procedure, the educational goals, the off-site consultants, the maintenance support staff, and often the identification of a potential future builder. Step 1 also includes the macro and micro site analyses.

While space here does not allow a detailed explanation of how this is accomplished, or of the other steps in the process (except Steps 3 and 5), it cannot be over-emphasized that the success of the project rests on the execution of the whole process and not just selected parts. For example, no matter how carefully a design team has understood and developed a workable set of general design goals based upon an understanding of the developmental needs of the children, there is a good chance that the project will fail if the team does not listen to (understand) the staff and the administrators. Of course, the reverse is also true. Or, a design team may complete a careful analysis of the existing site conditions, but not have a general understanding of the structure of the population, and because of this omission the physical solution may end up unusable. Finally, even though the design team succeeds in meshing the needs and developmental goals of all the specific groups it is working with, without a thoughtful articulation of those ideas into appropriate physical forms that are buildable by available construction teams within the specified budget, the project may end up as a beautiful model rather than an active, successful play environment.

It is true that, while equal importance should be given to each step in the design process when it applies to a specific problem, the ultimate effect of each on the built environment will usually vary. This is true because each problem contains unique circumstances that force the design team to value the results of the steps of the design process in relation to those circumstances. On one project, the site analysis may be a most critical step. On another, it may be of minor importance and understanding the administration's goals may be the key issue. In still another project, the initial feedback to the staff of the translation of the design principles into physical form might be the only way to ensure the future success of the facility. What the designer must realize is that no project tells the designer, in advance, what steps are critical; therefore, the design team cannot afford to neglect any one step in the design process.

The fact that all of the projects which have contributed to this work have been built at institutions is reflected in the design process. Children in institutional settings are 'captive', whether they only attend a centre two or three mornings a week, or whether they live in a residential treatment centre 24 hours a day. Institutions tend to structure the child's day into activity categories related to place and time, thus regimenting the play time. Conversely, the non-institutional play situation is usually visited only when the child decides to use it. Even in institutional environments where the children have the freedom to control some of their activities, it is probable that they will be routinely exposed to the play environment. Thus, institutional play environments must be complex enough or provide enough variety to generate and sustain interest, day after day. Keep in mind that the processes discussed herein were developed for this kind of situation, and not as universal guidelines for all play situations.

While it would seem to be necessary to write a profile of the children who have been a part of the development of this design process and design criteria, it is, in fact, impossible. Most institutions, while addressing certain categories of handicaps (e.g., physical, retardation), usually contained children with multiple problems. Therefore, the play environments could not address themselves to the specifics of certain handicaps, but instead had to address themselves to aspects of free play, social interaction and the condition of childhood in general, to be successful.

Age of the primary users, either chronological or developmental, like handicap, has proved difficult to generalize about. The projects which have led to these guidelines have been for children who usually were functioning developmentally between the ages of 2 and 10. While this clearly includes a wide range of physical and social abilities, it is assumed that it does identify most of the potential users who could benefit developmentally from interactions with creative therapy environments that encourage free play. It is true that groups of younger and older children may successfully use a developmental playground, but their sustained high use over time is unpredictable. Younger children appear to need the constant interaction of adults while older children, once they begin to involve themselves regularly in organized 'sports-type' games, need a different kind of physical environment, such as a playing field, to reinforce their major activities.

Step 2 of the Design Process: Formulation of Design Concept

For the physical designer, the act of creating a design concept is most difficult to explain. Discussions of concept often end up more mystical than rational. Therefore, this discussion will concentrate on the process prior to and after the act.

In any specific situation, people interact with the physical environment and create many behaviour settings. Every institution for handicapped children can be defined by its behaviour settings. Their relationships create a unique set of constraints the designer likes to label as 'the problem'. In Steps 1 and 2 the physical designer tries to grasp a clear understanding of that problem, but the designer does have certain limitations, particularly time and energy constraints. The designer is also never able to see the problem from all points of view. He is an outsider who views the problem from a remote and detached position.

The designer brings to each new problem a 'design past'. The 'design past' is composed of several parts: one that includes a professional education, formal and informal, that was aimed at teaching the translation of a problem into physical form; one that contains an understanding of how building materials should be properly used so that they will go together to be both structurally sound and aesthetically pleasing; one that contains sets of experiences that dealt with similar problems and solutions to such problems; and one that also includes a myriad of other information related to design and construction.

This past is an important attribute. In some ways it distinguishes the designer from others. It cannot be ignored, nor should the designer try to do so, because it is what makes a designer. If, however, the designer allows this professional past to affect his objective understanding of each new problem in Steps 1 and 2 of the design process, it will be detrimental. The designer must strive to look at each situation as if turned inside out and be able to see things in a new light. Only by separating the new problem from past experiences will it ever be really 'seen' and only when the eyes and mind are firmly fixed on the current problem can the designer let the past surface. To 'see' the problem and the hierarchy of critical issues of the subject at hand, the designer must become familiar with the children at the institution and their handicaps, the staff (teachers and therapists) and their ideas, the administration and its goals, the site and its constraints. Then, and only then, should the professional past surface.

Problem and past, therefore, are the ingredients in concept making. The screening of the problem through the past within the designer produces a concept. As it has been stated earlier, the designer cannot usually explain the mystical birth of the concept nor often recognize it at the time it occurs because initially the concept has not developed its unique personality. The designer works with it, and its individual character becomes apparent. The nature of concept for this designer is one which must be stated as a simple ordered graphic statement. The concept must be the distilled essence of the physical solution: 'the nature of the problem reflects what it wants to be', as architect Louis Kahn so beautifully stated.

Finally, for a concept to be valid and worth pursuing, the designer must above all believe in it. This does not mean that each concept is necessarily correct for a given problem, or that the designer as well as the future users should not be quite critical of it in review. It means that as the concept develops its distinctive form, the designer must absolutely, at that time, believe in it. Otherwise how can one go on, or suggest it as a solution to the future users?

It has been stated that the designer's professional past plays a significant role in concept formulation and the following design stages. But what is used to organize this fantastically complex lattice-work of information and ideas that have been retained? Within the lattice certain similar experiences join hands and reinforce each other by their successful applicability to many different situations. Eventually the parts of each cluster arise fused and become a generalizable idea. Idea clusters take on special significance for the designer and become unified into a cohesive set of ideas, or primary design criteria. The remainder of the lattice — scattered bits of information, fragmented knowledge, isolated thoughts — are also important to the designer because they help solve specific pragmatic problems. This second part of the past, stored like a bride's dowry trunk, might best be labelled the designer's 'legacy'.

The primary design criteria are important in concept formation to test the validity of a concept. They measure the applicability of the concept, because the designer must be able to incorporate these principles in the design development. Some designers believe that a good concept must include, as recognizable parts, the primary design criteria. For the author, however, the nature of the concept statement is at a simplified, generalized level and so related to the aspects of the specific problem at hand that it cannot do more than hint at the design criteria. In other words, the concept is born without the primary design criteria programmed as part of its DNA, because the problem conditions have no innate knowledge of them. This is why the designer must investigate each concept to determine if it has the potential and flexibility to embrace applicable design criteria. If investigation proves that it does not allow for this, the designer must discard the concept. This usually is a difficult task and the longer the designer holds onto an unworkable concept, the harder it is to get rid of it. Therefore, the designer must not practise self-deception, but must be painfully honest with himself/herself. One cannot fix up an unworkable concept just as one cannot fix up a cake baked with the wrong ingredients. Finally, concepts, in themselves, are never bad, ugly or immoral. When a concept is inappropriate, it is merely not the right one for the specific problem. The designer has synthesized it out of his past without the proper understanding of the problem at hand. It is like coming back from the market with oranges when the need is for apples because the problem was to bake an apple pie.

The next part of the design process, design development, contains the author's primary design criteria which have evolved from a series of design commissions dealing with both normal and handicapped children and are, in the author's opinion, applicable to all groups of children. These criteria are a result of many design decisions based upon a variety of diverse influences.

Step 5 of the Design Process: Design Development

Following the formulation of a concept, the designer must present that concept to the different user groups within the institution (Step 4). This feedback session, usually using abstract diagrams and models to portray the concept, 'tests out' the concept. It allows the users to determine whether the designer has understood the needs of the institution. Following the successful completion of this step the designer is ready to begin to evolve the diagrammatic concept into tangible physical forms. In design development, the primary design criteria are the important guidelines that facilitate this activity. The following nine primary design criteria are those used by the author:

1. sense of place;
2. unified environment;
3. variety of spaces;
4. key places;
5. multiple paths;
6. three-dimensional juxtaposition of parts;
7. non-objective spaces;
8. variety of materials;
9. loose parts.

Before discussing these design criteria it is approproate at this point
to introduce the comparable 'design principles' that were alluded to
in this paper's preface.

Design Principles

In 1976, Gary T. Moore and Uriel Cohen initiated a project in their
Architectural Programming and Design Studio (Team 699) in the School
of Architecture and Urban Planning at the University of Wisconsin-
Milwaukee to programme and design a play environment for the
St Francis Children's Activity and Achievement Center in Milwaukee.
St Francis Children's Center is an early education centre for children
with exceptional education needs and learning patterns that cannot be
accommodated in local schools. This project grew far beyond the
typical studio effort and resulted in a document that can serve as a
model for similar types of studies.

Team 699, with aid from the St Francis staff, delineated 14 specific
developmental goals that were directly applicable to the resident
population. These fell in the general categories of motor, cognitive and
social-emotional development.

The team soon realized that such categories do not define the
information in terms that can be applied to physical design solutions.
Early in their design process a number of design principles began to
emerge. To accept an idea as a design principle the team evaluated it to
see if 'the information would contribute to the provision of better
environmental settings for the fulfilment of developmental goals'
(Moore *et al.*, 1979, n.p.).

Thirteen design principles eventually were established. As the report
states, these should not be thought of as a concrete list of
commandments, but as a set of parameters that can be freely
supplemented as additional knowledge is discovered or quantified. Also,
it is realized that certain principles may prove redundant and should
be deleted.

All in all, it does represent a significant attempt to supply future designers with a set of design guidelines by which to measure their design solutions, and as such represents a significant step in planning play environments for special children. This brief summary does not do justice to Team 699's fine publication, nor should what follows be thought of as comprehensive explanations of each design principle, but rather as brief personal interpretations of them by the author. Because this paper was not done in collaboration with either Moore or Cohen some discrepancy may exist between their original meaning and these interpretations. While this was not intended, the reader is encouraged to consult the original text for fully developed explanations of the following design criteria:

1. *Continuity and Branching.* An environment should encourage the play behaviour to flow by providing a choice of options at decision or crossroad places.

2. *Imageability and Orientation.* An internalized 'reading' and understanding based upon the cues provided in a physical design allows the user to understand his location in space.

3. *Orderliness and Consistency.* An orderly visual organization of a physical environment reduces irrelevant stimuli and increases the potential for understanding.

4. *Paced Alternatives.* A physical environment should contain a wide variety of challenges to its users, thus providing the opportunity for each child to accomplish some tasks, but be stimulated by more difficult situations to strive for a higher level of development.

5. *Ambiguous to Defined Spaces.* A physical environment should provide a range of places from highly defined typological ones (e.g., playhouse) to non-objective, changeable (manipulatable) ones which encourage the users to apply their own creative imaginations.

6. *Variety of Spatial Experiences.* A physical environment should provide the user with a range of spatial experiences, from small, very enclosed spaces to large open ones.

7. *Range of Social Scale.* A physical environment should be designed in such a manner that it allows a variety of interpersonal experiences; from single to large group.

8. *Retreat and Breakaway Points.* A large and active social space should be designed to include various paths which provide an easy way out of (into) an ongoing activity. Retreat places, out of the active space but close enough to observe it, should also be provided.

9. *Repetition and Multiple Coding.* A designer should use the

redundant cueing of many sensory clues to define elements in the environment. Objects can be coded by colour, shape, texture, even smell and sound to clarify use.

10. *Clear Accomplishment Points.* A physical environment should be designed in such a way as to allow a child, regardless of disability, to have a feeling of environmental mastery over some portion of that environment.

11. *Loose Parts.* A play area should comfortably accept and contain a wide variety of 'loose parts', i.e., things that can be manipulated by the user.

12. *Emotional Release Areas.* Within a play area setting areas should be provided that allow children to express their emotional anxieties.

13. *Plants and Critters.* A comprehensive plan for a play-yard should provide opportunities for the users to interact with as wide a range of living things as possible.

It should be reiterated that this project and the resultant design principles were generated while the team was initially involved with one specific place and population, St Francis Children's Activity and Achievement Center. Nevertheless, one of the stated goals of the project was 'to generate a developmentally oriented and behaviourally based architectural program applicable to a wide range of exceptional education contexts and settings'. This they have to a large degree accomplished. They have not inferred that all these principles would be directly or equally applicable to every design situation. A comprehensive understanding of each unique problem, plus a delineation of the goals of each project, developed with the future users in the initial phases of the design process as recommended in this paper, should reveal information that will determine a hierarchy of applicability of these design principles.

Figure 17.1 relates the author's primary design criteria to the design principles. This is not to suggest that they are identical or interchangeable, but that aspects of both are theoretically related.

The following discussion of the design criteria will elaborate upon some of these aspects of comparisons.

Design Criteria

1. Sense of Place

The least tangible of the primary criteria, sense of place, refers to the over-all play environment image and, therefore, is the most difficult one

Figure 17.1: A Comparison of Shaw's Primary Design Criteria and Moore *et al.*'s Design Principles

No.	Primary Design Criteria (Shaw)	Design Principles (Moore, Cohen)	No.
1	Sense of Place	Imageability and Orientation	2
		Orderliness and Consistency	3
		Continuity and Branching	
2	Unified Environment	Continuity and Branching	1
3	Variety of Spaces	Ambiguous to Defined Spaces	5
		Variety of Spatial Experiences	6
4	Key Places	Clear Accomplishment Points	10
5	Multiple Paths	Paced Alternatives	4
6	Three-Dimensional Juxtaposition of Parts	Range of Social Scale	7
		Retreat and Breakaway Points	8
		Emotional Release Areas	12
7	Non-Objective Objects and Spaces	Ambiguous to Defined Spaces	5
8	Variety of Material Surfaces	Repetition and Multiple Coding	9
9	Loose Parts	Loose Parts	11
		Plants and Critters	13

to explain. It is the goal of the designer to create a solution that orders the specific constraints of the problem in such a manner that a prevailing atmosphere is transmitted to its users. This relates quite closely to the formulation of the concept and could have been as properly discussed in that section of this paper.

While each part of the area in a play environment forms a place for play to occur on, in, around and through, it is the over-all organization of these parts that creates the stage for the process of play through time, and that gives a sense of place to the whole. It infers that the individual parts are not only created to express their specific purpose, but must reflect an over-all order. In other words, it relates to a skeleton which is the framework that accepts the scattered bits of ideas and information and organizes them into a cohesive environmental statement.

While this criterion must be thought of in concept formation, it continues to be critical in design development. The designer must evaluate design decisions relating to the other primary criteria to ensure that the sense of oneness, order, place and image are not lost.

This criterion relates to the design principles of 'imageability and orientation' and 'orderliness and consistency'. The design principle of 'continuity and branching' is also concerned with 'sense of place' because it refers to over-all play-yard organization, but 'continuity and branching' more strongly relates to the next primary design criterion, 'unified environment'.

2. Unified Environment

Often play environments are composed of physically and spatially isolated pieces of play apparatus. Because they are isolated from one another, it is very difficult for children's activities to flow from one to another. Consequently, activity centres on the most complex pieces, while the less stimulating pieces of equipment usually receive little use. No balanced environment can be made up of elements that are all 'key' or high-use places. Every environment should have some elements that are stars and others that are supporting characters. The supporting characters can better perform their function if they are linked to the stars. The isolation of supporting pieces of equipment calls attention to their weaknesses, because isolated they are asked to perform in a star's role to sustain play. A play environment of all stars is like a meal made up only of rich, complex dishes. Great dishes need simple breads and salads to complement them in a well-designed meal.

When the users of a play environment are handicapped, the isolation of pieces of equipment increases the fragmented quality of the place. In repeated formal observations with normal preschool children, trainable mentally retarded children and physically handicapped children, research has shown that unifying the play-yard unified the play experience and increased significantly the time spent engaged with the physical structure of the space.[2]

Unifying the parts of the play-yard allows activity generated by the highly complex stimulating 'star' areas to flow naturally to supporting structures; thus, natural changes in use and variations of play occur. This criterion reinforces the notion that the whole, when it can be perceived (and hence used) as a whole, is much more stimulating than the isolated parts, which are perceived and used only as parts. Usually, the author's solutions physically connect as many of the elements of the environment as possible using pathways to lead to and from places, in such a fashion that they surround one or more central spaces. Thus, the built elements form the space-defining structure with understandable insides and outsides. This creates literal places and reinforces sense of place. Incidentally, research dealing with cognitive mapping by children using models of unified and fragmented play environments appears to indicate that the ability to develop and sustain workable cognitive maps may be related to the configuration of the play yard (Shaw, 1978).

When elements cannot physically connect, careful spatial relationships between them must be resolved. Linking physical structures links potential activities. Sliding naturally flows into jumping, climbing, hiding, swinging, etc. Unifying the environments gives the designer the key to manipulating the next specific design criterion.

3. Variety of Spaces

The word 'space' as used here means degree of enclosure. To many people the word 'space' means large, open areas (e.g., a ball field), while to the designer it usually means quite the opposite and connotes spatial boundary. In designing environments for handicapped children's play, the total area (i.e., the amount of land specified for the project) can be divided into many spaces of places that vary in size and feeling of closure. This will create a range of spaces, from small, very enclosed places highly defined by walls and ceilings, to large open places that lack clear spatial definition. Conversely, there should be large very well-defined spaces and small areas that lack specific spatial definition. Spatial definition can be literal (e.g., a wall) or implied. Implied spatial definition can be accomplished by a change in level, in surface material, in level of light, and even in noise level.

While it is possible to relate the size of a space to the number of children who will occupy that space, the designer should avoid this. While it is true that small enclosed spaces may be used a great deal of the time by one or two children playing and interacting quietly, one will often see many children packed into a small space 'telephone booth style'. A play-yard's spaces are just not used in predictable ways. Designers should always try to think of at least three different ways a space can be used to avoid the problem of making unconscious decisions in the design refinement that tend to limit the use of the space. Variety is a key word in creating a range of spatial situations. The specific problems of each unique design situation suggest where the emphasis should be placed, but each environment created should be carefully evaluated to check whether a variety of spatial situations has been created. Some spaces are static 'places'; others are active 'pathways'. Some spaces can be both, being used differently at different times. It is the unification of many different kinds of these two categories of spaces that provides a rich backdrop or landscape that will allow and support the occurrence of a wide variety of child-generated activities.

Earlier it was expressed that the conceptual organization of a scheme needed to be simple. The reason for that statement may now be more clear, for as the designer begins to develop the articulation of a series of spatial situations linked together, a simple overriding concept must exist that controls the placement of these spaces. If one does not exist, the result may be a chaotic environment that confuses the user. The designer's concept does not dictate the way in which an environment is to be used, but does establish a perceivable order.

Design principles 5, 'ambiguous to defined spaces', and 6, 'variety of spatial experiences', are clearly both similar to this primary design criterion. Usually the conceptual base will suggest that certain spaces are key high-use areas. This leads to the next design criteria.

4. Key Places and 5. Multiple Paths

These two criteria are discussed together because it is very important to establish their interrelatedness. Most standard pieces of manufactured play equipment have single functions and channel use into repetitive patterns. The standard slide, for example, has a ladder to reach to the top, a platform only big enough for one child, and a trough-like sliding surface. The child is directed to climb up, slide down, run around to the ladder, climb up, etc. If there are many children, they are expected to queue up and wait a turn (behaviour modification for later in life?). Because the slide sits by itself, no interaction is encouraged with the other isolated pieces of play equipment in the play-yard.

In contrast, well-designed play environments should enrich the potential for a variety of activities occurring on different pathways between the bottom of the slide and the return trip to the top. Big slides, as well as towers, falling pads, multiple tunnels, complex platforms and sand areas are some examples of potential key places in a comprehensive play environment. Key activity areas should usually be located so that their spheres of influence interact at neutral places (natural seams) in the environment. The reason this is suggested can be demonstrated by considering the act of simultaneously throwing two rocks in a lake. Each one sets up ripples. If they are thrown close together, the ripples negate the patterns of each other. The same thing will occur if two key activity, high-use areas are located close together: activities from each will clash. As the geometry of the concept is formed, the key areas are located and this determines the major spatial configurations. The design criterion 'key places' relates directly to the design principle of 'clear accomplishment points'.

The key activity areas must be resolved in the design to contain multiple methods, or paths to, through, over, under and around. The linking of support pieces of the environment to the key areas will begin to do this naturally. The nature of high-use activity areas infers that they contain a great deal of variety. Therefore, their pathways should be different in character. The design principle, 'paced alternatives', deals with many of the same issues as does 'multiple paths', but this author does not feel comfortable with the term 'degree of difficulty' which is used when describing 'paced alternatives'.

The term 'degree of difficulty' used when applied to the design of different pathways infers that the designer knows what is difficult for all the children who will use the environment. Observation has revealed that a steep slope may be easier to negotiate for some children than are irregular steps because of the nature of individual handicaps. It is better to be sure to create different options for approaches to key areas, than to guess the degree of difficulty.

Observation has also confirmed that many key activity nodes have elements that are group-gathering places well above the ground plane. This leads to the next design criterion.

6. Three-dimensional Juxtaposition of Parts

The game tick-tack-toe provides a convenient example. Played on paper it is a very simple game. Only a few variations of the opening move are possible. One soon gets bored with it. But envisage tick-tack-toe played on a 3-dimensional board, three sheets of clear plastic staked vertically with spacers to hold them apart, holes cut in each sheet to represent the standard 2-dimensional board and coloured marbles used instead of X's and O's. Now the simple game has developed complex and stimulating potential. A play-yard that has much of its activity occurring on the ground plane is like a 2-dimensional tick-tack-toe game. While it is true that some standard play equipment does allow the child to get above the ground, it usually supports only solitary activities rather than group interaction. A truly 3-dimensional play environment becomes a matrix of spaces, platforms and pathways juxtaposed so as to maximize interactions — physical, verbal and visual. The potential methods that can be used to change levels offer the designer a rich opportunity to introduce variety. Ramps can be steep or gentle inclines, smooth or rough, straight or crooked. Steps can be regular or irregular, large or small. Slides can be rolling or straight, wide or narrow, transparent or opaque, wet or dry. Ropes, cattle walks, tyres, poles, tunnels and ladders can also be used to change levels. This list is hardly exhaustive of the possibilities. A wide variety of paths allows children with handicaps to find those that relate to their abilities. More difficult paths present other challenges to be met as the child develops. This is very important. In an institutional situation, most children will be exposed to a play environment for many years. It must be complex and challenging enough to sustain interest over time.

Documented research mapping where children played in a unified play environment has shown that children played above the ground in groups a great deal of time. When children are only three feet tall, to be four feet above their peers is quite exciting.

When the previously discussed design criteria are combined, the resultant play environment should be one that is unified, composed of key activity areas, support spaces and multiple pathways — all juxtaposed three-dimensionally. Such a play environment ought to incorporate the three design principles that have yet to be discussed: a play environment that will support a 'range of social scale', with a configuration that includes 'retreat and breakaway points' and 'emotional release areas'. These three principles relate to the primary design criteria holistically. Since they define acts of the users, it is important that the designer grasp their relevance.

The designer needs to keep in mind that specific areas are not used for one purpose only. For instance, a particular place may at one time be a retreat place for one child, later it may be a gathering area for a group, while at other times during the same play period many different social activities may occur there. Places in playgrounds are usually multi-functional. This leads us to the seventh primary design criterion.

7. Non-objective Space

Playgrounds around the world are littered with abandoned, rusting rocking ducks and lonely, chipped concrete turtles. Adults use very little foresight in foisting these upon children. A lesson should be learned from children's construction. They seldom worry if their *ad hoc* collection of cardboard boxes and blankets resembles something specific. In fact, what is so nice about a box is that one moment it can be a jail, the next a palace, and later a rocket ship or the insides of a whale. The designer should think in terms of spaces as round, square, irregular, regular, bright, dark, big, little, etc.

The design principle, 'ambiguous to defined spaces', relates in part to this design criterion. It must be stated, however, that 'ambiguous to defined spaces' does recommend that some of the physical environment be designed in the form of literal spaces to encourage 'real life role modelling'. This author feels that such stage sets should be in the form of removable props. For example, a literal store front can be painted upon a piece of cardboard, roller shade, plywood, etc. and temporarily attached to a surface in the play-yard. Many such props can be designed. They can be used by the children or teachers to stimulate a variety of activities. Because they can be removed, they do not remain to influence an area when that is not desirable.

8. Variety of Material Surfaces

This is a natural continuation of the goals of variety discussed throughout the five previous principles, but needs stating as a primary design criterion. Material surfaces can be coded to specific body movements, for example, covering all similar ramped surfaces with one kind and colour of carpet; while this kind of multiple coding may help a designer organize a colour-texture scheme it should not be over-used.

This type of coded use relates to the design principle, 'repetition and multiple coding.' This author does not believe repetition and multiple coding can be successfully used as described; 'for example all objects that are large and cylindrical in shape being red in colour with a large "C" on them and having a surface that is rough to touch' (Moore *et al.*, 1979, n.p.).

Certain elements of a play-yard naturally multiple-code themselves. Sand, for example, has a texture, sound, smell, colour range and taste that signifies it as being sand. This is true for water, wood and most natural materials; multiple coding occurs in these cases without the designers' aid. To try to multiple-code for specific meaning all elements of the play environment is to organize the parts of the play environment into a rigid predictability that is not desirable for long periods of time. This also presents the problem of determining what objects are to be coded and which are not. Does it not lose meaning and be confusing for the user if in fact all things are not multiple-coded?

9. Loose Parts

This same term is used both as a design principle and as a primary design criterion because it so correctly defines an important ingredient in play. There is no question about the fact that every good play environment should contain manipulable elements. The variety they provide to the fixed background is critical to making an environment stimulating over time. There is somewhat of a question about who should provide loose parts. Many architectural visionaries foresee the exciting potential of movable buildings (even cities!) with plug-in and detachable parts, but presently the applicability of such concepts to parts of a play environment structure is impossible without sophisticated construction technology, high initial costs and even higher maintenance responsibilities. No one should ever think that a play-yard responsive to its users can be built without accepting maintenance costs, but when the structures are themselves movable, changeable, and considered loose parts, the owners should be made to realize they are accepting potentially great upkeep responsibilities. Of course, it is possible for the designer to design things that are movable within the environment, but the environment must be able to function without them so that, if they are permanently removed, the environment does not lose its meaning.

On the other hand, sand and water can be thought of as loose parts, easily renewable and controllable. These materials should be part of every play-yard. The supplying of loose parts (e.g., balls, blocks, toys, dolls) is an opportunity for the users (staff and children) to affect their environment. If places to store loose parts on play-yards are integrated into the designer's scheme, it increases the potential for them to be used spontaneously to reinforce the quality of activity in the environment. Storage areas also provide safe places to keep valuable portable elements after hours.

Conclusion

The design principle of 'plants and critters' is not considered by the author to be a primary design criterion. While it is clearly important to encourage handicapped children's involvement with many forms of living things, and the author has included both plants and animals as parts of design solutions, they have not been considered as organizing elements for projects. There are multiple problems created when plants and/or animals are introduced into active play environments, as well as the fact that local public health laws often prohibit them. Every institution should consider its whole environment as an adventure area and places should be created for various animals, as well as gardens of vegetables and flowers, but often these are best located some distance away from the active play area, where their presence creates another unique area with its own special sense of place.

In conclusion, the nine primary design criteria that have been discussed here are considered to be critical to the process of play environment design. During the design concept formulating stage, the designer must weigh the concepts against these criteria to discover if the over-all order is supportive of them. The specific conditions imposed by each 'problem' may lead the designer to stress certain criteria over others, but none can be omitted. During design development, the solution must be evaluated periodically to see if, in fact, the developing forms and spaces do physically manifest these criteria, because without them the resultant play environment will probably not be able to sustain high use over long periods of time.

The design criteria discussed here are also applicable to play environments for children free of handicaps. What makes the solution to a play environment for most handicapped children different from one for normal children does not lie in the design criteria, but rather in the execution of the parts so they respond to the particular social and physical needs of the users. In other words, the common bond of childhood is far stronger, and more important in designing play environments, than are the separating aspects of most handicaps.

Notes

1. Various design associates worked at different times with the author in creating the play environments and the design process outlined in this paper: John E. Page, Nan C. Plessas, David Smith and Daniel E. Williams.
2. 'A Child's Creative Learning Space', a research project by Leland G. Shaw and Mary F. Robertson, principal investigators, MH-20743, 1973—5.

References

Moore, Gary T., Uriel Cohen, Jeffery Oertel and Lani van Ryzin. 1979. *Environments for Exceptional Education*. New York: Educational Facilities Laboratories.
Shaw, Leland G. 1976. 'The playground: the child's creative learning space'. Unpublished final report to the National Institute of Mental Health.
———. 1978. 'A test using scale models of playgrounds to understand cognitive mapping abilities of preschool children'. Paper presented at the Annual Conference of the Environmental Design Research Association, Tucson, Arizona.

18 PLAY AND THE EXCEPTIONAL CHILD: ADVENTURE PLACE — A CASE STUDY

Clara Will and Michael Hough

The Adventure Place Concept

This paper describes a preschool assessment and treatment centre, called Adventure Place, for emotionally disturbed children in North York (a borough of Metropolitan Toronto, Ontario, Canada). It deals first with the centre's outdoor play programme and guiding philosophy and second with the playground that was built in response to the needs of the programme.

The types of difficulties presented by children who are referred to Adventure Place include emotional disturbance, behavioural disorders, developmental delay, speech and language disorders, learning disabilities, physical handicaps and functional retardation. A child may present problems in any one or a combination of these categories. The centre's enrolment also includes a core group of preschool children whose development is not impaired in any way. The emphasis in assessment and treatment is on relating to the 'total child' within as normalized an environment as possible; this requires the presence of 'normal' children. The programme is designed to respond to the *general* needs common to preschoolers, with the integration of more intensive specialized programmes relating to the *specific* needs of the individual children. The child's self-esteem is nurtured through relationships and through successful experiences which become gradually more challenging as he/she gains security and confidence. The multi-disciplinary team approach to helping the child within the family and the neighbourhood consistently recognizes this basic need of the growing child to develop a strong sense of self-worth.

The Adventure Place assessment and treatment programme was designed on the premise that play is the most powerful learning medium that the young child has. In the good play environment, many of the child's emotional, social, cognitive and physical needs can be met. In order that this environment can provide the optimum opportunity for learning, the play needs to be a joyful experience. This experience at the centre is both an indoor and an outdoor one.

During the first five years of the centre, the outdoor play area was a flat courtyard area with three sides adjoining the public school in

241

which Adventure Place rents facilities. Two small trees provided only a little shade. The play equipment and materials were stored inside the school building, which was locked after school hours. Each morning the staff carried out and set up all these supplies which made up the playground. Each afternoon the staff, with help from the children, dismantled the playground and carried all materials back into the school for safe-keeping until the following morning. At the end of each day there would not be a trace of evidence that anyone had been there that day.

Principles Dictating the Programme

The play programme on the unimproved site was based on criteria that became the basis for the design of the playground itself. The first criterion for the success of the improvised creative playground was strong leadership and commitment from one staff person who could organize the planning and also maintain good organization of the programme. The second criterion was an enthusiastic, energetic, competent staff who could be sensitive to individual needs and who would find joy in children's play. The regular staff were necessarily such people, and the teen-aged summer student helpers were carefully selected for these qualities. The third criterion was an appreciation of junk and scrap materials, an interest in scrounging and a willingness to scrounge. Much of the material that encouraged creative play was acquired very cheaply at rummage and garage sales. Some was obtained free from junk yards. Some was begged from parents, friends and neighbours, and a watchful eye was kept for good materials set out on scrap collection days.

The courtyard space was transformed each day into a playground environment that motivated the children to become involved. Consistent with the centre's philosophy of creating a normalized treatment setting, the outdoor play programme was planned to be suitable for preschoolers in general, rather than specifically for handicapped children. It was designed to encourage physical activity, skill development, expression of creativity, experimentation, socialization and self-direction through interesting, joyful experiences. The child could participate in any activity according to his/her own individual developmental level of functioning, but the opportunity for challenge was always there. Thus the adult did not limit the child's progress by placing expectations on behaviour and functioning according to the particular handicap or difficulty. Each child was encouraged gradually to become just a bit more involved without being unrealistically pressured. Each child's unique potential was respected as he/she was unconditionally accepted as a worthy person. Since these children with special needs require considerable assistance in learning how to utilize the play opportunities, additional student help was acquired in the summer.

The various play activity areas were consistently arranged in such a way that they could be easily identified and so that movement from one area to another was managed with ease. They were positioned to prevent quiet activities from being disturbed by the more active ones, and also to encourage integration of one activity with another in a free flowing manner (e.g., the junk box materials in the large activity area could become a fire station from which firemen could dash across the open area to the burning play house). The child in this environment is free to make choices, to initiate involvement and to change whenever he/she wishes. In response to the special needs of the Adventure Place children, adults would initially encourage the child to make choices and in some cases they would physically manipulate him/her through the steps in participation, always with the goal of increased motivation and direction on the part of the child.

As the children adapted to this structured environment with its safe, secure limits, they were able to become increasingly freer and more spontaneous in their play. Self-motivation and direction increased steadily. One could observe this general settling down and increased involvement begin to occur within the first week of the summer programme. From then on, the play would become more and more creative and the interaction would intensify. Aggressive children began to direct their energies away from anti-social behaviour in preference for interesting, creative activities. Withdrawn and anxious children began to venture forward little by little to explore new media and experiences. Children with severe communication disorders began to communicate non-verbally through play. As all of these things happened, the staff were able to decrease the extent of their direction and become involved in relaxed, joyful play. The integration of the core group of children into this total group contributed greatly to the general activity and fun. They provided modelling behaviour and enthusiasm which helped to motivate the children with special needs.

Programme Activities

The outdoor play programme was designed as follows (see Figure 18.1).

Figure 18.1: Design of Outdoor Play Programme

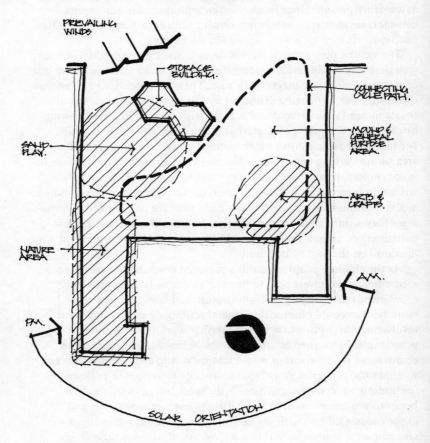

Large Sand Play Area

Water was available to this area so that rivers, lakes and dams could be made. This area allowed children the opportunity to get right into the sand and water with their bare feet. It was a good environment for social interaction and co-operative play. There was no limit to the degree of mess involved and it provided a valuable sensory experience. Children who found it difficult to allow themselves to become messy were not forced into the area, but they were encouraged by adults who modelled the play. Gradually, these cautious children began to involve themselves more.

Materials: sand, water, pails, garden-sized shovels, spades, wheelbarrow, wooden planks, old tin pots and pans, large toy dump-trucks, bulldozers, cranes, car tyres, etc.

Quiet Sand Area

A large sand box available mainly for the youngest children who preferred the less active play with smaller sand toys provided a good environment for solitary, parallel or co-operative play and also for one-to-one interaction between child and adult.

Materials: sand, water, small pails, shovels, spades, rakes, toy wheelbarrows, small planks, toy animals, small bulldozers, cranes, dump-trucks, tin cups, baking tins, pots and pans, sieves, whisks, bits of scrap materials.

Water Play

Splash pool area. Three plastic splash pools were arranged close together on a grassy area where the water hose and sprinkler were also available. This was a popular area with all the children who loved to play alternately in the pools, run through the sprinkler water and splash each other with the hose.

Water tables. Two water tables on legs (tubs on wooden crates could be easily used) were set up at a distance far enough from the pools to allow for more quiet, experimental play. The materials were alternated so that the child was not confused by too many choices at once. Now and then, detergent was added for variety and for experimentation.

Materials: floating toys, cork, funnels, plastic bottles, tin or plastic cups, pieces of hose, egg beater, whisk, sponge, etc.

Water play incorporated into the play house activity is described in the next section.

Play House Area (with integrated fantasy play areas)

This area, set apart from any other active play area, included the following.

Large tent for shaded living room, bedroom and dress-up area. Materials: child-sized cot, pillow, blankets, dolls, doll clothes, bed, blankets, plastic baby bottles, cushions, stuffed toys, dress-up clothes — including gowns, stoles, jackets, shoes, handbags, hats, wigs, jewellery, make-up — tall mirror, books, comic books, doll carriage, baby stroller, real suitcases.

Kitchen and dining area adjacent to the tent. The children were encouraged to carry sand and water into this area to mix in pretending to cook and bake. Foamy shaving cream was occasionally provided for added interest in mixing with the sand and water. All kinds of wonderful 'food' was prepared and served in this interesting area.

Materials: wooden stove, refrigerator (could be made out of crates), table and chairs, crate and basin for dish washing, dish-drainer, old tin pots, pans, coffee pot, muffin tins, baking tins, tin or plastic cups and plates, wooden spoons, egg beater, whisk, kitchen cartons, sponge, dish towel, detergent crates or table for work area, shopping cart.

Doll-bathing area adjacent to the kitchen. The dolls and associated materials were brought over from the tent and this activity could be integrated into the total fantasy play of the area.

Materials: basin, water, crate stand, table or crate for drying and dressing dolls, sponge, soap, towels.

Laundry area near the doll-bathing activity. Materials: tub or basin, water, crate stand, small scrubbing board, soap, clothes line and pegs.

Beauty parlour and barber shop area. This was placed a few feet from the previous areas so that it could be identified as a separate area, but close enough to be incorporated into the over-all fantasy play.

Materials: table or crate, chair, mirrors, old shirt smocks, combs, brushes, hair ribbon, hairpins, nets, curlers, wigs, toy shavers, shaving cream or substitute, make-up, cold cream, tissue.

Doctor's office. This area was also situated apart from but near the tent. This area was placed in the shade of a tree so that it would not be uncomfortable for the patient to be in the bed. A large wagon became the ambulance that brought patients into the doctor's office from all over the playground. One could frequently hear the 'siren' of screeching children as emergencies were attended to. Adults also became patients who had weird and wonderful operations performed.

Materials: cot, blankets, pillow, real stethoscope, doctor and nurse materials, doctor's bag, white shirts for smocks, white cardboard bands for hats, cloth bandages, plastic spoons, etc.

Other fantasy areas. Stores, fire stations, restaurants, etc. were created whenever the play initiated their existence, but they were not set up on a daily basis. Such areas could be organized on a weekly basis as themes.

Large Junk Play Area

In this area junk materials were set out to be manipulated by the children in any way they wished. Adults provided ideas and helped the children by moving some of the materials with them.

Materials: large cardboard boxes, tubes, barrels, wooden crates, car tyres, car seats, steering wheels, ladders, large wooden spool, planks, blankets and any movable junk material.

General Open Space–Gross Motor Area

This area provided the opportunity for motor and co-ordination skill development through jumping, bouncing, climbing, rolling, crawling, tumbling, throwing, rocking, sliding, lifting, pushing and running. It is important that the child have space for plain running.

Materials: trampoline, rockers, climber and slide, tumbling mat, skipping ropes, hoops, balls, bats, bean bags, basketball, tether ball, cardboard tubes, large blocks, wheelbarrow.

Riding, Pushing, Pulling Vehicles Area

The push-and-pull vehicles could be used anywhere in the playground area, but the riding vehicles need hard surfaces. Thus, there had to be a time made available for children to ride while supervised on the asphalt outside the courtyard fence. This arrangement was workable, but it did not enable the children to integrate the riding toy play with the other activities.

Materials: tricycles, bicycles, wagons, strollers, carts, riding cars.

Quiet Activity Area

This area was located far from the large activity area, but not too far from the play house complex. The child could retreat to this space for an interlude of quiet in the shade.

Materials: mat, shade canopy, pillows, stuffed toys, books, puzzles, paper, crayons.

Art and Craft Area

This activity was situated close to the school entrance for easy access to art materials and far enough away from the active areas to permit a quiet atmosphere. All sorts of art and scrap materials were on hand with paper, glue, scissors and drawing materials. Bright colours of paint and good brushes encouraged painting art. Much paper and large scrap pieces of cardboard boxes were also available now and then. Clay, plasticine and play-dough were media for fine-motor activities. This activity required only an abundance of interesting materials, a table area and a good area for working, and enthusiastic adults to provide inspiration and participation. Some of the art would be taped on the school wall for interest during the day.

Woodcraft Area

For the young child to enjoy woodcraft, real materials and tools are needed, but this also necessitates constant supervision. During unsupervised periods, the tools were put away and glue was used for wood sculptures. In both the art and the wood activities, the doing was more important than the excellence of the finished product. Each child's project was respected as a worthwhile expression of his/her unique individuality.

Materials: wood working-surface, bits of scrap wood, nails, real hammers and saws, glue, paint.

Snack Area

This was situated in the shade of one of the trees. Nutritious, rather than sugar, snacks were served, although occasionally popsicles, ice-cream, etc. were offered. Encouraging good nutrition is an important part of any preschool programme.

Activities outside the playground such as excursions, swimming at a neighbourhood pool and music activities inside the school were also included in this play programme. Music would also be enjoyed in the playground in singing, musical games, and by means of a record player.

Planting and caring for a garden would be an interesting addition to the play programme if vandalism were not a factor. Playing and caring for pets could also be added if proper care could be given to the animals after hours and at weekends. Young children with special needs can benefit from their relationships with and care of pets.

Design Principles for the Playground

The playground was conceived as a place of beauty and delight where teachers can help troubled children learn social, physical and creative skills according to their own special needs, in an atmosphere of sympathy and encouragement. The outdoor play programme had been in operation for some time before the playground was built. It had created the working envelope that was needed to enhance the programme. The design has therefore been dictated by the philosophy and principles described previously in this paper and by certain physical factors. These are summarized as follows.

The Child Makes the Playground

The playground must encourage creativity. What the child makes of it

Figure 18.2: The Playground is Created by the Children

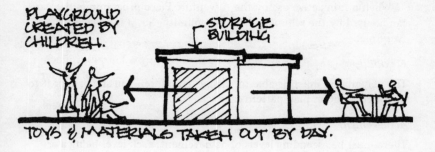

Figure 18.3: The Playground is Dismantled by the Children

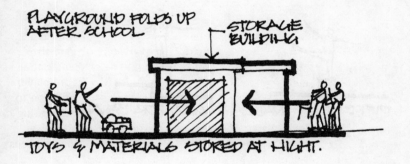

is according to his/her own choosing and needs. Its elements must therefore be open-ended and non-specific, offering unlimited possibilities for experiment. The playground unfolds when it is active; the child creates it and puts it away when he/she is finished. It is like a day-blooming flower: each day brings a new blossom.

The most intense and varied play is concentrated around the storage play structure and sand area. The structure stores play materials out of school and becomes a play area when the children are there. Dress-up, drama, sand and water play all happen within these open and sheltered places.

Extending from the structure is the play frame and associated sand areas which may be used for climbing, sliding, swinging, roof play and all kinds of sand play. It is a highly active means of moving from one activity to another. Canvas, cargo nets, ropes, tyres, can be provided as the programme may dictate in constantly changing combinations.

When not in active use by the Adventure Place programme, the yard can be used by the school and the community. So, it is a place for everyone.

Flexibility

The playground must be able to change as children and staff adapt it to their needs and as play patterns change.

Achievement

There must be ascending levels of achievement; each level being a natural growth from the one before and providing new goals.

Figure 18.4: Ascending Levels of Achievements

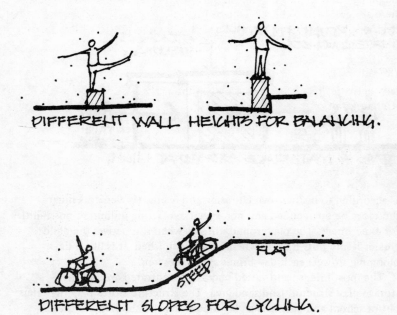

DIFFERENT WALL HEIGHTS FOR BALANCING.

DIFFERENT SLOPES FOR CYCLING.

Everything is Connected to Everything Else

Activities and elements of play must be related in a way that permits a natural flow from one activity to another. Continuity of experience between activities is important. The connection between one activity

Figure 18.5: All Activities are Connected to Each Other

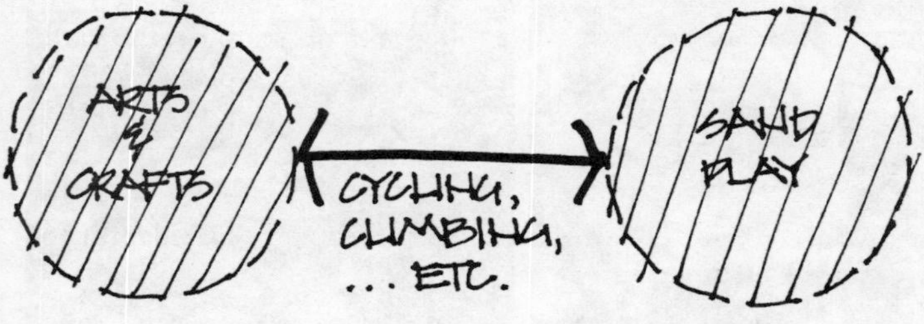

and another should itself be an activity that reinforces them.

Risk and Conflict

The playground should provide an optimum degree of conflict and risk. There are problems to be solved that help specific social interaction. Physical space is very important. Spaces that are too large inhibit social interaction and creativity in problem solving.

Diversity

Many activities take place in the playground, all of which require different kinds of space.

Figure 18.6: Some are Active and Require Large Spaces

Figure 18.7: Some are Reflective and Require Intimacy

Figure 18.8: Some Need Space for Construction Projects

Figure 18.9: Some are Natural Areas for Nature Study and Quiet Discussions

A Sense of Place and a Place for All Seasons

Every child reacts to the world outside of himself. Places that are beautiful, that have variety, that stimulate the senses of sight, sound, touch, smell and taste, are essential to learning and emotional health. Part of learning is being exposed to sunshine, rain, wet and dry, cold and heat, leaves and bare branches. Children with learning problems often forfeit these aspects of weather that normal children take for granted.

Site Influences

The elements of the playground are arranged to respond to wind and sun and to complete the enclosure of the school courtyard.

Summary

It is a curious, yet unfortunate fact that much of the best care and creative thought has been reserved for children with learning disabilities while normal children too often must fend for themselves in physically hostile play environments. Beauty and healthy environments are still regarded as desirable but dispensable luxuries, not as basic rights. Yet the kind of playground that Adventure Place required to fulfil its special programme is what any child needs for healthy emotional and physical growth. The difference, with the exception of some special equipment, is that disadvantaged children cannot seek out and assimilate life experiences on their own as normal children do. They need the help of devoted teachers.

The problem in much of what is designed for children is the uncontrollable urge of designers to be creative. One becomes uncomfortably aware that this is their greatest liability. A designer's role should be to encourage creativity in others by shaping the right environments for this to happen. That is all that can be done successfully and what has been collectively tried at Adventure Place.

Part Five

BEYOND THE PLAYGROUND

19 CRITERIA FOR CHILDREN'S PLAYTHINGS AND PLAY ENVIRONMENTS

Yrjö Sotamaa[1]

The Objectives of Environment Planning

The design of playthings and playing places is a part of environmental design.[2] The task of environmental design is to create physical surroundings of a high standard for human activity, play, residence, work, rest and leisure pursuits.

It is not enough, however, for the environments to satisfy only the immediate human, material — usually short-term — wants. To be of a high standard, the environment must be physically functional as well as harmonious, stimulating and humane — in a word, comfortable. A good environment accounts for the best of the historical heritage, social necessities, a creative interpretation of contemporary aesthetic values and the skilled exploitation of production processes.

The environment and its objects are long-lived compared to many products of society and culture. Their beauty may be enjoyed and their unsightliness and faults suffered by many succeeding generations, who often have no possibility of making further decisions about them. The environment and the objects included in it not only satisfy existing needs and create a new environmental culture, but also have influence on further needs and activities. The environment also has an influence on physical and psychic health. Therefore, high ethical, aesthetic and technical requirements must be set on planning products and the environment.

High standards in plaything design and environmental planning are generally viewed as economically impossible. Recently, however, many researchers, planners and economic spokesmen have started to emphasize quality factors as being central to social and cultural development, as well as production development strategy.

Playthings as Stimulants to Activity and Learning

The number and quality of stimulants that are directed towards a child decisively influence various possibilities for child development, among which the most important are persons and their relationships to the child. Also very important is the world surrounding the child and its objects, especially playthings (Koch, 1977, pp. 51a—b).

It must be assumed, as a premise of developmental psychology, that environmental factors do not directly determine development, but rather the child's activity, whereby the personality of the child is formed. The 'developmental' effect of playthings is not self-evident, but has a hidden potential, which attains its full meaning only when the child uses the objects.

A plaything is a message, a combination of symbols. An idea is sent and received. Reception is not a passive state, but, more correctly, the child 'decodes' the message of the plaything through his play activity in a manner characterizing the level of his development. If the playthings are correctly selected so that the child is stimulated into activity by them, the child receives the message of the plaything and reacts to it actively; the plaything has a noticeably greater influence on the physical and psychic development of the child than was previously assumed.

Playthings initiate 'early learning' and facilitate valuable 'early experience', which jointly form the basis of the whole childhood experience.

A developmentally correct plaything not only stimulates the playing child to learn and seek useful experiences, but also the child 'learns to learn'. If, on the other hand, he/she does not receive stimulation for activity, the child may 'learn not to learn'. The child loses the ability to learn. An unstimulating environment deprives the sense and weakens the ability to observe details and nuances. High-quality playthings and playing places must be considered to be essential from the viewpoint of the child's development, commodities which are as valuable as varied nutrition, undisturbed rest and clean air.

Playthings are a Part of the Total Environment

Playthings form a part of the environment and culture in which they are used. Their ability to arouse interest and to activate the child to action depend, in addition to the inherent interest of the thing itself, on other playmates, the environment and the culture. The environment also influences the content of the activity, the direction and its intensity. A toy reindeer in the hand of a small Lapp boy in the midst of Lapland's roadless backwoods sparks different thoughts and actions from the same object in the hand of an American boy on the 35th floor of a skyscraper in New York. A red toy ball in a shining white hospital room emits stimuli which differ significantly from the meaning which the same object receives in the centre of a playroom full of playthings or in the centre of a group of boys in a green field. An extreme example of the relative ability of the environment and its objects to spark interest and activity is offered by an experience from a certain children's home in Finland. In a room of children just under one-year-old were five metal baby beds and a polished plastic floor surface. That was all. In this environment the children lived from day to day. They were taken for fresh air out to the balcony, where they slept in the daytime. On the shining floor was a pile of colourful plastic playthings in which the children were not interested. Instead, they were very interested in food, above all its warm and sticky composition. Many of these children were excessively obese. They sought to compensate for a boring environment by eating (Laukka, 1979).

The examples depicted above indicate that the significance of devices is very dependent on the nature of their relationship to the rest of the environment, its ordering and its opportunities for activity.

The understanding and clarification of the tasks and requirements to be set for playthings and playing environments today requires, in addition to a child's internal developmental requirements (developmental psychology), the study of the condition of external, physical developmental prerequisites of residential and activity environments. The form, structure, colours, dimensions, fixed and mobile parts, and other physical conditions of the physical environment as well as the normative processes of the environment on activities within it are the framework which, together with the social environment, permit or prevent the development of the child's activity needs.

The Transition of Physical Requirements in Child Development

The very rapid industrialization, urbanization and technological developments which have occurred in the twentieth century and especially the latter half of the century have significantly changed the environment. This development, while it has increased the well-being of people in many respects, also contains numerous traits which cannot be held to be solely positive, especially from the viewpoint of children. The Finnish architect, Juhani Pallasmaa (1977, p. 1), pointedly depicts these changes in the nature of the city:

Although the quality of commodities increases constantly and environmental change accelerates, our living conditions become impoverished on several levels simultaneously.

The impoverishment of stimulant content is caused by the increasingly one-dimensional nature of functioning, the expansion of activity and building units, the over-rational formal ideals, the diminishing time factor, the vanishing of historical contrast and the natural vs. built-up environmental contrast, the mechanization of movement and the increase in speed, as well as psychic separation from the life environment through specialization and functionalization of the individual. Functionalization changes persons into passive resemblances of furniture, units to be used in a planned manner.

The impoverishment of our sensual environment is due partially to the attraction of our culture to deodorants, smooth surfaces and even temperatures and lights. On the other hand the sensual environment is impoverished by a dulling of the senses, a sensual din. Traffic noise covers delicate hearing experiences, exhausts prevent the recognition of fragrances, even lighting eliminates the transition of light and shadow and a levelling internationalism removes local variation.

The English recipient of the Alvar Aalto Award, Architect James Stirling (1978, p. 34), boils down what is, in his assessment, the central problem of the environment:

The architecture of our time is frequently simplified to flatness. The main causes of this are economic factors and commercialization. A very simple building is easier, faster and cheaper to build. But it transmits only one solitary image.

A built-up environment must have optimal stimuli so we may feel comfortable and our brains function well. This fact was first discovered through tests which studied what kinds of surroundings man could tolerate during space flights.

Strømmes (1978, p. 16) has noted that

When the amount of incoming information was decreased in the experiment space it was found that this was unbearable to humans to the extent that following the impoverishment of a certain field of stimuli psychic disturbances begin to emerge. This demonstrates that to function well the brain requires the labour provided by continuous information from the surroundings. The word information in this context means changing novelty. It is easy to demonstrate that the changing novelty unconditionally demanded by our brain is generally lacking in modern architecture. For example, having seen the first element on the left at the top in the facade of a block of flats one knows the shape and colour of all other elements in the facade.

The same is repeated in the building's interior, for example, when one has seen the corner of a wall in the flat, the appearance of the whole wall is known exactly.

This development process is even more frequently associated with a growing discontent, lack of personal identity, alienation and mounting crime.

In addition to the negative social and psychophysical effects, the ecological effects of rapid urbanization are generally known. Inaccurate premises in product and environmental planning have not adequately considered the needs of children and youth, as well as many other large citizen groups (e.g., the aged, the disabled). A consequence of a biased and indifferent attitude is the modern urban environment with its buildings and services — dangerous, insecure and non-functioning for a significant portion of users. The great advantages which would accrue to all from product and environmental planning which would accommodate the needs of the weakest users have not been appreciated.

From the viewpoint of the child, the features of the environment described above have the following effects: the scale and quantity of stimuli offered by the environment are reduced; the nature of stimuli has changed; the scale of the environment in relation to the child has been overwhelming; the living-space has diminished; and the nature of the city has become ever more technical, constituted of non-vital components. The changes are reflected in children's play which becomes one-dimensional, broken and of short duration; the play traditions are spare and new ones do not emerge. The general effect is the deterioration in the activity value of the child's life environment and the diminishing of the child's possibilities to be active.[3] The narrower the area of reality with which children come in contact, the plainer and more monotonous is their play.

What, then, are the effects of the surroundings and changes that occur upon playthings and play environments? More playthings of the kind which help children to understand the structure of the environment, its meaning for human activity and its many faceted principles of functioning are needed. Although playthings should not primarily be viewed as substitutes for the natural environment, they ought to play a compensating role for the profound losses related to the disappearance of the refined, slowly changing and delicate natural environment which has weakened the balanced and sensitive development of emotional, sensual, aesthetic and intellectual personality traits.

It is also a task of playthings to teach children to value and understand and, above all, to help internalize those characteristics which influence the enjoyability of the physical environment and which are in peril of disappearing before a life-style based on economically efficient urbanization and technical development.

Today's playthings and play environments can be criticized for being too ready-made. No opportunities remain for the child's own ideas. This is partly due to the fact that the planning society is in love with objects and environments finalized to the last detail. Less ready-made and less realistic objects and environments provide more opportunities for imagination than realistic objects and planned environments for predetermined activities. The child learns not only by looking and listening, but also by creating problem situations and influencing his/her environment. Work for thought and imagination is not provided by an environment which is too ready-made, nor by toys which cannot be manipulated in some way.

The general characteristics of a good play environment briefly may be defined as follows:

1. A play environment must be spacious. There must be a possibility to move and play expansive eventful games.

2. In its individual details, the play environment may, however, be small in scale.

3. The play area must not be barren. There should be slightly raised levels, pillars and corners, which old-style architecture created in abundance but modern construction, sadly enough, abhors. Comfortable surfaces such as furry carpets and worn wooden surfaces are also needed.

4. A play environment should contain changing and adjustable spaces. Children should be able to play train on chairs set in a row, sit in a large basket and make a slide out of a sofa-top or perhaps only crawl under a table.

5. The same requirements concern outdoor spaces: there must be space, a changing landscape and numerous small details such as stones, plants and ants, and there must be transformable space: the possibility to dig holes, build a hut and play games.

6. Only when the leading requirements for a sound environment exist do dolls, carriages and games in boxes find their proper role and place in a child's life.

One must become aware that the effort to make life simple in the extreme — the simplification of social wealth and diversity — leads to banal, monotonous and dead environments. The destruction of individuality also destroys productive and creative ability.

Structural Changes Reflected in Playthings

In addition to the physical surroundings, changes due to the structural development of society have occurred in the realm of individual growth. In the transformation of the family from a productive unit to a consuming unit, the opportunities for children to participate in work have been reduced. Compared to earlier times they are not provided with possibilities to have direct, personal, practical experiences in doing work, nor the diverse problems and experiences related to interpersonal co-operation. With increased mechanization, the transfer of production and services outside the home, and the satisfaction of needs occurring almost wholly with prepared products, the opportunities for practice of intricate and sophisticated hand skills are also reduced.

The educational demands created by the diversification and technical development of social activities and the transfer of teaching tasks to organized education are also reflected in the requirements of playthings.

As with requirements set for environmental changes, the tasks of playthings based on structural changes are aimed in several directions: playthings must play their part in teaching to understand and take advantage of new active opportunities created by science and technology; they must allow for experiences with various work tasks, alone and in co-operation with others; they must allow for the practice of hand skills and the adoption of valuable traits of hand workmanship practices.

Playthings and Games Analyzed by Content

The choice of playthings on the market is, in many ways, one-sided and limited. Their planning does not originate in the content of play, the developmental and growth needs of the child, but rather the selection of playthings is strongly controlled by commercial considerations.

A division of the types of play according to content is hopefully a better guide to someone designing and/or buying playthings than a list of existing and recommended playthings and play materials. A catalogue merely creates an inventory of playthings available at the moment and this is not far removed from a sales catalogue. The need for playthings, however, cannot be defined through a product list — this changes according to the ages of children and the conditions of time and space. It would, therefore, be most flexible to obtain playthings spontaneously

Table 19.1: Play Content Analysis in a Cultural Context

		Function games	Construction games	Role games	Games with rules	Didactic games
LIFE AS A MEMBER OF SOCIETY	**I SOCIAL SPHERE OF LIFE**					
	1. Various roles of members of society					
	— nurturing play			x		
	— playing house, housework and chores		x	x		
	— playing school, nursery, child health centre, zoo, circus, etc.			x		
	— dressing up as adults, being fine ladies, beauty contest			x		
	— war games and catching games, e.g. cops and robbers			x	x	
	2. Social rituals					
	— traditional ritual playing				x	
	— weddings, funerals, birthdays and annual holidays in play			x	x	
	3. Work and livelihood					
	a) imitation of events in environment			x		
	b) wider knowledge of cultural development					
	— professional roles			x		x
	— history and development of professions and trades		x	x		x
	— satisfaction of basic needs such as food and shelter in various cultures		x	x		x
	— the communications media and their development		x			x
	— development of communication, transportation and traffic		x	x		x
OBSERVATION	**II ORIENTATIVE LEARNING AND AESTHETIC EXPERIENCE**					
	1. Exercise of sense perception					
	2. Knowledge of nature					
	a) experience of affinity with nature and observation of natural beauty	x				x
	b) observation of natural phenomena and processes	x				x
	c) the adaptation of nature and environmental protection		x			x
	3. The aesthetic organization of the environment, decoration and decorating		x			x
	4. Organizing, constructing, planning		x			x
	5. Rules, systems, measurement, basic mathematics		x		x	x
EXPRESSION	**III PRACTICE IN EXPRESSION AND FACT-FINDING**					
	1. Oral expression	x		x		x
	2. Exercise, dance	x		x		x
	3. Graphic expression	x	x			
	4. Musical expression	x	x			
	5. Dramatic total expression and puppet theatre	x		x		x
	6. The elements of reading and writing		x		x	x

Note: The chart illustrates into what structural type the kinds of play fit according to content. Didactic games are open to pedagogic interpretation. It is also dependent on circumstances when parental guidance is needed.

Notes

I.1. In social games, children imitate adults and children older than themselves. In these, their own identities develop, as does the ability to put oneself in someone else's position. Children may feel themselves to be family members, fellow workers and friends. They identify with representative members of their own sex according to a model provided by adults. Through these games, children learn to behave in a group and become young citizens. Naturally, the children also absorb the unpleasant aspects of culture; thus, in social play, commercialized sex and violence also appear.

I.2. The adoption of standards in a community is emphasized in ritual games. Children love rituals even when their symbolic language is unknown to them.

I.3. A student of play traditions, Leea Virtanen (1970), has found that the only activity which children see performed by men in city courtyards is the washing of cars. The growth of culture in its working-life aspects can generally no longer occur through imitation. For this reason, the role of didactic games gains importance in the field of working games: these are games in which the guidance of adults is needed. Through play, children are able to review the history of mankind and become acquainted with cultural development through personal activity. Activities which are rather simple in themselves — such as fishing, the gathering of berries and mushrooms in the woods, acquainting oneself with a craftsman's trade, sleeping the night in a self-made hut, the preparation of food on an open flame, and the use of jungle drums as a communication device — are pedagogically first-class games.

II. Orientative learning occurs first of all through personal observation. An aesthetic upbringing is also dependent on a wealth of sense observation. This establishes clear requirements for a play environment. In a favourable environment, children may admire and study a living plant as a phenomenon, study its growth as a process, and influence nature actively themselves by caring for plants and animals.

III. In the area of expression and information gathering the reflected influence of culture is perhaps most strongly visible. The children live totally and do not differentiate between the form and content of expression, nor the seven forms of art. Also, the products of their imaginings are reflections of those cultural influences which surround them.

---

according to prevailing needs and occasionally to interject a creative question: are new playthings needed at all? Can playthings be made by the child and/or adult? Are appropriate playthings to be found, for example, in junk stores, hardware stores or in nature? With the aid of Table 19.1 (Laukka, 1979), it is in some degree possible to check if the opportunities allowed by the playthings and play environment are sufficiently many-sided.

The Consequences of Changes in Manufacturing Playthings

The manufacturing of playthings is becoming a significant branch of industry on a world scale. The value of world 'toy' production currently is estimated at nearly 15,000 million dollars (US), for which the United States accounts for approximately one-third. Plaything manufacturing will centralize and its value is expected to grow strongly during the coming years. The production and marketing of both indoor and outdoor playthings will, as a result of growth, increasingly adopt characteristic traits of product production and marketing.

With the constant increase in production volume and the continual increase in the selection and quantity of goods produced the market begins to become saturated. The competition for market among producers and products increases. This in turn leads to the growth of market centered thinking in production and product planning. As Scitovsky points out a development is visible in many areas of production, that manufacturers strive in product and services planning to play a safe bet by relying on marketing research revelations of unfulfilled consumer desires instead of innovative planning. At best this may slow down the birth of innovation and genuine progress in product design; at worst it can lead to the misinterpretation of consumer tastes and needs and the creation of mythical good taste (the average taste of the normal consumer), which is actually only accepted by very few (Bladen, 1974, p. 111).

The emphasis on marketing and excessive stressing of the commercial aspects has meant the birth of a superficially more stimulating and diverse play environment in plaything design. Actually, however, the superficial, bauble-producing, product-design outpouring from fashionable thinking leads to the impoverishment of values in the play environment. As discovered by the study on industrial product design carried out by the Foundation for the Year of Observance of Finnish Independence, 1968, design is still understood only rather superficially. It is considered as decoration of the product and environment, an anti-aesthetics view in fact, the purpose of which is solely to arouse the desire of people to buy the marketed product. Appearance, the determining basis and prerequisite of an aesthetic impression, therefore, acts as a lure; by changing it one can easily manipulate people's idea of products. Former generations of products are made to look aged, and by changing the appearance of products one can cause the planned obsolescence of products. A market-centred styling approach is the misuse of design and according to the study it conflicts, for example, with product safety (Coates, 1976).

Playthings as Reflections of Life-style

Playthings — as all man-made objects — reflect both intentionally and unintentionally, the society where they are created. Toys also express what we hold valuable and important, what we would like people to be like, for what we wish to bring up our children.

The plaything section of a large department store gives a clear picture of the commercialization of plaything design and the life-style supported by society. The dolls are all young and pretty female objects, automobiles have more status than transport objects. It is not always clear whether furry toy animals are cats, dogs or bears, so completely have they lost their natural qualities. In human and social activity, aimless wandering from place to place and warfare with modern devices are visibly represented. Despite the superficial appearance of plenty, one finds serious deficiencies in the selection. Toys have an impersonal 'multi-national' aspect; the connection with one's own culture, work, the man-made environment, nature and ordinary life is lacking (Laukka, 1979).

The above relates closely to the human desire to project values outward and the need for acceptance in the community through special symbols such as consumer goods. This is not in itself a problem. The problem arises when all kinds of knick-knack products are sold on aesthetic and prestige bases, or when people drive themselves spiritually or physically to the ground to gain prestige with material things piled around them.

This is a question which deeply influences the content of human life, as well as life-styles. It is also a question of life-style selection, choosing between will o' the wisps and more enduring values. Many of those who emphasize the fact that this is a question of free choice in matters of taste, however, strive to permeate a cheap material consciousness to the furthest reaches of awareness. Something of true humanity and the need for beauty which springs therefrom vanishes as a consequence.

Playthings are in a special position as related to other consumer goods in that the abilities of the conventional users of the device — the children — to assess and foresee possible dangers and protect themselves from them is less than is usually the case. Children are also exceptionally vulnerable to the temptations offered by marketing and advertising as

they are unable critically to approach marketing measures aimed at
them. The securing of consumer safety requires that, through legislation,
reliability in consumer goods in terms of health and economics should
be achieved: therefore, it should be possible to establish certain
minimum standards for consumer goods. Strict standards and
restrictions must also be developed for advertising.

The need for directives concerning the safety of playthings is
increased by the increase in the selection of playthings available, the
increased production and procuring of playthings, and the trend to
ever more complicated and technically advanced playthings accompanied
by, among other things, risk of accident.

The mass production of playthings also multiplies risk. Risk of
misfortune may extend to thousands, even millions of children. A
certain American firm was forced to take a million building sets off the
market when two children died after swallowing a rubber connection.
In speaking of safety, it must be emphasized that only physical safety is
not enough; psychic safety must also be considered. A toy must
function according to its planned purpose, for a toy which does not
fulfil a child's functional expectations of it through its designed
operation is a frustration. Frustration is not a positive development
supporting experience.

Failure during play due to an object may result in frustration leading
to compensation, for example, through aggression directed at the object
or something else happening to be in the vicinity. A model for
compensating behaviour due to frustration may also be passiveness and
alienation from play.

In this connection, it might be said that psychic security and the
positive contradiction which must exist between the external demands
of a child's needs and activities and internal development are to be
clearly differentiated. It should also be noted that excitement and
danger act as essential stimuli in creating active and intensive play.

Diminishing Choice of Materials

In addition to the above, a certain deficiency related to the mass
production of playthings has resulted in a diminishing choice of
materials. A mass-produced plaything's message lacks the maker's
interpretation and the mark of his hand. On the other hand, the
material of a mass-produced plaything illustrates the truths of industrial
society: specialized planning, division of labour in production,
standardization, quality control and internationalism, combined with the
professional skill and work of perhaps hundreds of unknown people.

The complicated message of the material reveals itself to the child slowly and with difficulty; the tasks of the educator increase correspondingly. The technical change processes of synthetic materials are rapid. Shall we be able to learn their characteristics at our own speed? The message of synthetic materials which are related to the material in various ways, its mode of preparation, its function and its content, is studied by few, but the results pass into the hands of many children. Synthetic materials are a non-renewable resource which must be used with discretion according to ecological principles. Synthetic materials are products of advanced technology. Plastic is difficult, if not impossible, to handle with simple tools. Moulds, heat energy, high pressures, etc. are needed. A plastic toy is difficult to transform and it may be impossible to repair. By directing a virtuoso execution of the work, plastic technology makes possible, sometimes without justifiable cause, the achievement of a perfectionist view of reality. A toy prepared this way leaves no room for the imagination, nothing to complement or adjust. With too highly planned materials, the child can be accustomed to be a passive consumer waiting to be amused (Salovaara, 1979).

The plastic revolution has been influenced by the basic factor that an object prepared from the raw material in mass production requires little human labour. A little plastic car ejects from an automatic spray moulding machine every sixth second, often totally finished. A tin car of the same size requires numerous work stages: cutting the form from a plate, the three-dimensional shaping of the plate, the surface treatment of the parts and assembly by hand. Plastic cars can be produced with a rental mould even in one's own cellar. A factory is needed to produce a tin car. The widespread use of plastic is based primarily on economic realities.

The positive aspects of plastic materials — lightness, pleasant acoustic characteristics, low heat conduction (i.e., it feels warm), as well as the expression of high technical ability — have not found sufficient natural application in playthings. In some plastic building sets, high quality has been attained and has received high evaluation (Lego, Fischer, etc.). They have something mathematically exact about them, which provides guidance in the acceptance of modern technology. Their pleasantly adhering and snapping connections are pleasant to touch. Plastic at its best is like Japanese polishing work and plastic is more pleasant than steel when put into the mouth.

In many instances, the expressiveness and prestige of plastic material has been increased by adding to it features of another material, for example, patterns reminiscent of the surface structure of leather. A borrowed characteristic has then been added to the content. Plastic playthings and the design of their form is in the hands of a few experts. The most natural form of expression for the material is sought, but it cannot be tested out in advance in the manner of handicrafts.

The testing of a material's possibilities through play can assist in determining a better understanding of the scope and limitations of the natural form of a material. 'The search for a natural expression for a material is a continuous frontier expedition in the land between the possible and the impossible.' The thesis of Eliel Saarinen (1948, p. 3) serves as a guide in the finding of natural form: 'In the search for form it is not wise for everyone to travel the same road.'

Instructional Quality Standards of a Plaything

The following are a set of quality standards for playthings:

1. A desirable plaything is an operative device and not an object of passive ownership.

2. A plaything is only one requisite of play. No plaything is instructional or 'explanatory' of itself as such without related direct or indirect guidance.

3. A desirable plaything transmits, however, a cue to instructionally correct play: positive social relatedness, the making of new observations, the practice of basic skills or the acceptance of rules.

4. A desirable plaything endures. It provides for the child an understanding of the way the object was made and characteristics of the material used therein. Ideal from the instructional viewpoint (though rare in modern times) would be the making of a plaything together with the child. One can also conceive that children become acquainted with the assembly-line production of playthings in a factory.

5. A desirable plaything attracts, via an aesthetic material, form, colour and expression. One cannot strive for perfection in this matter, however, since one object seldom fills all these requirements. A child may be attracted by such qualities in toys as the selective taste of adults finds cheap and common.

6. A desirable plaything contains aspects from cultural tradition and the present day. The child's view of man and the world are formed through play. Therefore, it is not a matter of indifference what views about the future adhere to playthings. The emergence of a child culture, however, is a prolonged and complex development and changes in play traditions occur slowly and capriciously. Therefore, one cannot assume

that with one blow the whole child culture can be renewed together with new kinds of playthings.

7. Play is an area of the child's independent activity, the autonomy of which should be respected. Children's games cannot be changed by compulsory means. Sound pedagogical ideals do not influence a child's behaviour, if they are strongly at odds with those norms which prevail in a child's home and environment. In the last analysis, the children in any case select their own toys.

8. Games and playthings imitate adult culture by exaggerating its external features. This leads to the caricature — like overtones often visible in games — in which the authority of children over adults, the various features identifying sexual roles, etc. are emphasized. An adult must see this playing behaviour characteristic of children with understanding on one hand, but 'without entering into the game oneself' on the other. The content of play should not be viewed as a direct imitation of the adult world, but an interpretation characteristic of children. A good plaything is a message from adult to child which the children interpret into their own language.

9. A plaything must always be received as a part of the whole formed by a play environment in which various possible interpretations are to be tested. The boundary between a plaything and play material is not exact. A narrow-minded pedagogical viewpoint could lead to an impoverished play environment.

10. A good plaything does not overload the joy of playing. It must always be remembered that play is primarily amusement. Apparently useless games without great pedagogical objectives can have a great liberating, therapeutic meaning.

Research and Planning of Playthings to be Improved

Despite individual sound examples, it may be said that the conscious planning of playthings and play environments is just beginning. In future, ever-increasing resources should be directed towards the scientific study of problems related to the child's environment and environmental design, as well as international co-operation, in an attempt at solving these questions. Designers, planners, decision makers, and manufacturers must also receive more information about children and their development.

Equally important is whether the society is willing to invest the necessary funds to realize the needs of children. In the Nordic countries at present, for example, notably more money is used for garages and parking areas than children's playing, co-operative and working needs.

Planners and decision makers know more about cars than children (Insulander, 1977, pp. 153–70).

Today – in addition to resources – plaything and play environment design problems relate, on the one hand, to the struggle against superficial and short-sighted thinking which stresses only technological-economic-commercial viewpoints and, on the other hand, to the control and application of an explosively expanding quantity of information. Also necessary is the prediction of coming needs and development forecasts as the children of today are, after all, the influential forces of the third millennium. Design and planning methodology is also to be developed: how to obtain and combine information, present demands and shape a physical solution which fulfils the demands. The field of design requirements should be expanded without bias for all ideas and all information.

Although adequate confirmed information is lacking for the time being about social, aesthetic and other quality requirements, concepts based on experience and observation concerning the nature of these requirements are available. The core of the problem, in fact, is in the attitudes about children held by the society and adults, concerning their growth conditions and the environment as well. If the mental and cultural content is missing from the environment, then everything is missing – this is the worst situation, when the environment is alienated from man. Environmental design is art, which requires both intelligence and heart (Ruusuvuori, 1979, p. 23).

Notes

1. This article is based on a project to determine requirements to be set for play environments and toys for children. The project was carried out as part of the agreement of scientific–technological co-operation between Finland and the German Democratic Republic in the years 1976–9. Participating in carrying out this undertaking were the Association of Finnish Designers (Ornamo) and Amt für industrielle Formgestaltung. The results of the project will be published in books called *Playthings for Play* and *Playgrounds for Play*. The former will appear in 1979 and the latter in 1981.

2. It is often difficult to differentiate between a plaything and a play environment. For this reason, these terms are intended to have a very broad meaning in this article and they will partly overlap. Nor, therefore, does the article differentiate between viewpoints on playthings and environments. It should also be noted that the term 'plaything' is used rather than 'toy' because of the inconsequential connotations of the latter term.

3. 'Activity value' is the ability of a plaything or environment to stimulate a child to play, work, demonstrate inquisitive behaviour and relate socially, that is, to encourage happy and free forms of development activity (Noren–Björn, 1977, p. 50).

References

Ahlin, J. and F. Krimgold. 1975. 'A planning process for industry', in Landestrom (ed.), *Part '74*. Stockholm: SIR, pp. 65–77.
Bladen, V. W. 1974. *From Adam Smith to Maynard Keynes*. Toronto: University of Toronto Press.
Coates, F. D. 1976. 'Human factors and the consumer: the aesthetic factor', *Ergonomics*, 19, p. 1.
Grosby, T. 1973. *How to Play the Environment Game*. London: Arts Council of Great Britain and Penguin.
Gutes Spielzeug: Kleines Handbuch für richtige Wahl. 1964. Ravensburg: Otto Maier Verlag.
Hayrynen, L. 1979. 'Sociological criteria', in Y. Sotamaa, J. Salovaara, K. H. Otto and K. Schmidt (eds), *Playthings for Play*. Berlin: AIF.
Insulander, E. 1977. 'Trust and security – co-operation and responsibility, social planning for children', in Y. Sotamaa and J. Salovaara (eds), *Criteria on Children's Playthings and Playgrounds*. Helsinki: Ornamo.
Kagan, M. 1974. *Aesthetik*. Berlin: Dietz Verlag.
Koch, J. 1977. 'Die Bedeutung des Spielzeuge für die Motousche und Psychische Entwicklung des Säuglings', in Sotamaa and Solavaara, *op. cit.*
van den Kooig, R. and R. Groot. 1977. *That's All in the Game*. Rheinstetten: Schindele Verlag.
Laukka, M. 1979. 'Pedagogical quality criteria', in Y. Sotamaa *et al., op. cit.*
Laurila, K. S. 1918. *Estetiikan peruskysymyksia*. Porvoo: WSOY.
Lehto, M. 1978. *Kuluttajapolitiikka ja muotoilu*. Helsinki: Ornamo.
Niiranen, P. 1979. 'Psychological criteria', in Y. Sotamaa *et al., op. cit.*
Noren-Björn, E. 1977. *Lek, lekplatser, lekredskap*. Stockholm: Liber Forlag.
Pallasmaa, J. 1977. *Suunnittelun ihmiskuva*. Hyvän huonekalun päivät. Helsinki: unpublished paper.
Pracht, E., M. Franz, K. Hirdina and G. Mayer (eds) 1978. *Ästhetik heute*. Berlin: Dietz Verlag.
Routila, L. 1972. 'Taide, Bieli ja taiteen kiali', in *Estetiikan kenttä*. Porvoo: WSOY.
Ruusuvuori, A. 1979. 'Arkkitentiniri tulea taas', *Helsingen Sanomat*, 11, p. 2.
Saarinen, E. 1948. *Search for Form*. Port Washington: Kennikat Press.
Salovaara, J. 1979. 'Material criteria', in Y. Sotamaa *et al., op. cit.*
Sotamaa, Y. 1978. *Muotoilu ja tuotesuunnittelun nuuttuvat vaatimukset*. Helsinki: Elinkeinahallitus.
———. 1979. 'Playthings in the Finnish consumption, trade and industry', in Y. Sotamaa *et al., op. cit.*
———, and J. Salovaara (eds). 1977. *Criteria on Children's Playthings and Playgrounds*. Helsinki: Ornamo.
———, J. Salovaara, K. H. Otto and T. Schmidt (eds). 1979. *Playthings for Play*. Berlin: AIF.
Stirling, J. 1978. 'Rakennuksella tulee olla ishteys ikmiseen'. Interview in *Suomen Kuvalehti*, April Helsinki.
Strφmmes, F. 1978. 'Asuinympäristössamme pitää olla ärsykkeitä', *Helsingin Sanomat*, 22 December.
Virtanen, L. 1970. *Antii pantti pakana*. Porvoo: WSOY.
Teollinen muotoilu. 1972. Helsinki: Sitra.

20 TOY LIBRARIES

Colin Pryor

Introduction

The growth of the toy library concept, with its emphasis on play and
parent participation, may be seen as the product of a particular
combination of academic, economic and sociological circumstances. Of
central importance has been the rapid expansion of research effort in
the area of children's play since the late sixties. A significant factor in
such investigations has been the application of ethological principles to
the study of parent—child interaction; such investigation (Schaffer,
1971) has produced much evidence as to the primary importance of play
in children's development. Importantly, and for the first time, it has
been recognized that parent and child appear to engage in a dialogue.
The parts they play are complementary but independent; and
negotiation in the main part takes the form of play. Play, then, has come
to be recognized as the vehicle whereby the meaning of the world is
passed to the child. It is also the vehicle whereby the child assimilates
and makes the world his/her own. As such, the importance of play has
been underlined by recent research efforts.

Academic legitimization of play, however, would not have been
sufficient in itself to promote the growth of play centres or toy
libraries. Two other factors coalesced with the research efforts of
psychologists and ethologists; the first was economic necessity. Forced
by the beginnings of economic restraint in the late 1960s, service
agencies looked toward more cost-efficient service delivery systems.
Parents were identified as therapists, and subsequently elevated to
assume increasing responsibility for the treatment of their child. The
recognition and use of parents as primary rather than secondary
therapists was particularly evident in behaviour management programmes.
Numerous research efforts showed that parents could be used as
therapists for their child. Underlying such studies was the fact that
agencies for reasons of necessity had to use parents as an easily
accessible and free source of manpower. The power and importance of
parents was thus realized.

The second factor, which in part grew from economic roots, was the
popularization and attempted demystification of psychology. Parents —
so long denied knowledge of what tests and curricula meant by obscure

274

language and jargon — began to press for more realistic and understandable services. They found allies in the academic world. Such writers as Eysenck, Lang and Skinner were gaining popular as well as academic recognition. In response, the service establishment sought to encourage and realize practical and more easily understandable service concepts. The supply of toys, and the use of these toys, as a base for explaining developmental concepts, had obvious appeal. Toys could be the tool with which the parent and therapist communicated, as well as the tool for the child's play.

In summary, toy libraries grew from an increasing awareness of the importance both of play and of parents. They grew from economic pressures to supply service with fewer resources, and from a movement to realize more practical and more understandable service concepts. To speculate as to the roots of the toy library movement is not, of course, to deny its validity or value. The pressure to supply service has increased, not decreased, and continuing investigation into the nature of developmental growth continues to point to the playful nature of learning. In this paper, therefore, the attempt will be made to isolate some of the practical functions which toy libraries may serve within a community and to explore some ways in which the toy library concept may unfold.

The Functions of Toy Libraries

While no one model may be proposed as uniform for toy libraries, the libraries with which the author has been involved have served the following primary and secondary functions. Primary functions have included:

1. allowing handicapped, emotionally disturbed, and normal children access to the enormous range of toys and equipment currently available on the market, and matching equipment to children's special needs;

2. seeking to help parents become more critical in their choice of playthings and promoting the understanding that play activities appropriate to their child's handicap can serve a developmental function (development to be interpreted as emotional or cognitive);

3. offering an informal meeting place within the community where parents can meet and gain support from other parents with similar problems;

4. making parents aware of the spectrum of services available in the community and, further, facilitating contact between parents and professionals;

5. lending toys to low-income families in which the purchase of suitable toys is impossible.

Secondary functions have included:

1. disseminating information about play, toys, and handicaps to other provincial agencies and parents in the form of audio tapes, slide packages, booklets, information sheets and video packs;
2. acting as a centre for social events for handicapped children and other children;
3. encouraging meetings between parents and those with expertise in specific areas related to child welfare and development;
4. offering resources for assessment to professionals in the community;
5. supplying toy manufacturers with information as to their products' usefulness and safety.

How a Toy Library Operates

In describing the operation of a toy library, it should again be stressed that no one pattern exists. What is described below is based on the operation of two toy libraries; one in Metropolitan Toronto and the other in Sudbury, Ontario. Families are usually seen every three to four weeks. Referrals to the library are usually self-referrals, although in some cases general practitioners have advised parents to join the library. To encourage membership, literature is disseminated in the community both individually through parents and professionals and through libraries, television shows and public service facilities. In the information pamphlets, the aims of the library are described with a clear outline of opening times and registration procedure. There is a small charge of two dollars to join the library; it is stressed there is no charge for loss or damage of toys, although membership may be withdrawn if there is sustained loss or damage. It should be noted that loss rates of toys to this time have been less than many book-lending facilities, running at approximately 6 per cent. Normal breakage of toys accounts for another 20–25 per cent of the toys in any one year.

Funding for the toy libraries cited above has come from both government and volunteer sources, although many libraries operate completely on voluntary contributions. It would appear that the concept is one which is 'visible' to funding agencies who can see tangible results from their contributions. A further avenue for funding has been toy manufacturers who give discounts and, in some cases, toys for testing in the library situation. The Surrey Place Library in Toronto cost $1,900 over two years, with a membership on average of seventy families. The Sudbury Library served some thirty families in its first year of operation and cost $900. The formula used for toy budgeting was as follows: if each family borrowed three toys at the cost of $5.50 per toy, the cost per family would be $16.50. Only three toys per family would not leave parents much choice when borrowing toys. In order that there be an adequate range of toys for families to choose from, the number of toys to be purchased was doubled. Thus the total estimated cost per family was $33.00.

Cost for storage space will, of course, vary from situation to situation. Some means of screening the child from exposure to all the toys should be found, however, as exposure to two or three hundred toys is for many children a profoundly disturbing experience!

How to Administer a Toy Library

Toy library administration includes the following activities:

1. An inventory is made of all the toys in the library, recording date of purchase, cost, place of purchase and name of the manufacturers.

2. A record is kept of the number of times a toy is loaned; the file records the parent's or the child's comment on the toy.

3. An intake file is made up containing information about each child's physical condition, e.g., sight, use of limbs, etc., and developmental ability.

4. Parents are required to sign a disclaimer freeing the library from legal responsibility for toys on loan. Parents also receive a copy of the library's conditions of membership.

5. Records are kept of parental visits to include advice given to parents, goals set and toys loaned. These notes enable continuity to be maintained both across different libraries and between sessions.

6. Receipts for all equipment, supplies and services are noted, and an ongoing balance sheet of the toy library's finances is maintained.

7. An information file relating to toy library events, manufacturers, toy shops, service agencies, etc., is maintained and made available to parents. A display board is useful in this respect.

8. Clear procedural guidelines for booking in the return of toys and their cleaning are essential. In terms of cleaning, the Surrey Place Library uses a phenolic germicide either sprayed or administered with a cloth.

9. A policy should be established with respect to buying toys. One

strategy is to buy toys in response to the requirements of the individual children attending the library. Counsellors seeing children should fill out requests for toys, giving the name of the toy and its approximate price. Separate requests may then be combined to make up a bulk purchase. When starting the library, it is inefficient — and in all probability disastrous — to buy a large number of toys without knowledge of the children who will use them.

Toy Library Play Sessions

The form which a session may take is left to the parents, who may wish to be seen individually or with another family. All sessions last for approximately one hour. During the session, the child is observed at play with the therapist and with the parents. Among other forms of analysis, a system analysis may be applied to realize information based on the input, output and feedback pattern observed in the interaction between parent and child (simple guidelines for this method of assessment have been developed (Pryor *et al.*, 1978)). The amount of advice offered to parents, both with respect to their interaction pattern and to their toy use, is variable. Some parents initially do not want advice and use the centre only as a source for good toys. This position is always accepted and no pressure is put on parents to accept advice. During sessions, toys are also chosen for non-handicapped siblings and they, too, may be observed at play, both with their parents and with the therapist.

In summary, sessions have three common goals:

1. Parents are encouraged to explore their child's interaction pattern with themselves and his/her developmental abilities in finer detail. Simply, they are encouraged to sensitize themselves to those aspects of their child's behaviour which may not previously have seemed important.
2. Parents are encouraged to think sideways about toys, to step beyond their obvious use and explore what a particular toy can do for their child.
3. The importance of play is stressed, particularly the importance of parents as play therapists.

There seem to be two aspects to the above goal: parents are in a unique position to potentiate their child's environment for meaningful and productive play, and to become involved with the child as a serious and sensitive other player.

Who Can Run a Toy Library?

In Great Britain, where the concept originated, there are over 500 toy libraries. The great majority of these are run by parents and professionals on a volunteer basis. The training and background of those who run the library may be expected to influence the services offered. The author's own experience suggests that it is advisable to include on the staff someone with training in developmental psychology or a related field. This person may serve as a consultant or counsellor within the library system. It would seem essential that all voluntary staff used within the library should undergo some form of orientation to the administration of toy libraries, and to the concept of play as a tool for developmental growth. In some instances, systems for the realization of developmental goals may be used as an integral part of play sessions. If training is not offered, there is a danger that in the eyes of the volunteers the lending function of the library may become the only reason for its existence. It cannot be over-emphasized that the purpose of the toy libraries is not only to lend toys, but also to use them as a means of teaching and promoting parental awareness of developmental issues.

Toys are a vehicle to involve parents, not an end in themselves. As such, staff should be aware of current theories concerning development and play, and should further be able to communicate these theories to parents. Put simply, toys provide both a source for debate (we have all played and feel able to comment) and a means to communicate (explaining the function of a mobile and its possible uses crosses what for most people is the formidable word concept barrier of professional jargon).

Future Trends

To this time, the majority of toy libraries both in North America and in Europe have been low-budget voluntary organizations. As such, they have often fallen on the periphery of service provision, to be encouraged for the reasons stated in the introduction, but not absorbed into the main body of service delivery.

It may be expected that toy libraries will gain in importance as their value in involving and attracting parents is recognized. For example, increasing evidence points to the lack of parenting skills as a primary cause of child abuse, yet the very parents who abuse their children are often the least likely to attend parent skill classes or formal programmes.

Toy libraries might fill this gap; their informality and the prospect of easing the family budget by borrowing toys may reach parents who would previously not have become involved in service provision.

As non-threatening information centres and as referral agents, toy libraries could become the first step in a family use of other children's services.

In addition to their value in helping parents enter the service system, toy libraries with their emphasis on play may be expected to encourage new forms of assessment practice based on ethological procedures. To observe children at play is essentially an unstructured activity. The child is not presented with a task to be solved as in normal psychometric practice but rather the product of his own free association with his play materials or parents is observed. The movement to observation from more prescriptive techniques of the 'do this' variety is important and may be expected radically to affect the nature of children's assessments. Toy libraries, then, are based on notions of assessment which are not traditional, and as such they may be expected to result in the realization of new observational assessment procedures.

With the increasing placement of handicapped children and adults within the community, toy libraries are well placed to act as centres for integration. Toys and the provision of a pleasant informal environment may be important factors in drawing handicapped and normal children together. Parents who might otherwise avoid bringing their normal children into a play situation with a handicapped child may, under their own child's pressure for access to the toys in the library, involve themselves in the library activities. This is clearly a crucial first step. Toy libraries can be expected to assume a 'honey-pot' role, attracting and holding children and families who might otherwise avoid contact with the handicapped.

Within a future of economic restraint, it would appear the borrowing of toys for many families may become an attractive alternative to toy ownership. The relationship of toy libraries to toy manufacturers may change and it would seem likely that commercial profit-making toy libraries will appear with fixed membership costs and a guaranteed selection of toys. Parents might join such libraries perhaps on a yearly basis, either paying a lump membership fee or a set cost per toy; further services offered by the libraries could include play assessments and ongoing play counselling. Toy libraries may, therefore, become an alternative way for manufacturers to promote and sell their products.

In summary, toy libraries are well suited to serve an important function in the community. They are an attractive and non-intimidating place for parents to meet and as such they serve the purpose of encouraging parents to use other more traditional services.

In addition, by lending toys to both normal and handicapped children, toy libraries promote the integration of the normal child with his handicapped peers; such integration is of increasing importance with the return of the handicapped child to community settings. It would seem, therefore, that while economic and academic factors have played a significant role in the success of the toy library idea, the concept itself has real merit, both from the developmental perspective and with respect to parent/child appeal.

We all play, and as such feel comfortable with a service where play is the basic medium of interaction and exchange.

References

Pryor, C., W. Filipowich and M. Sevink. 1978. 'Play interaction differences between normal child/mother and retarded child/mother dyads'. Paper presented at the Seventh World Congress, International Playground Association, Ottawa.

Schaffer, H. R. 1971. *The Growth of Sociability*. London: Penguin.

21 FITNESS AND PLAY

Peggy Brown

Introduction

Does children's play promote growth and fitness development? What
is physical fitness and why should children be fit? How can parents,
educators, play leaders and concerned individuals enhance children's
vigorous play experiences? The following paper discusses these questions
and examines some current attitudes toward fitness play (physical
activity).

The Need for Fitness

Few would question the right and need of children for vigorous play.
Children's lives are filled with spontaneous, joyful movement; they
respond totally to their world with their heads, hearts and bodies. Most
people feel that the child's need for exercise is met by his/her natural
play instincts. Recent research, however, in several countries would
indicate the opposite: many children are 'growing up old' (Sarner, 1978)
with poor levels of physical fitness and limited capacities for both
physical work and vigorous play. Many parents, educators and play
leaders are concerned. Does children's play promote growth and fitness
development? How fit should children be? What are the implications
for their future?

In days gone by, adults and children toiled in physical labour: they
worked and played hard. Today, automation and mechanization reduce
the amount of physical activity in an individual's life. Post-industrial
society is characterized by emotional stress, poor eating habits and the
overuse and abuse of cigarettes, drugs and alcohol. Most people's lives
are sedentary: driving instead of walking, watching instead of
participating. The consequences include an increasing incidence of
psychological distress, obesity, fatigue, heart disease and other
degenerative ailments. Health care costs are staggering. For example, in
Canada, total health costs have increased from $2 billion in 1960 to over
$7 billion in 1978. An unknown — but large — proportion of this
amount can be attributed to the life-style described above.

Similarly, many children have adopted inactive life-styles. Children's
natural play spaces have become city slums and the population explosion
has reduced available space for play areas. Opportunities for physical

activity have been reduced: many children are bussed to school; the average Canadian child today spends 26 to 30 hours a week motionless in front of a television set; spontaneous vigorous play has been replaced by organized sports leagues where more time is spent on the sidelines than playing; and physical education and outdoor recreation programmes are given low priority in times of budget restraint. The results are alarming: children who are unable to complete four simple fitness measures, an increase in postural defects and obesity, and an increased use of medication for emotional problems.

The effects of deprivation of the opportunity for natural activity in programmes with disadvantaged children are even greater. It has been observed that for the slow learner, the under-achiever and the child from the inner city and crowded suburb, vigorous physical play is important not only for physiological growth and fitness, but for social and intellectual development.

As Piaget suggests, activity facilitates thinking, learning and emotional growth. Success in physical play builds confidence, independence and self-esteem.

Children also grow in social status with physical play. Studies show that those children who score high on physical/motor traits tend to be extroverted, sociable, dependable and tolerant, prone to be leaders and popular with their peers.

In today's society a child must be able to cope with stress, over-stimulation and mobility. With the exhilaration of effort comes knowledge of relaxation, release of tension and a sense of oneness with oneself and nature.

Children denied vigorous physical play miss out on the opportunity to reach their optimum potential and to succeed physically. The life-style pattern of inactivity is established; and as adults they will be more susceptible to health problems associated with sedentary living. Physical fitness is an integral part of children's total well-being. Fit children have the ability to carry out their daily tasks with vigour and still have ample energy left to play or to cope with frustration or emergencies.

Much of a child's development is due to inherent growth factors. Normal children follow a sequential orderly progression when learning movement patterns. Growth and progress, however, are subject to environmental influences which can impede or help children obtain the upper limits of their mental or physical potential. The development and maintenance of physical fitness depends on health status, nutritional status and the amount of physical activity. Prolonged, vigorous physical activity — a prime aspect of play — is the vehicle for developing physical fitness.

Individuals who work with children need more than a knowledge of developmental psychology and motor patterns. If effective play experiences are to be designed, they must also understand physical fitness and the effects of training on fitness development.

The Dynamics of Fitness

Physical fitness is perhaps better understood by looking at its basic components. Each of these components is greatly influenced by physical activity.

Strength

Strength refers to the maximum force a muscle or group of muscles can exert against a resistance; e.g., the ability to lift a certain weight, once. Four factors affect muscle strength in maturing children: increased size, maturation (one extra year can usually improve strength 5–10 per cent), the development of sexual maturity, and the amount of use the muscles have. Bailey (1972) showed that there is little difference in strength development between young boys and girls when weight is held constant. With the onset of puberty, however, boys normally develop added strength. Another study of Canadian girls aged 13–14, who were in fact competitive swimmers, showed that they were unable to pull their own weight off the floor, i.e., do one chin-up. This lack of strength becomes a major obstacle in learning some sports skills. For example, young skiers become quickly frustrated if they are unable to lift themselves up after a fall.

Muscular Endurance

Muscular endurance refers to the ability of a muscle group to perform repeated contractions against a lighter resistance; e.g., the ability to perform repeated sit-ups is a measure of muscular endurance in the abdominal area. In the 1950s and 1960s, the Kraus–Weber minimal test of fitness administered in the United States showed that 50 per cent of the children failed to complete the four test items. One of these test items was the ability to perform a single sit-up. These same researchers have determined that 80 per cent of the low back pain suffered by American adults today is due to poor abdominal muscular development and a lack of physical activity.

Children must develop adequate muscular strength and endurance to ensure good health and correct posture. The minimal level entails the ability to lift one's own weight by climbing 2 to 3 metres up a rope. When muscles are not used, they become flabby and weak and atrophy in size. Muscular strength and endurance are developed by play which involves resistance: resistance of body weight or parts (chinning, calisthenics, climbing, push-ups, rope climbing, parallel bars), resistance of another (wrestling, tug of war), resistance of inanimate objects (carrying, pulling, pushing). There should be no fear of developing muscle-boundness. This type of activity changes the shape of the muscle, enhancing strength, speed of movement and appearance. Active children have firmer and stronger muscles and less adipose tissue. Hence, they are more likely to succeed in sport and motor skills.

Flexibility

The third component of fitness, flexibility, is a measure of the range of motion in the joints. It is an important factor in determining how well a child can move and perform activities without injury. The ability to touch one's toes is an example of a simple measure of flexibility. Typically, young children perform well on flexibility tests, with a marked difference in favour of girls, a difference which increases with age. This flexibility, however, is quickly lost with advancing age and an inactive life-style.

Play activities which enhance flexibility include stretching, bending, twisting, dance, creative movement and gymnastics.

Cardio-respiratory Endurance

Cardio-respiratory endurance, considered to be the best index of overall physical condition, refers to the operating efficiency of the heart, blood vessels and lungs, and the ability of the entire body to continue activity for prolonged periods. A run of some distance is an example of cardio-respiratory endurance. Cardio-respiratory endurance can be assessed by an exercise stress test which determines aerobic power, that is, the ability to get oxygen to the working muscles. This vital process determines a child's level of stamina and general level of energy or fatigue.

Since the measure of aerobic power is a measure of the ability of the body to move and do work, aerobic power normally is expressed per kilogram of body weight. When expressed this way, Bailey's (1972) longitudinal study of children in Saskatchewan, Canada, showed no consistent increase in aerobic power with age, but a levelling off at a young age and a decline in the teenage years. He therefore concluded that

For the ordinary Canadian child (not athlete), physical fitness as expressed by aerobic power seems to be a decreasing function of age from the time our children get behind a desk in schools. (Bailey, 1972, p. 17)

Goode (1976) studied students in a Canadian junior high school from November to February and showed that the students' aerobic power declined over those four months. He stated: 'Surely this is the only subject area in which a decrease in capacity occurs as a child goes through school.' Observations on American children produce similar results.

It should not be expected that children have the aerobic power to handle their weight as compared to adults. They have less power reserve, lower biomechanical efficiency and a lower haemoglobin concentration than adults; in addition, the pre-puberty growth spurt of young males may account for a temporary decline in aerobic power.

Studies in Sweden and Norway show a slight increase in aerobic power over the same age group (Astrand, 1975). One should be cautious of a comparison, as these studies are cross-sectional in nature and subjects are not randomly selected. Hermansen and Oseid (1970), however, in a 3-year longitudinal study on 20 Oslo boys, showed increasing values in aerobic power. Despite the problems of international comparisons, it does appear clear that in countries where physical activity has high priority and is organized for all students both during and after school, the fitness of their children is impressive.

Typically, boys score higher than girls in measures of aerobic capacity. This is due to several factors: the hormonal influence and body weight gain, the development of additional adipose tissue in girls, and social pressures which dictate that as a girl gets older it becomes unfeminine to perspire or take part in vigorous activity.

Vigorous play experiences improve the efficiency of the heart, lungs and blood vessels and effectively increase a child's energy level. Any large muscle activity which causes the heart to beat faster improves cardio-respiratory fitness, e.g., running, cycling, tag games, dancing, skating, skiing, swimming, water-polo, rugger, European handball, skipping, soccer.

The key to cardio-respiratory development is the quality of the exercise. The movement must be sufficiently intense to elevate the heart rate to at least 150 beats a minute to be maintained for 15 to 30 minutes. In a study of a typical basketball gym period, a student's pulse was found to be over 150 for only 1 to 2 minutes. The rest of the time was spent standing around, changing, or lining up in squads.

The Implications for Fitness Programming

The implication for teachers and play leaders is clear. Free play and movement education *is* important, but guided play and a planned programme to increase a child's physical fitness is essential. Children need to develop sport skills in carry-over activities (such as swimming, skating, cross-country skiing, badminton and tennis) that will increase their fitness as children and prepare them for active enjoyable recreation pursuits as adults. A guided play period or physical education class should always involve 10 to 15 minutes to vigorous movement for all involved.

It is important to recognize that levels of exercise affect each child differently. The principle of individual difference applies in fitness development and should be respected. Children should be allowed to move at their own rates and experience physical success as they progress.

Various studies have shown that regular physical activity improves all aspects of fitness — muscular strength and endurance, flexibility and cardio-respiratory endurance. It is also important for body structure, specifically bone growth and the maintenance of proper body weight. Excess weight is a problem for over half the adult Canadian population (Nutrition Canada, 1973) and is a growing concern for children in industrialized countries.

Mayer (1977), in his studies of the Boston area, has shown that the proportion of obese children has grown in the last 20 years from 12 per cent to 20 per cent. More importantly, he has shown that overweight youngsters normally do not eat more than normal-weight children, but that they exercise less.

Daily activity is essential to balance caloric intake and output. Obese children tend not to join in vigorous play and they need constant encouragement to participate. The tendency to put on additional weight increases over the winter months when they have less opportunity for vigorous outdoor play. Fat children suffer from poor self-concept and from discrimination among their peers. They normally grow into fat adults and, as such, are susceptible to the many health problems and shortened life span associated with obesity.

With nutrition and behaviour counselling, and participation in non-competitive, enjoyable play activities, obese children can learn to become thin. The involvement of parents in the process is essential. By adopting an active life-style, characterized by good nutritional habits, the entire family grows healthier and happier.

Regular physical activity is essential for the development of physical fitness. Motor development and performance-related functions are also important for the growing child. Power, agility, speed, co-ordination, balance, and gross-motor and fine-motor movements develop largely as a result of maturation and practice. It is not enough to say that children will develop on their own if protection is simply provided. The child needs an environment based on the opportunity for exploration, manipulation and guided physical play.

When Dr Thomas Tutko (Sheehan, 1975, p. 13), a sport psychologist, was asked by a fitness leader which sport a student should be in, he replied 'Just ask him. Have him rate all the activities and choose the one he likes best.' The fitness leader was surprised: 'Shouldn't we test for suitability, measure the child's body type, strength and flexibility? How can he rate a sport he's never experienced?' The point is that he cannot. He must experience it to find an activity he can enjoy for a lifetime. Young children learn to jump by jumping; they learn motor and sport skills by having the opportunity to practise them. At the same time they acquire an understanding of movement and a love of vigorous activity which they can carry into their adult life.

Some children today are beginning strenuous physical training at a very young age. Many wonder if this will have negative effects on a growing child. Eriksson (1971) and Astrand (1963) conducted detailed studies on top female swimmers aged 12 to 16 who had been training for several years, some of them 28 hours a week. A complete evaluation of their physical and mental health revealed the following. The girls had increased aerobic power and increased dimensions of heart volume, blood volume and vital capacity. They showed advanced growth, good or superior intelligence; they were extroverted and energetic. It is interesting that their families were found to be close and actively involved in sport and physical recreation. The researchers wondered about their future; therefore, ten years after the girls had stopped training and were busy with careers and motherhood, they were re-evaluated. Although their aerobic power was drastically lowered due to a lack of activity, the larger than normal dimensions of the heart and lungs remained unchanged. Several of them volunteered to recommence training and showed a quick return to their previous high aerobic power.

These findings indicate another interesting hypothesis: does a lack of excess of strenuous exercise during the growing years affect the ultimate adult complement of cells and hence the functional capacity to perform as adults? This study and other studies would seem to back this hypothesis, although more work is needed in this area. One might argue that the swimmers had superior heart and lung capacity by natural endowment which contributed to their success as swimmers. Other studies by Eckblom and Saltin seem to indicate that fitness pursued in youth improves adult capacity (Bailey, 1972). There are still questions to be answered, but it is known that a certain amount of exercise is important for normal growth and probably for future capacity.

Attitudes to Physical Play

From the young child's point of view, movement means freedom, discovery, safety, a means of communication, enjoyment, sensual pleasure. Vigorous play is an absorbing and enjoyable activity in its own right.

What happens? Many children and adults begin to look upon physical activity with displeasure. Negative attitudes toward fitness play are a social, historical and personal phenomenon. Some examples of these negative attitudes are as follows:

1. 'Fitness demands a conformance to elite athletic standards.'

Every child, whether a natural athlete, or disabled, has a need and right to reach his or her optimum physical potential. Play experiences should stress maximum participation, a recognition of individual differences and reinforcement of individual successes. Children need to understand basic physiology and fitness principles, and to develop confidence in their bodies.

2. 'Fitness requires a "train through pain" attitude. Physical activity is only important as a means to an end.'

Accepting vigorous play as fun for itself could be the most significant factor in positively influencing fitness development. The autocratic, formal, militaristic approach to physical play experiences evokes automatic, frightened responses. Adults need to re-assess their attitudes toward work and play and to provide leadership which accepts physical play as children do. They must re-learn to accept the legitimacy of physical play and to drop their inhibitions about running, jumping, perspiring, or rolling down hills.

The separation of mind from body and work from play is a philosophical tradition, a typical value of western civilization. Sheehan (1975, pp. 33–4), cardiologist and running guru, expresses a new philosophy:

Play is the priceless ingredient in any successful fitness program. Play is not just fun and pleasure. It has to do with human need. Fitness is something that has purpose but no meaning. Play is something that has meaning but no purpose; fitness is a bonus in play, and people are finally learning how to play.

3. 'Winning isn't everything, it's the only thing.'
This quotation, attributed to American football coach Vince Lombardi, often typifies the adult attitude in sport. Too often children are seen as mini-adults. Adults organize and control their games into competitive structures and teach them that the value of sport lies in winning. Adults forget that the child is there to participate and have fun; that involvement is reward enough.

A seven-year-old baseball and hockey drop-out expressed it this way (Orlick, 1976, p. 23):

Q. Why did you stop playing hockey?
A. I started not to like it. I quit because I never got to play. All I did was sit around. I was always at the end of the line in hockey and baseball.

Orlick (1976), in *Every Kid Can Win*, recommends a change in emphasis in children's sport. Based on extensive interviews with children, he clearly shows that children are afraid to participate in competitive sport due to the fear of personal failure and the stress of winning. His novel co-operatives games, in which all children must co-operate to succeed, are extremely popular with children and build positive behaviours. With proper guidance, children develop the 'we' of team sports and learn that everyone has something to contribute.

4. 'Girls are too delicate.'
Despite women's liberation, many females grow up learning that perspiration and vigorous play is unsuitable for women. Girls still encounter discrimination in sport. In a recent highly publicized case in New Jersey, Marie Pepe filed a legal suit when she was refused a position on the Little League Team. When the court demanded that she be allowed to play, a furor of resignations resulted. The male Little League Officers even voted to suspend all play in the whole state if the decision was carried out.

Young girls are the mothers of tomorrow and their attitudes greatly influence their families. Bailey (1972), in his study of the fitness of

Canadians, has shown that the poorest level of fitness in Canada exists among females in their teens and 20s. The (Canada) Royal Commission of the Status of Women has recommended that girls be provided equal opportunities with boys to engage in athletics and sports activities.

Orlick (1976) has pointed out that mothers are extremely sensitive to the needs of children in sport. Women need to take more of a leadership role in sport for children and to participate in vigorous play for their own sakes and that of their children.

Establishing Priorities for Physical Play

Physical Play as a Priority in the Schools

Children spend a large part of each day in school, where good facilities and strong leadership are available. The school, then, should be the prime setting for providing positive physical experiences. Instead, in many countries, physical play is given the lowest priority in terms of scheduling, professional preparation and emphasis. A comparative overview of the amount of time allotted to physical education in various countries shows that Canada is far behind other countries; for example, Denmark allots twice as much curriculum time to physical education and East Germany three times as much. Anything less than daily physical activity fails to understand the total child and is not in keeping with a recommendation of the UNESCO Council: 'An individual, whatever his role in society, needs in his growing years a balance of intellectual, physical, moral and aesthetic development which must be reflected in the educational curriculum' (International Council of Sport and Physical Education, 1964).

In Vanves, on the outskirts of Paris, an attempt was made to provide that balance. A one-third approach was initiated: the students had 4 hours of academic work in the morning, while the afternoon was devoted to physical activity, art, music and independent study. One to two hours a day were spent in physical activity. Initially, the parents were worried that their children would slip academically or become sick as a result of spending so much time out-of-doors at sport. Ten years later, in 1961, the programme was evaluated. The health, fitness, discipline and general enthusiasm of students were all greatly improved and their academic performance often surpassed children in conventional programmes (McKenzie, 1974).

It is the responsibility of voters, parents and educators to establish the priority of physical education in the schools. Beyond this, teachers and curriculum designers must understand the child's need for play. Most people can report a school experience where gym or recess were cancelled because they interfered with the 'work' of reading, writing and arithmetic. Children need to learn sports skills — not to win glory for their school, but to be better equipped to play. Fun should be brought back into the physical education curriculum.

During the early years, young people acquire the motivation, understanding, skills and attitudes necessary for effective adult living. Recreation skills should be provided in lifetime sports and fitness play (skiing, skating, etc.).

Every physical education and health class should further a child's fitness development and knowledge of himself. Each child should be given the chance to succeed physically and to understand that physical play is essential, important and fun.

Physical Play as a Priority in the Community

To provide effective fitness opportunities for all requires time, money and political pressure. In recent years, organized groups such as the International Playground Association have effected great changes in play spaces for children. Traditional sterile playgrounds have been replaced by structures which challenge a child's creativity while developing fitness and motor skills. There is still, however, much to do in facility development. For example, why do many school gymnasiums, pools and rinks remain locked and unused outside of school hours? Why are fitness trials allowed to be built with apparatus that is too high or unwieldy for a child to use? The city of Ottawa, Canada, has shown what can be done to provide fitness and recreational opportunities for the whole family. Simply closing a parkway to automobile traffic on Sunday encourages thousands to cycle; flooding and cleaning a downtown canal allows many more to be active.

More important than facility development is the training of play leaders in the community. A recent report from London, England, concludes that 'Skilled leadership is vital and the (adventure) playgrounds flourish most where parental and local community interest and involvement are high' (Inner London Education Authority, 1978, p. 9).

In many European countries children have ready access to recreational clubs, competent leadership and coaching. The following examples are from Sweden:

640 boys between the ages of 7 and 12 are members of the Västeras Wrestling Club, and train for a couple of hours once or twice a week in the Sports Hall, or in one of the gymnasiums at the various local

youth clubs. Thirty per cent of these boys are from immigrant families. Västeras is an industrial town, and a large number of Finns, Italians, Yugoslavs and Greeks work there. Eine Ranta is mother to two of these young wrestlers, Petri and Risto. The family comes from Finland.

'Wrestling means holding each other, touching each other. The boys establish contact without words. When they wrestle, it doesn't matter that they speak different languages, they have a physical contact, which breaks their isolation. I think this means a great deal to our immigrant boys.'

The latest development is that a group of Västeras girls have asked to join. . . .

It all started five years ago on 'Ockero', a municipal area in Stockholm, where the teen-agers got together in two evening groups and danced. It spread to the school-children, and by 1973 there were four folk-dancing groups for 7 to 12 year olds. The adults thought the children were having such fun at their meetings that they also started to dance. A cautious start was made with courses in old-time dancing on four islands. Now they have a society, with a full four hundred members.

But you can't go dancing every evening, so the children have the further alternatives of gymnastics, volleyball, handicrafts, radio, jazz, gymnastics, drama, swimming and table tennis. (Arlemalm, 1975, p. 66)

Physical Play as a Priority at Home

The environment of vigorous physical activity is conducive to a healthy life-style. A family that spends its Saturdays out cross-country skiing and weekends camping is not exposed to the negative attributes of sedentary living. Parents must be aware of a child's need for vigorous activity and share that enjoyable activity when possible.

Conclusion

Children model the attitudes and actions of parents, teachers and other significant adults in their lives. It is not enough to provide positive fitness play experiences for children. Adult attitudes are communicated by what adults do in their own life-styles. A sedentary adult who smokes and overeats projects these values. A life-style involving active fitness and recreational pursuits is full of fun, exhilaration, relaxation and play. Eric Nesterenko, a former Canadian hockey star, describes the joys of physical activity:

> I still like to skate. One day last year on a cold, clear crisp afternoon, I saw this sheet of ice in the street. Goddam, if I didn't drive out there and put on my skates. I took off my camel hair coat, I was just in a suit jacket, on my skates. And I flew. Nobody was there, I was free as a bird. I was really happy. That goes back to when I was a kid. I'll do that until I die, I hope. Oh! I was free. (Kidd, 1978, p. 386)

The young child has an instinctive need for physical activity. Exercise gives instant and exhilarating effects — a natural legal high. The child plays because it is fun; the child seeks out physical activity for its own intrinsic pleasures.

As leaders of children, it is the responsibility of adults to help the child understand those values and to provide guidance and opportunities for physical activity: for the sake of fitness development, growth and play.

As individuals, adults must learn to share those values and an active life-style: for the sake of our own fitness, health and enjoyment of play.

References

Arlemalm, I. 1975. 'Free time activities for children aged 7 to 12', *Current Sweden*, 66.

Association for Childhood Education International. 1968. *Physical Education for Children's Healthful Living*. Washington DC: Association for Childhood Education International.

Astrand, Per-Olaf, I. Engström, B. O. Eriksson *et. al.* 1963. 'Girl Swimmers'. *Acta Paediat. Scand.* Suppl. 147.

———. 1975. *The Child in Sport and Physical Activity*. Stockholm.

———. 1975. *Health and Fitness*. Ottawa: Fitness and Amateur Sport Branch, Health and Welfare Canada.

Bailey, Donald. 1972. *The Saskatchewan Child Growth and Development Study Report No. 9*. Saskatoon, Canada: The University of Saskatchewan.

———. 1972. 'Exercise, fitness and physical education for the growing child', *Proceedings of the National Conference on Fitness and Health*. Ottawa: Health and Welfare Canada.

———, R. Shepherd, R. Mirwald and G. McBride. 1973. 'A current view of cardiorespiratory fitness levels of Canadians', *Canadian Medical Association Journal*, III, July, pp. 25–30.

Brower, Jonathon. 1978. 'Children's play should be returned to children', *Arena Review*, 1, 1, pp. 27–9.

Canadian Association for Health, Physical Education and Recreation (CAHPER). 1976. *New Perspectives for Elementary School Physical Education Programs in Canada*. Ottawa, Canada: CAHPER.

Eriksson, B. O., I. Engström *et al.* 1971. 'A Physiological Analysis of Former Girl Swimmers.' *Acta Paediat. Scand.* Suppl. 217. 68.

Goode, Robert. 1976. 'The physical fitness of our school children', *Education Canada*, Winter, pp. 26–31.

Hermansen, L. and S. Oseid. 1970. 'Direct and indirect estimation of maximal oxygen uptake in pre-pubertal boys', *Acta Paedeat, Scand.* Supp., 217, p. 18.

Inner London Education Authority. 1978. 'From five to fourteen: a report on leisure-time needs', *Playtimes*, 6, pp. 8–9.

International Council of Sport and Physical Education. 1964. *Declaration on Sport*. Paris: UNESCO, Place de Fontenoy.

Kidd, Bruce. 1978. 'Intrinsic benefits of physical activity', *Ontario Fitness Leaders Manual*, I, pp. 1–32.

Kindl, M. and P. Brown. 1978. 'A program to treat childhood obesity', *Modern Medicine of Canada*, 33, 5, pp. 662–6.

McKenzie, J. 1974. 'One-third physical education', *CAHPER Journal Supp.*, 40, pp. 69–72.

Mayer, Jean. 1977. *A Diet for Living*. New York: Pocket Books.

Nutrition Canada. 1973. *Nutrition: A National Priority*. Ottawa: Health and Welfare Canada.

Orlick, Terry. 1976. *Every Kid Can Win*. Chicago: Nelson Hall.

President's Council on Physical Fitness and Sports. 1976. 'Physical fitness practices and programs for elementary and secondary schools', *Physical Fitness Research Digest*, 6, p. 4.

Sarner, Mark. 1978. 'Growing up old', *Canadian Weekend Magazine*, 3 June.

Sheehan, George. 1975. *On Running*. Mountainview, California: World Publications.

22 BEYOND COMPETITION: ORGANIZING PLAY ENVIRONMENTS FOR CO-OPERATIVE AND INDIVIDUALISTIC OUTCOMES

Peter K. Jensen and Harvey A. Scott

In Praise of Play

Play, as Huizinga (1950) has pointed out, is a cross-cultural universal, expressing in an almost unlimited variety of ways the primal biological urge to move, explore, discover, risk, test, master, create and — of paramount importance — have fun. At its very roots, it is free, spontaneous and creative. In its more structural forms, it becomes games, dance and other art forms. At its most institutionalized rule-bound form, it is sport. Play, however, is justifiably an authentic end, a way of being, in and of itself.

It is, however, useful to analyze play and the kinds of functions it serves for the individual, his community and the greater society. If play is so important, it is necessary that the factors that modulate play behaviour and manage them be dealt with so that they may facilitate rather than inhibit play. A vast amount of literature is developing which clearly outlines the importance of play in the socialization process. The whole area of sports sociology investigates the many other important social functions of play and sport. The success of such television programmes as 'Sesame Street' and programmes for disadvantaged groups such as 'Head Start' have forced those in education to recognize that playful behaviour is very often motivated by the desire to learn and is accompanied by positive feelings of enjoyment and much learning (Ellis, 1973).

The play of young children, however, is most often thought of as preparation for adult life. Most developmental psychologists hold the view that play affords children a miniature world in which they can test skills and explore themselves. They stress that a great reservoir of responses (upon which children can later call) are developed, which children can utilize when specific situations are met. Play, then, is a miniature laboratory in which children are protected and allowed to experiment. Children carry on play activities as long as they are interested in them and are stimulated. They terminate the activities when they are tired or not interested. It is only adults who are under the compulsion of completing a formal task or of meeting set requirements.

Problems in the Playpen

The regulation game, a 30-minute half, seven innings — these are all adult-imposed structures upon the play situation. So, too, is the insistence that soccer balls are to be kicked, hockey sticks are to be used with hockey pucks, and volley balls go over nets. Play is very quickly robbed of its potential for both the satisfaction of individual human needs and the positive contribution it can make to the development of the participants' community and society. Play potential is limited by the cognitive structures of those who direct children's play and by the physical structures that are designed for play experiences. The child is not viewed as a whole, living, vibrant, creative organism, but rather as an imperfect adult. It follows, therefore, that the adult demands are always right and the children conform precisely and exactly to the adult rules of the game, ways of using equipment, etc.

At the root of the problem is an over-emphasis on achievement, which most frequently is expressed in competitive play experiences provided by adults for children. The disproportionate use of competitive play environments, such as is often witnessed today, may be dysfunctional for both society and the individual. It should be made clear, however, that it is not being advocated that all competitive programmes be abolished. Rather, the position taken by Tutko and Smith should be adopted:

> I'm not against competition. Everybody *likes* to win, but there is a vast difference between competing for the fun of competing, and regimenting everything with only one goal in mind — to produce an elite champion. (Tutko and Bruns, 1976, p. 56)

> This discussion is *not* intended to suggest the elimination of competition. It is intended to advocate more emphasis on cooperation, less forcing of children into competitive situations, and a critical examination of the real effects of competition to try to have it serve more constructive ends than it has in the past. (Smith, 1976, p. 8)

It is suggested that play environments and programmes be organized in line with the joint needs of the participant and his/her community. As will be indicated below, such competitive environments are entirely appropriate for certain participant groups whose needs and objectives are met. For others, however, it is suggested that settings and programmes must be selected, modified, and/or created to meet co-operative or individual needs. The traditional games of Canada's indigenous peoples provide some valuable beginnings in this regard. Equally useful are some of their adaptations of European competitive games into a more co-operative mode.

Over-competition — which creates such a highly competitive atmosphere that positive harm rather than benefit may come to children — is not the only concern. Several by-products of the system are also major problems:

1. the selection of only the best players rules out experiences for the vast majority;
2. the effects of these programmes on the self-concepts of those who do not succeed may lead to fear of failure and the 'ego secure' spectator in a non-participant role;
3. the 'unfreedom' of a play environment which requires a player to specialize at one position prevents him/her from developing a whole range of skills (two obvious examples are the 'stick to your wing' philosophy of most hockey coaches and the current emphasis on team systems in minor league soccer); and
4. the physical size of the adult sports environments (e.g., 10' basketball hoops) may have a discouraging effect on young children.

It should be reiterated that an anti-competitive play experience for children is not being suggested here. Rather, it is felt that the frequent inappropriate use of serious, competition-oriented play environments is a major problem. It is recognized, as Mead (1961) has pointed out, that competition, co-operation and individualism are each healthy and necessary modes of social behaviour in all societies. The extent of each will vary from society to society, but some balance is obviously required in the learning and use of these three modes. The disproportionate use of competitive play environments, such as is often witnessed today, is dysfunctional for both the individual and the society. It is probable that North American society is not as competitive as many would suggest, and that co-operation has at least as much utilitarian value as competition in performing an adaptive role for the child. Rather, it seems that the emphasis is too strongly in the direction of competitive play experiences.

One might be so bold as to suggest that there is an interesting moral conflict here as well. It is naive — and in some instances a case of 'functional blindness' — to insist that play and games programmes are value-free. Each organizer and coach, and indeed playground designer, works from a value structure which becomes an inherent part of the end-product. To deny this is simply to avoid a very important issue. It is also apparent, upon examination of the lives of individuals who have exhibited a high level of both moral and emotional development, that there exists a hierarchy of values. Dabrowski (1964),[1] in his theory of positive disintegration, has justifiably made the point that such individuals (e.g., Christ, Gandhi, Thomas More, Abraham Lincoln) would be in complete agreement as to the make-up of such a hierarchy. There is no question, at least in the minds of the authors, that co-operative behaviours would rank at a much higher level than competitive behaviours. To be more specific, sharing, assisting and working-with rank above most of the behaviours evident in a highly competitive children's games programme. This is not to say that it is unethical to coach, design, or otherwise be connected with such programmes. It is merely suggested that it is essential for all involved clearly to establish a hierarchy from which they are operating. Many competitive sports coaches are excellent in both the skills and the humanitarian behaviour that they stress. There is much co-operation and sharing evident on many successful sports teams. These people are extremely skilled at what they do. Others, who are not so skilled, cannot operate as effectively from the framework; therefore, in the sections that follow, ways of changing the rules of the game, or indeed constructing new games, that help channel the child's experiences in more positive directions are suggested. Because these games are designed with co-operative outcomes in mind, they provide an easier structure for coaches and teachers through which to achieve these ends.

Putting The Player Back In

Given the state of affairs discussed above, what can recreation educators, planners and programmers do? Play, particularly in the bureaucratized form of sport, often takes on the aura of the religious and seems to put itself above criticism and change. If, until recently, one had tried to suggest changes in the rules or structure of children's sport, one would have been met with great resistance, if not outright hostility. The authors have felt those frustrations and would like to share an approach that has been developed through trial and error and an exchanging of ideas.

The Design and Programming of Play Environments

Traditionally play was basically left to the player; hence, his/her

Figure 22.1: Designing Play Environments

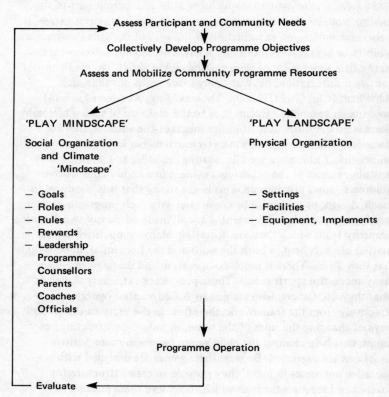

informal programming met very directly his/her felt needs for play. In recent years, however, outsiders have become heavily involved with intervening in play, often with the result that the play environments lose touch with the objectives of the player himself. The most blatant form of this is adult involvement in developing overstructured and overly competitive sport. Unfortunately, not infrequently, adults are involved vicariously to meet their own ego needs to win, with the result that what should be free, spontaneous, creative play becomes a very distorted form of sport where winning is the only thing. Play is too vital a human, social process to be left to the whims of this misplaced minority. Paradoxically to the very concept of free play, in order to return it to the player and the realm of the spontaneous and free, it is necessary carefully to plan play environments and programmes. Hopefully, someday this will not be necessary.

The design and development of any social environment involves a simple ongoing, planning, operation and evaluation loop as suggested in Figure 22.1. While there is nothing very startling about such a simple management by objectives framework, it is remarkable in so far as it suggests how little systematic thought has been given, until very recently, to providing play opportunities.

Assessing Play Needs

One of the striking and disheartening features of community play and recreation programmes of just a few years ago was their narrowness. Unfortunately, despite the great improvements being made by many centres at present, there are still many communities that identify community recreation with competitive sport. Such programmes will often be aimed at only the pre-pubescent boy and are comprised of ice hockey and baseball. This is beginning to change. Basically, people need their definition and view of play and recreation to be broadened. Most practitioners are unaware of the many needs, other than the competitive urge, that can be satisfied in play. Herein lies the role of exposure programming in new or modified activities and leisure education in general. People will not choose other programmes or actively support play reforms until they see their possibilities and potential.

Community people directly involved in programming are the key opinion leaders and therefore the first whose horizons must be broadened before any positive changes can begin. One of the roles of recreation professionals should be to provide them with conceptual frameworks for assessing the breadth and quality of their present programmes. Maslow's (1970) categorization of needs provides a useful tool for this purpose. Figure 22.2 suggests how Maslow's basic categories of human needs may be operationalized as recreational or play outcomes. This 'programme needs checklist' allows the practitioner to assess existing play programmes, facilitating the identification of shortcomings or unmet needs in the participant community. The framework also requires the breakdown of the community into specific need groups by age, sex and special characteristics. Many design and programme problems arise primarily out of conceptual confusion and tunnel vision as to what play and recreation is or could be. A quick perusal of framework brings home to the play organizer both the potential and thus the shortcomings and achievements of their programmes. Again it is worth emphasizing the dual role of recreation professionals: that of educating and bringing people to an awareness of new play possibilities and of enabling them to assess their needs more fully.

Figure 22.2: Play Needs Programme Checklist

Needs	Programme Objectives	Young Child	Child	Youth	Young Adult	Adult	Seniors	Special Groups
Physiological	Fitness, health, relaxation							
Safety	Safety, skills, knowledge							
Love and belonging	Friendship, socializing, acceptance, sharing, helping, co-operating							
Esteem self	Self-identity, growth, independence, self-confidence							
Public	Status, recognition, mastery, excellence, competition							
Self-actualization	Self-fulfilment, peak experiences, creativity, freedom							

Source: Adapted from A. Maslow, *Motivation and Personality* (Harper, New York, 1970).

The need to bring the player and the community play organizer into the planning process has already been implied. A community development approach is, therefore, advocated. If the doers are not involved early on in assessing their own needs and setting programme objectives, commitment to the programme will be questionable. This is particularly true in dealing with 'sacred' areas such as sports modification. Opinion leaders in both participant and organizer camps will need to be clear as to the paths to be taken if they are to convince the large community groups.

The present North American value system indicates a clear choice for emphasizing co-operative and individualistic needs in play-setting programme development. Although the feeling may not be widespread, there appears to be a small but significant trend in community opinion in this direction. Again, a circular relationship can be seen between exposure to play featuring co-operative outcomes and their acceptance and a recognized need for such programmes. In this regard many players, parents and play organizers seem often to have felt a vague uneasiness with 'competition only' kinds of recreation programmes, yet have not been able to identify any alternatives. Many recreation professionals are involved in this process of creating alternatives to the 'winning is the only thing' kind of programming. Notable in this regard is the work of Orlick (1975, 1978a, 1978b).[2] Following Orlick, it is felt that sharing, helping and self-discovery are possible outcomes of play programmes.

The Social Organization of Play

The actual socio-psychological structuring of the play social climate (or 'mindscape') will now be examined. It is well to remember that the play and game worlds are small, more or less self-contained micro-worlds, with their own more or less unique social system and culture. Each may be likened to a stage with its own cast of characters, plot — vague or formalized — rewards and punishments, and various props. In more psychological jargon, it may be usefully construed as a behavioural environment with general goals and specific objectives, a network of interacting roles, with rules, rewards, punishments, etc. Obviously play environments will vary from 'worlds' of almost complete freedom and role creativity to those of organized competitive sport where the social organization is tightly specified and controlled.

Again, the key question here is whether all aspects of that play programme and setting as a social world line up with the programme objectives. Unfortunately, in North America most play environments

Figure 22.3: Play Environments as Reflective of Programme Objectives

1. Participant needs and objectives	What are the characteristics, needs and objectives of the participants and their community?
2. Play goals or processes	How well are programme objectives expressed in goals *or* ongoing process or 'drama'?
3. Play positions and roles	How well do the various roles in the social world reflect the needs and objectives of the programme?
4. Playing script, rules, guidelines, time	How well do the rules, formal or implicit, serve to reflect the specific programme objectives? Is programme time in time with participant's needs?
5. Rewards and sanctions	How well do the reward and punishments encourage the desired outcomes?
6. Leadership	How well do the role presentations, leader characteristics and needs reflect the programme objectives? Are the leaders, counsellors, coaches, officials, etc., all there for motives congruent with the programme?
7. Settings and facilities	Are the physical settings and facilities conducive to achieving participant needs?
8. Equipment, implements and props	

Source: Adapted from Murray Smith, 'A preliminary case for classifying sports environments by participant objectives', *CAHPER Journal*, 41 (Sept.–Oct. 1974), pp. 27–30.

and virtually all of the sports environments have been strongly modified in tune with the dominant 'business as usual', win-oriented model of commercial/professional sport. Canadian children's hockey is a most notable example and apparently minor soccer football organizers are concerned that a similar process is leading their game to the more marketable professional model with its emphasis on violence and winning at all costs. Smith (1974), a noted Canadian physical educator, has developed a typology for sports environments categorized by participant objectives. His rationale and suggested characteristics of the social environments for each type of environment have been generalized and adapted here to provide a framework for analyzing, modifying and designing play environments by objectives (Figure 22.3).

The Physical Setting or Play Landscape

Often overlooked in planning is the need to match physical environment, space and implements with programme objectives. Until recently, most adult sports environments were seen as directly transferable and appropriate for children of all ages. Obviously, the capability of young players to develop in and enjoy soccer or basketball in environments designed for adults would seem to be limited. None the less, the struggle to modify to mini-soccer and biddy-basketball took some considerable effort. Both field size and ball size have been reduced. Still, many communities and children's leagues today are unaware, ignore, or reject these innovations. China, it may be noted, is far ahead of the North American society in the physical modification of play environments.

A number of important examples of play innovations are outlined below. It is worth noting that those practitioners searching for alternative play environments must be prepared to look in a variety of sources. Noteworthy in this regard are the many fine modifications and ideas for creating new activities from play and games activities of aboriginal peoples.

Work in the Canadian Arctic has led the authors to the realization that the original people of Canada have much to teach both about co-operative values to live by and about play activities that gently teach people how to share and get along while honouring the individual's right to do his/her own thing. Any number of co-operative or friendly competitive games might be cited here. A simple example is the moose-skin ball game of the Hareskin Indians of the Great Bear Lake Regions of Northern Canada. In a simple keep-away type of game, men and boys take on women and girls in a friendly tussle for a moose-skin ball roughly the size of a tennis ball. The aim is to keep the ball in the air by volleying it to a team mate. Males and females engage in friendly wrestling for the ball amidst a continual ring of laughter. There are no winners or losers, just players. This same sharing spirit is beautifully expressed in their circle dance. Everyone in the settlement participates in a simple two-step to the sound of the drum and song. Both play activities are all-inclusive and a simple celebration of the common good and communal good luck in hunting or fishing. Their play and their values are in painful contrast both to Western society's eliminate, exclusive, competitive forms of play and to the same features in that society itself.

The Inuit modification of competitive baseball to a total community

Figure 22.4: A Comparison of the Three Games

	Conventional	Bobby Hull	Silver Seven
Objectives:	Entertainment	Growth, fun, participation, learning	
Environment:			
Participants:	Adult professionals	(a) 5–6 years	9–10 years
		(b) 7–8 years	
Roster:	18 players	6	7
Playing area:	Full ice	1/3 ice – cross ice	full ice
		1/2 ice – lengthwise	
Ice time/60 mins:	20 mins	60 mins	60 mins
Positions:	Fixed	Rotate positions	
Body contact:	Allowed	Not allowed within 10 feet of boards	
Scores, points:	Statistics important	No scores kept	
Inter-community competition:	Yes	No inter-community	Limited inter-community
Leadership responsibilities:	Winning; motivation; changing lines; 'the coach'	Tying skates, warming hands, praising, skill teaching, encouraging, 'the helper–counsellor'	

participation happening is another example. This version of baseball sees everyone playing, from young children to grandparents. Players enter and leave in a game that may extend from noon to noon under the midnight sun. Again no one wins, no one loses, and everybody gets his turn.

Implementing Alternative Programmes

If the participants and community opinion leaders have been involved in the programme from the preliminary planning stages on, the job of recreation professionals will be almost done. One key is to multiple programme, i.e., make sure that the needs and objectives of a wide variety of participants are met. For example, if one were introducing an alternative hockey programme in a community, it might be wise to offer the conventional one as well. While this may appear to be a compromise, it may allow the alternative programme to survive where it might not otherwise.

In general, however, innovative programmes are much better received than one might expect. It has been found, for example, that co-operative programmes are well accepted at both the kindergarten and elementary school levels. Again, involvement of the leaders and participants is the key.

An Alternative Programme Experience

The following is a brief outline of an example of an innovative play or sports programme, in this case hockey, to illustrate how the above framework might be used. Figure 22.4 outlines three innovations, two of which are labelled 'Bobby Hull', and one 'Silver Seven'. Silver Seven is an advancement back to the hockey of 40 years or so ago.

Co-operative Games Programme

Orlick is the main pioneer in the development of co-operative games. These games, in some cases from Inuit peoples, all have one thing in common: no losers — the participants are the winners.

A recent research project assessed the ability of co-operative games to change children's free play behaviour (Jensen, 1978). The children in all three schools in which the games were played (two pilot studies and the research) thoroughly enjoyed the games. The teachers found them easy to teach and all expressed the desire to continue to use them. They found the games encouraged behaviours which were most congruent with establishing desirable learning environments. A lack of co-operation between teacher and student and student and student makes an effective learning environment most difficult. The results of this research are not startling and certainly will do little (unless implemented on a world-wide basis immediately) to reduce the possibility of another world war. The children did, however, co-operate with their playmates more frequently during free-play periods in the game-playing experimental phases of the experiment when compared with baseline measures. It is not the intention to present here a scientific paper (that will be done elsewhere), but merely to emphasize that such games work, they are fun, and the children love them.

Notes

1. The whole area of play, games, sport and emotional and moral growth is one that needs more investigation. Most North Americans tend to lean to Kolberg's theory in this regard. We would strongly recommend Dabrowski's theory as one that possesses tremendous potential in this regard. At the time of writing, two books of his are being published. Most of his works have been published as papers in Polish. The only available English written work to date that presents the theory is Dabrowski (1964).

2. Terry Orlick, from the University of Ottawa has, in our opinion, been the leader in the development and implementation of co-operative games. They are best outlined in two recent publications. The third publication written along with Cal Botterill provides background information and justification for changing current competitive programmes from the mouths of children who have dropped out.

References

Dabrowski, K. 1964. *Positive Disintegration*. Boston: Little, Brown.

Ellis, Michael. 1973. *Why People Play*. Englewood Cliffs, New Jersey: Prentice-Hall.

Huizinga, J. 1950. *Homo Ludens: A Study of the Play Element in Culture*. Boston: Beacon Press.

Jensen, Peter K. 1978. 'Increasing cooperative social interaction between kindergarten children in a free play setting'. Unpublished doctoral dissertation, University of Alberta, Edmonton, Alberta.

Maslow, A. 1970. *Motivation and Personality*. New York: Harper.

Mead, Margaret (ed.). 1961. *Cooperation and Competition Among Primitive Peoples*. Boston: Beacon Press.

Orlick, Terry. 1978a. *The Cooperative Sports and Games Book*. New York: Random House.

—. 1978b. *Winning Through Cooperation — Competitive Insanity: Cooperative Alternatives*. Washington, DC: Hawkins and Associates.

— with C. Botterill. 1975. *Every Kid Can Win*. Chicago: Nelson Hall.

Smith, Murray. 1974. 'A preliminary case for classifying sports environments by participant objectives', *CAHPER Journal*, 41 (Sept.–Oct.), pp. 27–30.

—. 1976. 'Sport and physical activity as possible factors in the child's psychological and social development', *CAHPER Journal*, 42 (May–June), pp. 6–13.

Tutko, Thomas and William Bruns. 1976. *Winning is Everything and Other American Myths*. New York: Macmillan.

23 DEVELOPING THE FULL CAPACITIES OF CHILDREN THROUGH THE EXPANSION OF NON-FORMAL EDUCATION PROGRAMMES

Bernard Zubrowski

Educating All the Capacities of Children

Educating in the fullest sense of the term means the shaping of both mental and sensori-motor capacities. In contemporary Western society, one becomes educated by entering an institutional system so that this system will assist in the growth of these abilities and give direction and form to them. Today, schools are seen by most people as the main institution which educates. Any time a new study reveals that children are deficient in certain areas of knowledge, or are lacking in skills, it is the schools which are called upon to correct this deficit. On the contrary, it can be argued that various institutional arrangements promote certain kinds of learning, and that no one institution is capable of educating all the capacities of a person.

Certain educators and psychologists maintain that school is only one kind of learning experience, a specialized situation which promotes the use of abstract symbol systems for verbal and mathematical analysis and communication. Other capacities, particularly those related to the sensori-motor capacities, are utilized in a limited way in schools. This seems to be the case particularly in using non-verbal modes in developing intuitive knowledge of the world; that is, the ability to detect patterns through the various sensual modalities, and to comprehend the totality of an experience and its relation to past experience.

Education of the Intuitive Capacity

In his book, *Psychology of Consciousness*, Ornstein discusses at length the differences between these two ways of knowing the world. He states that the first involves analysis and logic, especially verbal and mathematical. It is predominantly the processing of information in a linear manner. Most schools concern themselves with this kind of thinking. The other mode is more holistic and relational; it tends to process information simultaneously. He cites recent findings in the area of brain research which indicate that, in fact, the two halves of the brain seem to function in a similar manner.

309

The education of intuition calls for a different approach and process than that which is ordinarily practised in schools. Ornstein studied the practices of certain esoteric psychologies in depth, particularly that of Sufism, and found that practitioners played at various crafts, especially those dealing with movement, in spatial visualization and the use of the entire body and senses in detecting changes in the environment.

Institutions Which Help in the Development of the Intuitive Capacity

Arts and crafts, environmental education and certain approaches to the teaching of science are among a range of experiences which enhance a way of knowing the world other than the rational and the linear. Each of these areas is given some attention within the school programme, but it is of a minor nature and of a limited orientation. More often than not, they are used to teach the basics, rather than being another mode of personal expression and another way of knowing the world.

Traditionally, museums, performing groups in theatre and dance, and related cultural institutions have functioned as the major avenue by which children experience arts, crafts and science in a more personal manner. There also exists a wide range of programmes for children that happen in community and neighbourhood centres such as settlement houses, multi-service centres, boy's clubs, the YMCA and community schools. Unfortunately, both kinds of institutions suffer from a limited public image. The cultural institution is too often looked upon as a form of entertainment and, if it is taken more seriously, accusations of elitism arise when programmes are designed for limited audiences (to maintain a quality experience). Programmes of neighbourhood agencies are seen as recreational, meaning that children are kept off the streets and are given captivating activities which will provide constructive outlets for their excess energies. In both situations it is not acknowledged that environments and games teach, or that play with materials is a form of learning, different in nature, but just as valid as that found in the classroom. It is this type of environment and form of learning which is conducive to the development of intuitive thinking.

Change and Growth of Non-formal Education

This general lack of recognition of the value of play on the part of educational administrators as well as the general public is short-sighted, because there are great social changes happening which have serious implications for the caring and education of children. The number of single-parent families and the number of situations where both parents work has increased dramatically in recent years. This has caused a great demand for child care which is not being fully met. Early childhood programmes have only recently received serious attention, while after-school care has not been dealt with at all in many communities. When there are efforts in this area, it is usually the neighbourhood centre that initiates and carries out the programme. Parents who have children in this kind of programme are wanting more than custodial care; they are also seeking an enjoyable and enriching experience for their children.

Another important change is the increase in leisure time for people of all economic levels. As a result, there has been a growing interest in the arts and related areas. A recent Harris survey did an in-depth look at public attitudes toward the arts. It revealed that many more people are attending museums and cultural performances and would like to see their children have more direct participation and instruction in a wide range of arts and crafts activities. What was perhaps most indicative was a feeling that public revenue should be supportive of the arts.

The Conflicting Roles of Arts in the Schools

Growing out of this changing attitude towards the arts has been an increase in the implementation of 'arts in education' programmes in schools. Most of these emphasize the role that the arts can play in teaching the basics — reading, writing and arithmetic. If these programmes attempt to emphasize the personal growth aspect of such experiences, there results an inherent conflict. This can be illustrated in the area of creative writing. A student writes about his/her own personal experience or creates stories that are projections of personal feelings. A teacher evaluates these writings in terms both of creative expression and of how the student has conformed to standing grammatical usage. In this situation, the total effort is being evaluated. For children, it is difficult to separate these two kinds of critiques. From the child's point of view, his personal efforts are being judged.

There are several ways that teachers and school systems have attempted to resolve this conflict. For instance, a friend of mine once related how her son's writing improved greatly through the efforts of one of his teachers. The creative expression, by which the child's fantasies and feelings are projected, was discussed by this one teacher while another teacher dealt only with grammar, logic and spelling. In this manner it was made clear that what he had to express was separate from how he said it. Of course, in poetry or related kinds of literature the two are very closely intertwined. The important consideration in this and similar cases, however, is that the beginner starts from a very personal context and, therefore, is very sensitive to evaluation. Although much effort in recent years has been given to humanizing schools, the overwhelming emphasis is still on the acquisition of basic skills, rather than creativity and personal growth.

Community Education in Boston

If the functions of cultural institutions and community centres were to be expanded and redefined, it might be helpful to examine what sort of programmes and services for children could be offered. For example, Boston and its surrounding communities can be assumed to be representative of other urban areas in the United States. There is a wide range of programmes offered to children in Boston, but at present these are limited in scope and accessibility. The most popular type of programme is the recreational programme in which competitive sports are emphasized. This, however, is changing. In recent years, there has been an increase in gymnastics programmes, as well as karate and the martial arts. In addition, there has been an increase in the number of professional dance groups which offer courses to children and adults. A trend has been growing for some time in which physical exercise is becoming a more individual endeavour, the emphasis shifting from competition to personal growth and aesthetic expression.

Several agencies which have traditionally served children after school hours (such as boys' clubs and YMCAs) have also expanded their programming to include the movement activities mentioned above, as well as crafts. For instance, over the past five years several boys' clubs have been running a Discovery Programme which invites children to participate on a drop-in basis in simple arts and crafts and science programmes. They do not need to sign up ahead of time and there are generally no fees attached. Recently, this programme was given national recognition by receiving an award from the national organization citing especially the social development of the children participating in these programmes.

Other agencies such as neighbourhood houses and community schools have taken a similar approach in offering a mix of programmes in which children can participate in crafts and science, at both introductory and in-depth levels. These agencies have particularly felt a need to offer the drop-in type programme to reach a wide range of children. Some have been able to enhance this experience by developing a full-scale community arts programme in which courses are offered by professional artists. This arose out of a recognition that children also needed to experience growth and mastery in a specific area.

Many cultural institutions have attempted to expand their audiences, especially in low-income areas. Much of this effort has taken the form of programmes at the neighbourhood centre. When necessary, however, children have been bussed to the sponsoring institution. Currently, the Boston Zoo is working with three neighbourhood agencies on an after-school basis, in which children come to the zoo for introductory programmes, allowing them more opportunity to become knowledgeable about the animals than would have been possible in a casual visit. The Museum of Science hosts members of two boys' clubs on Saturdays for an extended look at certain exhibits and an opportunity to participate in 'hands-on' science experiments. For the past five years, the Children's Museum has worked with a large number of community groups, training programme leaders in arts, crafts, science, and in the implementation and design of informal community programmes. Also, a recent informal survey of other cultural institutions around Boston has indicated that there is a strong institutional interest in increasing accessibility for children through after-school programmes.

The Complementary Roles of Community Centre and the Cultural Institution

What has become apparent over the past five years in working with a diverse number of neighbourhood agencies is that their programmes provide for certain needs of children which are not being fully met elsewhere. Perhaps the most important factor is that these programmes provide a location where children can gather and hang-out with each other. Experience has shown, however, that certain kinds of organized activities are needed to establish a context in which personal relationships can develop among children. It has also been found that children attend these programmes seeking relationships with adults. In fact, programme leaders feel that lending a sympathetic ear and giving emotional support to children is their most important function. Because of the importance attached to this function, the activities offered are selected more for their entertainment value than as an occasion for meaningful conceptual learning or the acquisition of skills even though that potential exists. Some of these children would like to do in-depth exploration, and programme leaders have recognized this need for mastery. There have been various attempts to accomplish this, but most neighbourhood agencies lack the financial and educational resources to offer continuing programmes of an in-depth nature.

At the same time, cultural institutions are attempting to provide this same kind of programme, but are lacking the intimate kind of atmosphere that is usually found in neighbourhood centres. Some institutions do offer programmes which allow for exploration in a very personal way but, because they are usually so brief, there is little chance for growth in interpersonal relationships. The human and material resources that cultural institutions can bring to neighbourhood programmes are significant and can fit nicely with the kind of learning that happens in neighbourhood centres.

It is clear that deliberate collaboration would be beneficial to all groups concerned. The word 'deliberate' is used because, in the past, such efforts have happened by chance and were not carefully thought out, especially in terms of the relationships between institutional settings and the type of learning that occurs in those settings.

Future Development: Bring the Cultural Institutions and Neighbourhood Centre Closer Together

What is needed is a development plan that examines how the resources of both types of institutions can be integrated into a broad programme which would act as an environment which encourages personal growth at the same time as it develops the capacities of intuitive thinking. Careful planning would have to be done to ensure that the play-like and personal atmosphere continues to be the essential ingredient of any effort to bring this collaboration about.

This planning would involve a number of considerations. Various types of collaborative relationships would have to be examined, tested and evaluated. The over-all goal in such an effort would be to generate two or three models that result in effective co-ordination and quality programmes. Some of the questions that might be considered would be:

1. Should children come to the institution or the specialists go to the neighbourhood centre?
2. What would be the length of the special programme?
3. How would these programmes be financed?
4. What would be the relationship between the general and special programme in terms of content?

This last question is important, for it deals with the complex problem of how the activities of the programmes shape children's behaviour and growth. What would be needed is an arrangement whereby the activities in the drop-in programme or after-school child-care programme would become the introductory experience on which specialists could expand. These introductory experiences would try to preserve that special social atmosphere of nurturing, and would serve as a way of exposing the children to a variety of modes of expression and explorations. Hopefully, this would give that initial impetus of motivation, making the child want to explore further a specific area.

Once this motivation becomes evident, neighbourhood programme leaders can act as brokers in getting children to a specialist who can capitalize on that interest and extend that introductory experience. Museums, zoos, theatres and dance groups would become the vehicles to carry this out. For instance, in the general programme, children could do very simple theatre games and skits. Those who have enjoyed it and want to pursue it further could do so with a visiting theatre person who comes to the centre twice a week to work with small groups of children. In science, explorations could be done with batteries and bulbs making simple circuits. Further exploration could be done at a science museum or nearby university where more sophisticated equipment is available and a knowledgeable person is available to guide the children in more in-depth exploration.

If all of the above were carried out, a solid foundation would be established for the development of a system of education complementary to that of school. It would attempt to meet the needs of a growing number of parents who are looking for enriching experiences for their children after school and would allow for a balanced development of mind and body.

CONTRIBUTORS

Shani Beth-Halachmy, BA, MA: PhD candidate, Division of Educational Psychology, Department of Education, University of California at Berkeley, Berkeley, California.

Doyle Bishop, PhD: Professor, Department of Recreology, Faculty of Social Science, University of Ottawa, Ottawa.

Peggy Brown, BA: Fitness Consultant, Fitness and Amateur Sport Branch, Health and Welfare Canada, Ottawa.

Mavis Burke, BA, MA, PhD: Education Officer, Curriculum Branch, Ontario Ministry of Education, Toronto; Chairperson, Ontario Ministry of Education Committee on Multiculturalism.

Catherine Cherry, BA, M.Ed.: Consultant, Ontario Ministry of Culture and Recreation, Toronto.

Walter Filipowich: Behavioural Adviser, Behaviour Management Program, Sudbury and District Association for the Mentally Retarded, Sudbury, Ontario.

Shelley Gordon Garshowitz, BA: Consultant in Programs and Leadership Training and Group Recreation, Toronto; Staff Member, Eastern Co-operative School, United States of America; Staff Member, Recreation Workshops Cooperative, Toronto.

Michael L. Henniger, BA, PhD: Assistant Professor, Department of Curriculum, Instruction, and Media, Southern Illinois University, Carbondale, Illinois; Regional Vice-President, Illinois Association for the Education of Young Children.

Michael Hough, Dip. Arch, M.L. Arch: Principal Consultant, Hough, Stansburg Associates Ltd, Toronto; Adjunct Associate Professor, Faculty of Environmental Studies, York University, Toronto.

Ellen Jacobs, BA, M.Ed.: Assistant Professor, Department of Education, Concordia University, Montréal.

Claudine Jeanrenaud, PhD: Associate Professor, Department of Recreology, Faculty of Social Science, University of Ottawa, Ottawa.

Peter K. Jensen, BPE, MA, PhD: Athletic Director, Glendon College, York University, Toronto.

Joyce Knowles, BA, Dip. Ed., DCP: Principal and Director of Studies, Castle Priory College, Wallingford, Oxfordshire, England.

Jan Kubli, BA: Play Co-ordinator, Paediatric Department, Charing Cross Hospital (Fulham), London.

Ethel Bauzer Medeiros, BA, IP, MA: Full Professor, Department of
    Educational Psychology, Instituto de Estudos Avançados em
    Educação, Fundação Getulio Vargas, Rio de Janeiro, Brasil; Vice-
    President, World Leisure and Recreation Association, New York.
Lanie Melamed, BA, MA: Conseiller pédagogique, Centre for Continuing
    Education, Dawson College, Montréal; Part-time Lecturer, School of
    Social Work, McGill University and Department of Applied Social
    Science, Concordia University, Montréal.
Dorothy Jane Needles, B.Arch.: Consultant in 3-Dimensional Learning,
    Board of Education, Borough of Etobicoke, Etobicoke, Ontario.
Nancy L. G. Ovens: Senior Lecturer, School of Community Studies,
    College of Education, Edinburgh.
Colin Pryor, PhD: Programme Director, Oaklands Regional Centre,
    Oakville, Ontario; Consultant Psychologist, Sudbury and District
    Children's Aid Society and Sudbury and District Association for the
    Mentally Retarded, Sudbury, Ontario.
Harvey A. Scott, BPE, MA, PhD: Professor, Faculty of Physical
    Education and Recreation, University of Alberta, Edmonton,
    Alberta.
Mayah Sevink: Behavioural Adviser, Behaviour Management Program,
    Sudbury and District Association for the Mentally Retarded, Sudbury,
    Ontario.
Leland G. Shaw, B.Arch., M.Arch.: Professor, Department of
    Architecture, College of Architecture, University of Florida,
    Gainesville, Florida.
Yrjö Sotamaa, Int. Arch.: Head, Department of Interior Architecture
    and Furniture Design, University of Industrial Art, Helsinki, Finland.
Otto Weininger, BA, MA, PhD: Professor, Department of Applied
    Psychology, Ontario Institute for Studies in Education, Toronto;
    Co-Editor, *The Journal of the Canadian Association for Young
    Children.*
Paul F. Wilkinson, BA, MA, PhD: Assistant Dean (Academic) and
    Associate Professor, Faculty of Environmental Studies, York
    University, Toronto.
Clara Will, BA: Executive Director, Adventure Place, Faywood Public
    School, North York Board of Education, Toronto.
Robert Woodburn, PhD: Director, Rethink Ltd, Kitchener, Ontario;
    former Consultant, Ontario Ministry of Culture and Recreation,
    Toronto.
Thomas Daniels Yawkey, PhD: Associate Professor, Early Childhood

Faculty, The Pennsylvania State University, University Park,
Pennsylvania; President, Pennsylvania Association for Childhood
Education.

Bernard Zubrowski, BS, MST: Bricoleur-in-Residence, The Children's
Museum, Boston, Massachusetts; Instructor, School of Education,
Boston University, Boston, Massachusetts.

INDEX

adventure *see* playgrounds; –
Education Concept 206; –
Place 241–53

age differentiations   94–6, 97, 107,
117, 120, 122–3, 136, 139,
140

Aiello, J. R.   136

Allen of Hurtwood, Lady Marjory
27

Altman, I.   119, 121, 122, 123, 125,
126, 129, 131

America, North   27–8, 171, 279,
298, 303, 305

Ames, A. H.   119, 120

ANOVA variance   137

Ardrey, R.   123

Arendt, Hannah   34

Ariès, Philippe   37

Arlemalm, I.   293

arts and crafts   19, 29, 247, 291,
310, 311, 312, 372

Ashley, Brian J.   148

Astrand, Per-Olaf   286, 288

autonomy   60, 80, 82, 127, 130,
132, 219, 220, 271

Avison, Margaret   39

Bailey, Donald   284, 285–6, 289,
290–1

Bakker, C.   124–5, 131

Bakker-Rabdau, M. K.   124–5, 131

Barker, R.   135

Barnes, K.   100, 103

'battered child syndrome'   38

Bender, B. G.   88

Berlyne, D.   73, 76

Bernal, J. F.   210

Bernstein, B.   60

Beth-Halachmy, Shani   135–42, 316

Biber, B.   47–8

Bishop, Doyle   73–84, 316

Bladen, V. W.   266

Blurton Jones, N.   135, 136

Bormuth, J. R.   60

Boston   287, 312–13

Botterill, Cal   308n

Boyd, Neva L.   172, 178

boys   107–8, 113, 114, 136,
138–41, 293

Brazil   32, 33

Britain   28, 63, 145, 154, 156,
194, 198, 279

Britton, James   187

Brower, S. N.   123, 124

Brown, A. L.   97–8

Brown, Peggy   282–95, 316

Bruns, William   297

Buhler, C.   104–5

Burchenal, Elizabeth   176

Burke, Mavis   200–9, 316

Caffey, John   38

Camus, Albert   33

Canada   11, 14, 17, 23, 24, 28, 63,
172, 200, 201, 202, 203, 241,
282, 283, 285–6, 287, 292,
304, 305

Caplan, Frank and Theresa   20–1,
22

Castle Priory College   151, 155,
157–8

Central Mortgage and Housing
Corporation   25

centres, assessment   241–53;
community/neighbourhood
310, 311, 313–15; Concordia
University Child Care – 129,
132; day-care 11, 119–34;
information 280; St Francis
Children's 229

Chace, C.   73

Chapin, F. S.   119

Cherry, Catherine   63–9, 316

Chevalier, Michel   28–9

China   305

Coates, F. D.   267

Cohen, Uriel   229, 230

Collard, R.   100

communication   45; problems
152–3; *see also* language

competition   296–308, 312

Connolly, K.   135, 137

control   79–83

Corbin, H. Dan   63

319